Medicine, Science and Merck

P. ROY VAGELOS

LOUIS GALAMBOS

CAMBRIDGE
UNIVERSITY PRESS

PUBLISHED BY THE PRESS SYNDICATE OF THE UNIVERSITY OF CAMBRIDGE
The Pitt Building, Trumpington Street, Cambridge, United Kingdom

CAMBRIDGE UNIVERSITY PRESS
The Edinburgh Building, Cambridge CB2 2RU, UK
40 West 20th Street, New York, NY 10011-4211, USA
477 Williamstown Road, Port Melbourne, VIC 3207, Australia
Ruiz de Alarcón 13, 28014 Madrid, Spain
Dock House, The Waterfront, Cape Town 8001, South Africa

http://www.cambridge.org

First published 2004

Printed in the United States of America

Typeface Sabon 10/13 pt.   *System* LaTeX 2_ε [TB]

A catalog record for this book is available from the British Library.

Library of Congress Cataloging in Publication Data
Vagelos, P. Roy.
    Medicine, science and Merck: the first three careers of Roy Vagelos / P. Roy
Vagelos, Louis Galambos.
        p.   cm.
    Includes bibliographical references and index.
    ISBN 0-521-66295-8 (hc)
    1. Vagelos, P. Roy.   2. Physicians – United States – Biography.   3. Medical
scientists – United States – Biography.   4. Physician executives – United States –
Biography.   5. Merck Sharp & Dohme.   I. Galambos, Louis.   II. Title.
    R154.V34A3   2003
    610′.92–dc21
    [B]   2003051233

ISBN 0 521 66295 8 hardback

To my wife, Diana, who helped me throughout my career and brought happiness to our entire family

– Roy Vagelos

To the memory of my wife, Jane, and to my four wonderful daughters

– Lou Galambos

Contents

Preface

As the retired chief executive officer of a major U.S. multinational firm, Roy Vagelos has already received a lifetime allotment of public attention. Whether it was standing before financial community experts to explain the past, present, and (I hoped) future of Merck & Co., Inc.; or testifying before a congressional committee in defense of the National Institutes of Health budget; or announcing Merck's gift of a new drug with the potential to eradicate river blindness – I spent years in the media limelight, receiving more than my share of newsprint, magazine pages, and TV coverage. Now, however, almost a decade after that highly visible life ended, I have collaborated with Lou Galambos on a book that has allowed us to reflect on all three of my careers: in medicine, science, and business. Along the way, we have tried to provide a balanced perspective on two important professions and on an industry, pharmaceuticals, that has aroused a tidal wave of controversy in recent years.

When Lou suggested that we collaborate on this book, I initially resisted. I was then in my last year on the job at Merck and didn't have time to reexamine the past – especially what seemed at the time to be the distant past of my family, my education, and my first two professional careers. But I was finally convinced that we could do the job expeditiously if, following recorded discussions concerning the events of my career, Lou drafted chapters and I edited them. As we got down to work, I became intrigued by the task, but mine was an action-packed retirement that left very little time to devote to editing. I was serving as chairman of the Board of Trustees at the University of Pennsylvania, and then I added the chairmanship of Regeneron Pharmaceuticals, Inc. These responsibilities, in addition to serving on several corporate boards, kept me quite occupied. Later, I took on the presidency of the American School of Classical Studies at Athens and the chairmanship of Theravance Corporation. So a decade passed in writing a book about a life that was lived in fast forward.

To make that life understandable, we've introduced you to several generations of the Vagelos family. As will become obvious, there is here some celebration of a Greek heritage and the American systems of education and political economy. We are not apologetic about those larger dimensions of our society. Close families, a marvelously open educational system, and a business environment attuned to competition, professional accomplishment, and innovation created a setting that enabled the son of an ice cream and candy maker to help millions of people in the United States and abroad live longer and better lives. In one country alone, the People's Republic of China, the introduction of the world's first recombinant DNA vaccine will eventually allow that nation to break the deadly hold of the hepatitis B virus on its population. Knowing that, one sleeps well and writes a book that appreciates the American institutions – public, nonprofit, and private – that make this society so creative.

With time to reflect, it is also possible to write a book that exposes some of the institutional warts on the American system and explains where Roy Vagelos fell short of his own goals. We have tried to do that throughout. If we seem harsh about judging Hillary Clinton, we hope our readers will agree that we have been just as tough about Roy Vagelos's several careers. In doing so, we have not tried to address all the questions raised since 1994 about medicine, the biomedical sciences, or the pharmaceutical industry. All have come under intense fire. All have changed. All have continued to attract worldwide attention as the AIDS pandemic ravages developing societies and resistant forms of bacteria and new viruses threaten our lives. What we have provided is a general response to these serious problems. We have urged our society and its leaders to nurture a system that will enable the United States and its pharmaceutical industry to be as flexible and innovative in the future as they have been in the past.

In writing this book over several years, we have received a great deal of help and advice. Our families have been supportive and tolerant. In matters large and small, they have supported our efforts, put up with our egos, and demonstrated an infinite capacity to love. Roy is particularly indebted to his wife, Diana, his son Andrew, and his sister Helen Barnes, all of whom spent much time improving the manuscript. Diana also selected all of the photos included in the book. Cambridge University Press has been an ideal publisher, and Editor Frank Smith has exceeded even his high standards in bringing this book into print.

Developmental Editor Carol Shookhoff provided us with expert advice about every aspect of the manuscript. In Roy Vagelos's New Jersey office, Diane Taylor has given us enthusiastic support, as has Elizabeth Kafig, a research associate of Lou Galambos's at Johns Hopkins University. Diane and Elizabeth's enthusiasm and organizational skills allowed us to make the great leap from records and recollections to a book manuscript. At Merck, from the top down, we have received assistance and backing for this endeavor. Particularly helpful were Senior Vice President and General Counsel Kenneth C. Frazier, Vice President Jeffrey L. Sturchio, and Archivist Joseph Ciccone. They helped us improve the manuscript while leaving to the authors the job of interpretation and analysis. That of course makes us responsible for any mistakes – a burden we gladly accept.

Roy Vagelos
Louis Galambos
June 2003

1 | *The Making of a Physician*

My life is in many ways the classic American dream: poor immigrants come to the United States and work very hard; their children receive an excellent education and lead a better life. I was born just before the start of the Great Depression, in October 1929, in Westfield, New Jersey, where my Greek father and one of his brothers owned a shop that sold candy, ice cream, and snacks. In the next few years, times were hard for all of us, but we were cushioned from the worst effects of the economic crisis by our family. Children now grow up in a society less supportive than mine was even in the harshest days of the 1930s.

In elementary school I was a cutup who entertained the other students – but not of course the teachers. They were interested in teaching Pindaros Roy Vagelos (they wouldn't use my nickname, Pindo) to read and write in English, goals that seemed formidable to a first-grader who spoke only Greek at home. I was a slow learner. I wasn't interested in learning. It was much more fun to fool around and tease the other kids. Besides, I had recurrent ear infections that made it difficult for me to hear. Since my last name begins with a "V," I sat in the back of the class, where it was hard to hear even when I was healthy. I got used to not paying attention to the lessons, although I was clever enough to pretend to work when the teacher was watching.

My sister Joan, fourteen months older than I, was a different kind of student. She learned to read early and loved it. My specialty was wasting time. Nevertheless, Joan and I were very close because we went through school together and shared the harsh years of the depression, when our family was forced to move repeatedly into smaller and smaller apartments to survive financially. Joan and I did everything together (except read). We always went to the movies together, we learned to ride bikes and swim together, and we took music and Greek lessons together. I was afraid of the dark upstairs, so she would go with me. When we went fishing, she always put the worm on the

Vagelos family outing, 1930. Roy's mother and father at left with Roy (far left) and Joan.

hook for me. Our younger sister Helen, born nine years after me, was also a quick reader, but she had a different life. By the time she came around, the depression was fading and life became better for our family and Joan and me.

The year 1936, when I was in first grade, was an especially difficult one for the family. My father and his older brothers had settled in Westfield, an affluent bedroom community about an hour's drive from New York City. My father and his oldest brother owned the Westfield Sweet Shoppe located on Broad Street in the center of town. Like many other Greek immigrants, they gravitated to the candy and small restaurant businesses because they were largely uneducated and restaurant startup costs were small. They could thrive with minimal English, making up with hard work and warm personalities what they lacked in education and language skills. The Westfield Sweet Shoppe was modestly successful, providing our family with a very nice four-bedroom house on a wide, tree-lined street a few blocks from the store. But the hard times of the 1930s didn't spare New Jersey. Some of the shop's former

Roy with his sisters Helen (left) and Joan (right).

customers were now out of work and finding it hard to pay for their food and rent, let alone for ice cream and candy. In addition, my father had invested in real estate in Westfield and bought stock on margin. When the market collapsed, he had to sell the real estate to cover his losses.

I was quite aware that times were tough because, in 1936, we lost our house. Business was so poor my father couldn't pay the mortgage on both the store and our home. Since the store was our only source of income, we moved into an apartment above a drugstore in Cranford, about two miles from Westfield. Gone was my sunny bedroom. Now I had to sleep on a sofa in the living room. I felt as though my life had lost all sense of order. We couldn't go visit the store for ice cream, candy, and sodas anymore because we now lived too far away. We changed schools and neighbors. In Westfield, three of our relatives had lived within one block of our house, and several other relatives and other Greek families lived in town. In Cranford, no relatives were nearby, and we were the only Greeks we knew. This was a new world for us.

I remember it like it was yesterday. My parents, Herodotus and Marianthi, never discussed their financial problems in front of me, but I absorbed every sign of urgency in our family. My father and his older brother Thucydides tried to keep the Sweet Shoppe going by cutting expenses and working longer hours. My father took off only a few hours from the store on the weekend to spend time with us. My mother grew very anxious. She talked about jobs she needed to get outside the home and was short-tempered when I pestered Joan. When I fooled around, she would sometimes break into sobs, and I grew frightened about these disturbing episodes.

Around this time, my mother, who had stayed home before I entered school, took a job ironing clothes in a laundry. After a full day there, she came home and made elaborate evening dresses for the few women in that part of New Jersey who could still afford them. My mother, an expert seamstress, could make a fancy dress from any pattern and fabric supplied by a customer. People loved her work, and although her hours were long and the pay poor, she was able to bring in some income as my father struggled to sustain the family. Joan and I watched, trying not to upset my mother. We had jobs too. I washed the windows and swept out the store and the sidewalk in front of our business. Once a month, I polished the Sweet Shoppe's wooden tables, chairs, and booths. I actually enjoyed being around our family business and took pride in doing adult jobs.

* * *

Family and business were intertwined, as they were for many of the families that came to America from Europe in the early years of the last century. The Vagelos family came from the village of Eressos on the island of Mytilene, the ancient Lesbos. Grandfather John Vayos Vagelos

John Vagelos, M.D. (P. Roy Vagelos's grandfather).

had died of typhoid fever in 1898 while serving as an army physician in Denizli, Turkey. His widow, Aphrodite, had then returned to Eressos with her daughter and five sons, the oldest of whom was Thucydides. The fourth son was Herodotus, my father.

Although they could farm and raise goats on the family property in Eressos, Aphrodite's sons recognized that their holdings would never support a family of seven. Thucydides was the first to leave in search of economic opportunity in America. In 1901, at age fifteen, he bought passage to the United States with help from a relative and sailed alone carrying a note to a family friend who was to meet him at the dock in New York City. But the friend never showed up. Thucydides, who spoke only Greek, wandered about the strange city for a couple of days holding a note in English that directed him first to Connecticut and then to New Jersey.

Eventually, he found his way to the home of Stratis Mitchell, another Greek immigrant, in Westfield, New Jersey. Transformed at Ellis Island from a Michaeledes to a Mitchell, Stratis had settled in New Jersey, learned how to make candies, and launched the New York Candy Kitchen in Westfield. He needed help, and Thucydides needed a job. Together, they built a successful small candy business that became the Vagelos beachhead in America.

Thucydides was determined to help his brothers leave Mytilene and to make their passages easier and safer than his had been. He met Homer and Phillalithes (who soon became Philip) at the dock in New York and helped them set up their own candy shop in nearby Wood-bridge, New Jersey. Next in age and next to come was Herodotus, who was born in 1890 and named after the world's first historian, Herodotus of Halicarnassus. After finishing the sixth grade, the most advanced schooling available in Eressos, Herodotus had apprenticed to a shoemaker. Good with his hands, he enjoyed the ancient and honorable craft of making shoes to order, but when he arrived in America at age eighteen, he learned that shoemakers spent most of their time repairing worn, smelly shoes. He quickly decided to find a new calling to accompany his newly anglicized name, Roy, courtesy of the Ellis Island officials.

After apprenticing with a candy and ice cream manufacturer, he joined Thucydides at the New York Candy Kitchen on Elm Street (just around the corner from its later site on Broad Street) in Westfield to run the manufacturing wing of the tiny enterprise. The business, like most

N.Y. Candy Kitchen delivery truck. Roy Vagelos (at left) and helper.

of the Vagelos brothers, changed names, becoming the Westfield Candy Kitchen and later the Westfield Sweet Shoppe. There, Herodotus introduced a major new product line, homemade ice cream, that became popular in Westfield, then in Woodbridge, and finally as far away as Plainfield and Elizabeth, New Jersey. In Westfield, everyone seemed to know just when the freshly made ice creams were ready. The police always dropped in to sample his latest creations. Thus, this transplanted Greek – Herodotus at home, Roy to the customers – became something of a local personality by way of his high-calorie confection.

By the early 1920s, the brothers were doing very well in Westfield. Stratis Mitchell had returned to Greece permanently, leaving the shop in their hands. By 1922, all five Vagelos brothers, including the youngest, Emmanuel, were settled in America, all running small businesses producing, retailing, and to some extent wholesaling candy and ice cream. All five returned to Eressos to marry in the Greek style. For immigrant Greek men, marriage was arranged by their relatives – sometimes to good effect, sometimes not. The bridegroom was expected to have launched a successful career, acquired some money, and established a home in America. By the early 1920s, Herodotus met all three conditions. He had built a house in Westfield, near the Candy Kitchen, and by the standards of Eressos, he was a wealthy man and a desirable thirty-five-year-old bachelor.

He returned to Eressos, met his fiancée, Eleni, and together they began the elaborate preparations for a formal wedding in the Greek Orthodox Church. These were festive affairs attended by virtually the entire population of the village, most of whom were related. In the summer of 1925, Eressos celebrated the marriage of Eleni and Herodotus, but shortly afterward, the young bride became ill and died in a matter of months. Herodotus spent the next six months in Eressos as a widower growing a long gray beard while he mourned his loss. (Vagelos men get prematurely gray hair, as I can attest.)

As he prepared to return to the United States, several villagers, unwilling to see this energetic, well-to-do, young compatriot leave the island a bachelor, approached him about arranging another wedding with one of their daughters. Herodotus decided he should indeed marry again, but this time, he took matters into his own hands. While preparing to marry Eleni, he had visited a special dressmaking shop for wedding clothes in the port city of Mytilene and met an adroit, attractive seamstress. He had been so taken with Marianthi Lambrinides that he boldly invited her to the wedding, but she of course refused his invitation. Now a widower, he persuaded Marianthi and her family that she should marry him. On January 17, 1926, she and Herodotus John Vagelos, his mourning beard neatly cropped, were wed at the island's capital in a beautiful white church overlooking the Aegean Sea. They sailed to America a month later.

Marianthi, like her husband, had Turkish connections. She had been born in Smyrna (now Izmir), Turkey's second-largest port city, which had a large Greek population that dominated the finance and commerce of the region. In 1922, war broke out between Turkey and Greece, and the Turks of Smyrna began to loot and burn the city. The Greek population fled for the coast, Marianthi's family among them. Some of the Turkish soldiers they encountered helped them, but some robbed them; others killed Marianthi's uncle and two men from her family's party in front of their children. At the waterfront, pushing their way through terrified crowds, they boarded the last ship out of Smyrna. For the rest of her life, my mother feared and distrusted Turks.

Her family had lost all its possessions except for a few clothes, but fortunately her entire immediate family – parents, three sisters, and two brothers – survived and escaped to Mytilene. There, she worked in the dressmaking shop where, three years later, she met the man who became her husband.

* * *

Herodotus had a sentimental streak. He remained loyal to people and even to objects long after they lost their value. He refused to move his new wife into the house he had built for Eleni. He had a second house built in Westfield, and in the meantime, he and Marianthi lived with Thucydides, his wife, and their daughters. The ice cream and candy business was prospering, and soon after moving into their new house, Herodotus and Marianthi started a family of their own.

Their first child, Joan, was born on July 23, 1928, and their second, Pindaros Roy Vagelos, on October 8, 1929 – just three weeks before the stock market crashed. My grandfather had named his sons for notable ancient Greeks: Thucydides, the great historian of the fifth century B.C.; Homer, the poet; Phillalithes, the great soldier Philip of Macedon. Another brother, who died during the typhoid epidemic of 1898, had been named for the poet Pindar. My father gave me that brother's name, Pindaros. In Greek style, my father's "American name," Roy – the anglicized version of Herodotus – became his son's middle name.

Since Pindaros – pronounced "PIN-da-ros" – was a bit long for everyday use, I became Pindo to my family and friends. That's what they call me even today. But my teachers insisted on using Pindaros even though they found it hard to pronounce. They weren't the only ones who butchered the name, and finally I asked my father what I should do. "Use your father's name," he replied. "Use Roy." I was a bit concerned because it was not a Greek name, but I became Roy and simplified my education.

At school I needed all the help I could get. I had barely survived the first grade in Westfield, receiving an E (on a scale of A–F) in spelling and a D in reading. Music, which I still love, was my only strength, and I hadn't yet mastered reading when I squeaked through the second grade. I was among the weakest students in the school and I knew it. So did my father.

I can now look back and see that while hovering on the brink of school failure, I was actually learning a great deal about life at the Westfield Sweet Shoppe and at home. From an early age I understood how hard you had to work just to hold your own. Being part of an extended family, I also knew something about community and interdependence. We celebrated all of the Greek holidays at home, and these occasions brought together all of the aunts and uncles, cousins and spouses.

Easter is the most holy day of the Greek Orthodox Church. During Lent, our family observed the ritual of fasting and ate no meat. During Holy Week, the week between Palm Sunday and Easter, we ate mostly vegetables and a few animal products such as milk or cheese. On the Saturday before Easter Sunday, my mother prepared red Easter eggs, special Easter pita, and a special soup, *patsa*, made with tripe and other sheep organs mixed with egg and lemon (*avgolemono*) laced with garlic.

Easter eve was spent at church in Newark, at that time the only Greek Orthodox church near home. Just before midnight, the priest, accompanied by special music, would intone, "Christ is risen," and everyone in church would light a candle. The congregation then poured out of the church to break the fast. Milling around on the sidewalk, everyone cracked his or her own red easter eggs against someone else's. The winners – those whose eggs stayed intact – congratulated the losers and circulated among the crowd, cracking other eggs until their own eggs broke. The cracked eggs were then quickly devoured along with Easter breads. Then it was home to enjoy the *avgolemono* soup, or *patsa*, on this very happy and festive occasion. The next day, Easter proper, families gathered together. For us, it meant all the American Vageloses joined under one roof or another to share a feast of roast lamb with many side dishes and wonderful desserts.

Christmas was equally festive but quite different. We didn't go to church on either Christmas Eve or Christmas Day. However, Greek families in the United States, including mine, quickly adopted the Christmas tree, a tradition entirely unknown in Greece, along with the idea of Christmas presents and a celebratory party. In Greece, the big celebration was on New Year's Day, when people exchanged gifts, danced, and sang with their relatives and friends.

At all our family parties, everyone spoke Greek and ate Greek food: roast lamb, special homemade breads, and fresh salads with olives. Appetizers included *keftedes* (meatballs made with red wine, garlic, and oregano), pickled vegetables, and stuffed grape leaves (filled with either meat or rice and spices). The desserts – all made with honey – were baklava, *galatoboureko*, *koulourakia*, and *karethopita*. The appetizers were accompanied by *raki* (Turkish for ouzo), a colorless grape distillate flavored with anise. With the meal, the grownups drank Greek wines, both white and red. As the evening wore on, the adults would begin to sing Greek folk and love songs, many of which described the islands they had left years ago.

These Greek family traditions were central to our little community. Watching my father help other members of the family come over from Greece taught me important lessons about our responsibilities to others. Even during the worst years of the depression, when we were just scraping by, Herodotus and Marianthi helped their relatives in whatever way they could. Like many other American immigrants, they considered themselves fortunate to be in a place where people could build new lives and had access to greater economic opportunities. They sent money and packages of clothing to those who were still in Greece. Over time, my father arranged the passage of other relatives to America, meeting them at the dock, housing them for months, and helping them find work, homes, and even mates. He offered advice, mediated disputes, and lent relatives money when they needed it. When we had a guest bedroom, it was always occupied by newly arrived Greek relatives or friends. All the guests ate with the family and learned about this country from my parents, who had themselves only been here a few years.

Dad, who was easygoing and good natured, nevertheless had a strong set of beliefs that he repeated to us frequently. America, he said, is the most wonderful country in the world. If you work hard, you can achieve anything here, and the role of the immigrant is to work very hard so the children can get an education and lead a "better life." The Greek culture and language, he told us many times, needed to be preserved in our community and family. Greeks are inherently smarter, more able, more efficient, and harder working than Americans. I, of course, believed him until I was about twelve, when I began to notice that all other immigrants said the same things about their own group. Nevertheless, we heeded my father's admonitions, and my parents never socialized with Americans. It was shocking when my sister Joan defied my father by dating and ultimately marrying an American. All ten of our cousins, who had been born and raised in America, married into Greek families. Me too. Although it is important to work hard and plan your future, my father explained, fate and luck play a role in every life. It is important to help others in the Greek community. Family always comes first. Friends come and go, he said, but your family will always be with you.

***

In 1938, we moved back to Westfield to a two-bedroom apartment over a furniture repair shop next to the railroad tracks. Finally our lives settled down a bit. My parents continued to work very long hours, and money was still tight. After a few years in the Westfield apartment, our finances – along with those of many other Americans – began to improve even more, and the family was able to move to a small house on Walnut Street. There, we had a big garden. My dad was proud of his huge red tomatoes, which he shared with others by the boxful. We raised chickens for food, although sometimes weasels broke in and ate them, and later, during the Second World War, I raised and bred rabbits to supplement the family larder. After reading several books about how to do this, I built a large six-cage hutch for them. I fed and tended my animals, but when we needed meat, my father had to take over the job of killing the rabbit selected for dinner.

After we moved back to Westfield, our maternal grandmother, who had moved in with us when she could no longer live independently on Mytilene, helped with the cooking. Despite the hard times, my sister Joan and I were able to continue the music lessons we had begun while living in Cranford. My violin lessons and Joan's piano lessons each cost one dollar a week, and my father also paid twenty-five cents a week for our Saturday Greek lessons taught to six of us from the Westfield community by a traveling teacher.

Our family was close, and some of my strongest memories come from the Westfield Sweet Shoppe. The luncheonette had two distinctly different components. One was the store on Broad Street with its candy cases, soda fountain and booths, and ice cream freezers. My uncle Thucydides, his wife, Elpiniki, or their daughters, Irene or Effi – all of whom were fluent in English – greeted the customers at the door. My dad ran the manufacturing operations in a little two-story factory in an alley off the main street. The downstairs held all the ice cream equipment, including a huge cylindrical drum in which fresh milk and cream were heated to be pasteurized. The mixture was then cooled by circulating ice water through a jacket around the pasteurizer before being piped into the ice cream machines. My dad would add sugar and sliced and mashed fresh strawberries, peaches, or other fruits or flavorings (chocolate syrup or vanilla or coffee extracts) as the mixture was churned. Eventually, the ingredients became ice cream that was poured into five-gallon receivers, which were carted into a walk-in freezer. From there it went to the Broad Street store or was delivered to other retailers, including my uncles Homer and Phillalithes. As a little boy, I was allowed only to watch my dad and his helpers perform this miraculous operation.

Upstairs, however, my dad made his candies, and there our whole family plus our relatives contributed to the magic of transforming large slabs of chocolate and bags of sugar into confections: chocolate candies with centers of caramel, roasted nuts, delicious creams, and, my favorite, peanut brittle. Wearing a crisp white apron, dad would heat sugar and sugar concentrate in a large copper kettle. In another kettle, he browned the peanuts and then tossed them into the molten, caramelized sugar. Next, he poured the hot mass onto a large steel table, where it quickly cooled and was broken into irregular chunks. More than fifty years later, I think I could still make his style of tasty, fresh peanut brittle.

His candy business really boomed on the holidays, and his Easter and Christmas candies were the best. Everyone in the family pitched in at those times. My dad showed us how to work the hot materials and protected us with big white aprons and heavy gloves. At Christmas, we made multicolored ribbon candy and red-and-white candy canes from scratch, twisting and pulling the mixture by hand. One year, when I was about fourteen, we made an enormous candy cane, about five feet long, as the centerpiece for the store's Christmas window decoration. We then realized we could sell it if we could figure out how to price it. My entrepreneurial instincts were aroused, and I suggested that we raffle it off for about a nickel a chance. Customers loved the raffle, and we made far more money than we could have by selling the giant candy cane outright.

Easter candy was the most fun. We poured molten chocolate into tin molds to make chocolate rabbits and hollow eggs, which were then elaborately decorated with hand-piped swirls of white, pink, and yellow frosting. We were proud of these candies, and so each Easter, hoping to build his business, my dad invited the children and teachers from our grade school to tour the little candy factory and gave each one a sample to take home.

Like my dad, I preferred making things to selling them. Luckily, the two brothers' personalities fit the dual needs of the business. Thucydides, the salesman, read the newspaper and interacted with the customers. Dad largely stayed in the factory, wallowing in ice cream and candy, making the stuff of children's dreams.

* * *

All during my childhood, Dad delivered ice cream to homes, where it was served for dessert after big dinners on Sundays and holidays. I was always delighted to tag along. We drove our red truck up to the large houses with fancy lawns and gardens, found our way to the back door, and dropped off ice cream stored in a pail of ice. On holidays, the ice cream was shaped in fancy molds – turkeys, Christmas trees, and rabbits. The only people we saw were the kitchen help, who were all on a first-name basis with my dad.

Saturdays, however, Dad insisted on being free to be with us, and he would fully stock the store with ice cream and candies so they wouldn't run out. During the school year, we would visit Greek friends and relatives for coffee or dinner, storytelling, and reminiscing. In the summer, we would often go on family outings. At the last moment, I would be sent to get "gas money" from my uncle. He would take fifty cents from the cash register, and that would buy us enough gas to fight through the horrendous weekend traffic to the Jersey shore. Our red delivery truck also served as our family car. At dawn, Herodotus and Marianthi would fill the truck with excited children, sandwiches, and fruit, and we would head to the beach at Asbury Park, Point Pleasant, or Belmar. My father was the only Vagelos brother who could swim, and he enjoyed the beach almost as much as we did. We kids – my sisters and any cousins who were available that day – loved everything about these days at the shore – swimming, running around, being free from the shop, and being with our parents when they were relaxed and paying attention to us. My dream was to spend more than one day at the beach, staying the night at a beach cottage or motel perhaps. In the late 1930s, however, we could spend only one day. But to make up for this, on the way home Dad would stop at a favorite food stand where we would indulge in a hamburger and a Coke. These were the only times we ever ate out as children, but it was heaven after a long day in the broiling sun. Contented, I usually slept the rest of the way home.

* * *

While I was learning important things about families, communities, and work, those lessons in life weren't making me a scholar. I was an able young musician, playing my violin in the school orchestra and singing in the chorus. But, if anything, that encouraged me to think of myself as an entertainer. My older sister was doing very well in school, and the contrast between the studious Joan and the comedian Pindo only made me look worse. During our toughest depression year in Cranford, Joan had become an avid reader. She retreated every moment she could into the books the drugstore downstairs gave to her when they remained unsold. Resentful, I hid her books, but to no avail. She was stronger than I was, and she tickled me until I either confessed or we aroused our mother's ire.

While all this was going on, Herodotus remained gentle but firm. He kept telling me about relatives whose sons had received scholarships to college. He spoke of the advantages of working with a pen behind a desk instead of working long hours on one's feet in a store or a factory. Gradually, I began to get the picture and started to concentrate more of my energy on schoolwork – especially when I discovered that mathematics came easily to me and that my spelling was not too bad. Reading was still a problem, however. Herodotus and Marianthi were obviously pleased when I displayed a new enthusiasm for education, and that encouraged me to channel even more time and effort into class work. I didn't, however, become a loner. I still had plenty of close friends even though I no longer made them laugh in class. We played touch football after school, and I found I preferred studying with my friends rather than alone. My academic performance improved steadily, and to my surprise I found myself among the top group of students at Roosevelt Junior High School.

About that time, my father and his brothers began to fight bitterly over the business. They had diversified to accommodate the growing Vagelos clan. Thucydides had continued to manage the Westfield Sweet Shoppe, while Herodotus handled the production. But now Emmanuel and his wife had started to prepare and serve sandwiches and hot meals at noon and dinners in the evening. This arrangement was successful at first, but as their business started to pick up in the late 1930s, the three brothers began to disagree about how to share the profits. After cooperating informally for years, they found it necessary to bring in lawyers and formalize the organization in 1941. My father was horrified, but he felt he had no alternative. The family gatherings became less frequent and smaller, which was very sad for everyone. Two years later the split had widened, and my father sold his shares to Thucydides. He and Marianthi bought their own business, Estelle's Luncheonette, from another Greek family who had saved enough money to retire. So we moved once again, this time from Westfield to Rahway, a working-class town just five miles away.

For me this move was providential. It threw me into the hands of Miss Brokaw, who was the immediate source of my first epiphany. Miss Brokaw, an algebra teacher at the high school in Rahway, was young, enthusiastic, and interested in her students. When she saw that without much effort I could consistently score one hundred on her tests, she began to make me feel that I could do something important in life. She constantly challenged me with extra homework assignments, and I responded to that positive pressure by doing exactly what she had in mind. I kept ratcheting my performance up another notch as I learned the excitement of meeting the serious intellectual challenge of an advanced algebra curriculum. Thus, final traces of the clown were erased in math class right there in the public high school in Rahway, New Jersey.

Oddly enough, a second aspect of this transformation took place at Estelle's. Through high school, my sister and I continued to work at the family's luncheonette. My mother ran the kitchen, Herodotus was out front making sandwiches and handling the cash register, and my sister Joan waited on tables. Even my grandmother was occasionally pressed into service peeling potatoes – a task she clearly felt was beneath her. By the time Helen turned ten, she too was assigned regular hours at Estelle's. I split duty between the kitchen, where I peeled potatoes and washed dishes, and the fountain, where I was a soda jerk. My parents spent long hours there, and the family had dinner together at Estelle's every night except Sunday, when the place was closed. My dad taught me every aspect of running a small luncheonette from preparing the dinners and making sandwiches and sodas to washing the dishes and floor. It all had to be done, and it was all done by family members (later assisted by part-time waitresses when the business picked up).

When I was working the fountain and helping with the tables, I got to know our customers, especially the people who worked for Merck & Co., Inc., the big pharmaceutical company that was Rahway's leading business. Merck was only a few blocks from Estelle's, and many of its scientists and engineers regularly came over for breakfast, lunch, or dinner. Several of them impressed me with their intelligence and ability to talk about different ideas. I wanted to understand the things they talked about and to be educated like them. They talked about interesting chemical reactions I didn't understand. The chemical engineers discussed costs and efficiency and the purity of their products, and for the first time I saw people excited about their work. I decided I wanted to be like them and do work that improved people's lives.

The common language seemed to be chemistry, but the level was way over the head of a high school student. I found the rote experiments of high school chemistry dull and could see no relation between what I was doing and the processes discussed by the Merck engineers. But I knew enough to understand that a knowledge of chemistry was necessary to undertake the kind of work – making medicines – I was hearing about at Estelle's.

I started to see an interesting path opening ahead of me, and it was made possible only by going to college. Less than a third of my Rahway high school classmates would go on to college, but I was now determined to be part of that elite group. For some years, my father and Miss Brokaw – separately and in their own special ways – had been marking that trail while they waited for me to realize what I needed to do. Now I did, even though I still wasn't certain where higher education would lead me. All I knew was that math and science, especially chemistry, were my strengths. When I was in high school, my parents became convinced that I had inherited my grandfather's medical interests and abilities. But the conversations of the Merck researchers were all about chemistry, and that was the science I targeted.

Once I had a clear goal in mind, and once I understood that academic success in high school was essential to winning a scholarship to college, I turned up the intensity of my school work another notch. I concentrated especially on the courses that prepared for a technical career: math, physics, biology, and chemistry. I had to work every afternoon at Estelle's, so I couldn't play varsity sports, but I took part in intramural games and continued to play the violin since I could schedule my own practice sessions. Most of my intellectual energy was, however, now focused on science.

* * *

By the time I was a senior at Rahway High School, in 1946–47, I was class vice president and an honor student on a fast track in science and mathematics. Academic accomplishment brought out a fiercely competitive streak in my personality, which is something I can't remember having when growing up in Westfield. It was something I would never lose in the years that followed. If anything, it became even stronger as my career unfolded. At this fork in the road, Joan and I took different paths. I am certain she was smarter than I was (her studies came easily to her, while I had to work hard), but the Greek tradition was powerful and we adhered to it. Young men who could make the grade took college preparatory classes. That's what I did. Young women, assumed to be headed for marriage, took secretarial classes. That's what Joan did. Much later, Joan returned to school and graduated from college, but in the 1940s, in our corner of Rahway, New Jersey, talent was less powerful than ethnic tradition.

In my senior year in high school, I applied to three universities: Rutgers, the University of Pennsylvania, and Johns Hopkins. Hopkins, which had a sterling reputation in science and medicine, interviewed me at a hotel in New York City. Upon discovering that neither of my parents had attended college, the interviewers asked if I had any questions. When I said no, they promptly sent me back to Rahway. Fortunately, Rutgers and Penn were more tolerant of the sons of Greek immigrants who ran a luncheonette. Both accepted me and offered scholarships – a full scholarship at Rutgers and only a half at Penn. I knew, however, that Penn offered more courses in chemistry and had a more distinguished faculty. Penn's program prepared students better for graduate school and medical school, and it had one of the great schools of medicine right on its campus. Rutgers had no medical school, and so I chose Penn, which offered everything I wanted in a university.

* * *

I had never seen the Penn campus before my parents drove me and my single suitcase down to Philadelphia in September 1947 and dropped me at the gate on 37th Street and Woodland Avenue. Excited and apprehensive, I entered a phase of my education that would reshape my life. Beyond the gates were dormitories built around large quadrangles of green lawn. The classrooms and laboratories that absorbed my time over the next three years sprawled on both sides of Woodland Avenue, which divided the campus. I knew very soon that I had made the right decision in choosing Penn. I found exactly what I was looking for, including the opportunity to set my own pace and to explore the many new areas of science that intrigued me. I was particularly excited by a course in organic chemistry given by Professor Alan Day. Organic chemistry dealt with the molecular building blocks of all living organisms, and I found it exhilarating to study that process. Although others found the course very tough, I was so intrigued by learning how new molecules were formed that I did exceedingly well and immediately enrolled in an advanced course on the same subject – also taught by Professor Day. From that time on I was solidly hooked on chemistry.

I was not drawn to literature and the humanities because, in part, of my earlier difficulty in mastering English. Even today, fifty-five years later, I see the effects of those grade-school problems on my life. I still rarely read for entertainment. In addition, I had always found it difficult to memorize things and had run into trouble with poetry and history. During high school I could think my way through a complex problem in math, chemistry, or physics, but I could not memorize a poem, dates, or the names of various parts of a dissected frog. My problem was so obvious that, when the principal asked me to give the valedictory address, he suggested that I read it rather than speak it without notes as others traditionally did.

In the Penn science classes, memory was not critical, and I could analyze my way through problems – probably faster than most others did. Here I began to hit an intellectual stride that I managed to maintain for the rest of my life. I became an addict. When I found major intellectual problems to solve in chemistry, or physics, problems that sustained my interest, I became energized. I learned how to concentrate, to stay focused for longer and longer periods of time. I found I could carry a heavier-than-normal course load and still excel. Did the immigrant Greek background, the hardships of the depression years, the memory of my mother bent over her sewing, my father's long hours in the shop, have anything to do with the kind of high-energy drive for achievement I was exhibiting? I believe they did, as they have for many other immigrants in America. Studying late at night, I would sometimes remember how hard both my parents worked and reflect on the difference between their lives and those of our customers at Estelle's.

The only significant break in my schedule was rowing. My father thought sports were silly and childish, but I knew I wanted to do athletics in college, when I no longer had to work at the luncheonette. During my senior year in high school, I had swum and played basketball regularly, and the summer after graduation, I spent long sessions lifting weights and doing calisthenics to get myself in shape for college sports. At Penn I rowed the whole time with the lightweight crew and served as stroke oar in the eight-man racing shell. I could do this partly because rowing was a sport in which students started at a beginner's level because most high schools didn't offer it. Prep schools did, but the number of prep school graduates in the Penn class of 1950 was quite low.

The discipline of rowing in a racing shell – the physical exertion and team coordination – fit my personality. During my freshman year, we were undefeated the entire season. Since I hadn't been able to do serious sports in high school, I felt I had achieved what had been a distant dream. My teammates became my closest friends. The team rowed together every day except Sunday, we ate together at the training table at Franklin Field, and we partied together after races. As a sophomore I was selected for the varsity boat and spent my remaining years at Penn training and racing at every major university that had competitive rowing. I became well acquainted with Harvard, Yale, MIT, Brown, Cornell, and Princeton. Rowing proved a great entrée to life outside academics. From rowing I learned the benefits of being in peak condition, the importance of teamwork and team leadership, and the positive impact physical fitness could have on my intense studies in chemistry. After I rowed, my concentration was always better.

Other than rowing, however, I focused on my studies and was able to graduate in three years. Today many students plan their careers before they leave high school, but I was so completely immersed in my courses and my rowing that I didn't worry about where all that would lead me. Then, as graduation loomed, I suddenly had to decide what I was going to become when I left Penn. I hurriedly started to talk to friends, some professors, and my family. Judging from these conversations and my own reflections, I concluded the top two contenders were graduate training in chemistry or medicine.

I loved chemistry. Organic chemistry in particular had continued to be incredibly exciting, and I wanted to pursue a career in which I might make important intellectual and practical contributions to this field. But my family heritage intervened. My father talked about my grandfather, who, after graduating as a physician from the University of Athens in 1881, spent his life healing people in both Greece and Turkey. Medicine, both Herodotus and Marianthi argued, would maximize the potential impact of my knowledge of chemistry. The connections between the two were pretty vague for me at that time, but I thought I might put chemistry to work in understanding disease, and so I got more and more excited about medicine.

The core of medicine as a profession was practical help. The Vagelos household had always had a strong tradition of giving a helping hand to family members and close friends. Inside my head I heard my parents and relatives saying, "You have to do things for others." This was the kind of deeply grooved voice that stays with you for an entire lifetime, and now it guided me away from chemistry and toward medicine. Medicine would enable me to satisfy my addiction to serious intellectual challenges while also learning to heal others.

Fortunately, I had time to enroll in several courses in biology. They were required for admission to every medical school, but I hadn't taken any since I seemed to be drifting toward graduate work in chemistry. But now I was headed for medical school, and I didn't change course again. My family was extremely proud of this and of what I had accomplished at Penn. They were especially proud when I was inducted into Phi Beta Kappa, the national honor society, and admitted to Columbia University's College of Physicians and Surgeons. Their son was pointed toward an honorable profession, and that was important to the Vagelos clan.

* * *

But then in the fall of 1950, my triumphant march through academia came to an abrupt halt. At the College of Physicians and Surgeons (P&S to us), I quickly rediscovered academic anxiety. I found that I was launching my study of the ultimate biology – the anatomy of the human body – with the least possible preparation. What I had mastered at Penn was problem solving in science, my strength, but medical school's basic introduction to human anatomy required memorization, my weakness. I was deeply distressed and uncertain what to do. Returning home at Christmas break, I was on the edge of failing this basic course, and I contemplated ending my medical career before it began. Fearful of failure, I nevertheless returned to New York and survived my first year in medical school by grinding my way through anatomy.

I then spent the summer at home in Rahway working as an intern for Merck & Co., Inc. – my first stint there. Years of listening to company engineers talking hadn't taught me how to spell the company's name because when I applied for a position, I wrote to "Merk." Luckily, the company hired me anyway and put me to work checking the toxicity of drugs and screening for new antibiotics. I would like to claim that the work engaged my imagination, planting a seed that would bear

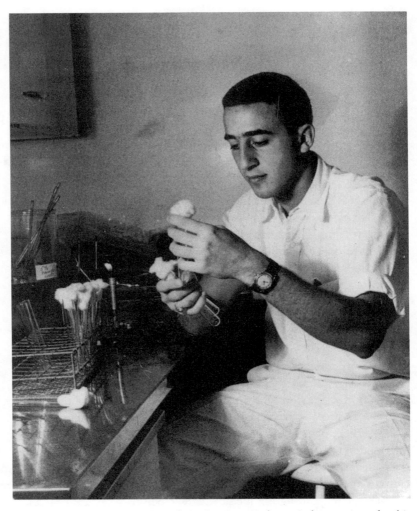

Roy as a summer intern at Merck & Co., Inc., Rahway Laboratories, after his first year of medical school, 1951.

fruit many years later when I devoted twenty years of my life to developing new drugs. That would be dramatically satisfying, but it wasn't like that at all. I enjoyed working with various individuals in the lab – professionals like those who had impressed me at Estelle's. I was in the lab of Dr. Harry Robinson, who had been involved in the early work leading to the discovery of streptomycin, the first antibiotic effective against tuberculosis. He had an M.D. as well as a Ph.D., and he seemed to me to have a thorough understanding of almost every important medical and scientific subject from how bacteria grow to the latest treatment for infectious diseases. But the personal relationships couldn't make up for the nature of my daily work. At first I found it interesting to see what went on at the Merck laboratories, but the routine, almost mechanical nature of the research soon left me bored. The screening involved carefully controlled, repetitious tests (called assays) to find out if a particular substance was active against bacteria. You could do these tests for a year or a decade and find nothing of value. Even though I knew that the Merck laboratories were widely respected as a state-of-the-art operation, the rote tasks they assigned me were deadly dull. After that summer, I had no intention of ever returning to Merck or any other pharmaceutical company. The only positive result was to make medical school and a career in medicine look even more attractive.

During the following years at P&S, I became deeply engaged in mastering medicine. I became especially interested in cardiovascular disease and began to contemplate a career in clinical cardiology, treating patients who had suffered heart attacks or strokes. In the back of my mind, however, was the idea that biochemistry, or the chemistry of living things, might provide the basis for understanding much of cardiology and of the rest of medicine. I had come to believe that all diseases (other than infectious diseases) resulted from aberrations in the body's chemistry, which was a new idea at that time. If biochemistry, when fully developed, was going to be the Rosetta Stone of modern medicine, then I might be able to fuse my intense interest in basic mechanisms at the chemical level to my growing love for clinical medicine. This left me contemplating two different career tracks and experiencing a tension that would finally be resolved a few years later in a different setting.

The second-year program at P&S focused on the diagnosis and treatment of disease. We studied pharmacology, pathology, and bacteriology and began to explore clinical medicine and surgery. My coursework that year went exceedingly well. I was very impressed by the faculty and my classmates for their enormous capacity to understand what was known about diseases and their deep dedication to patient care.

In my third year, I encountered the legendary Dr. Robert F. Loeb, chairman of the Department of Medicine. This towering figure was coauthor of the *Textbook of Medicine* used in many medical schools and revered at Columbia, where it was the bible for both faculty and students. Loeb had an encyclopedic knowledge of all of medicine and had done important research on Addison's disease and diabetes. He was certain that there was only one way to diagnose and treat any disease – his way. He went to considerable trouble to be absolutely confident that every P&S graduate left school with a solid grip on Loeb's essential knowledge.

The Loeb program began at his first meeting with our class of 125 students. He had already memorized all of our names and faces, and so he called on us by name, leaving no doubt in our minds that any slip on our part would be recorded. We had already heard many Loeb stories and knew that he was a terrific diagnostician. But we also knew he had a sadistic streak that emerged when he did medical rounds. Marching through the open wards of the Presbyterian Hospital, Loeb fired a constant stream of questions at the six to eight nervous students trailing behind the master.

Stopping at each bedside, Loeb expected the target of his inquiry to instantly produce *the* correct answer about the patient's malady. Sometimes students froze, unable to remember information they knew very well. When a student hesitated, Loeb seemed to enjoy ridiculing him or her. Some broke into a sweat and began to stutter. Sometimes Loeb's rapid-fire questioning and derisive comments were so overwhelming that the women students broke down and cried, embarrassed in front of their patients and peers.

Terrified by these encounters, we learned the Loeb medical dogma extremely well. I survived his rounds relatively unscarred. I perspired heavily several times, but I neither stuttered nor cried and was able to answer most of his questions. In fact, I enjoyed clinical medicine so much that I began to set my sights on internal medicine, which involves diagnosis and treatment with medications, still possibly leading to a subspecialty in cardiology.

The path to internal medicine grew even more attractive during our fourth year, which was entirely clinical and introduced us to pediatrics, neurology, gynecology, and obstetrics. Now we were beyond the reach of Dr. Loeb, who concentrated his sharp wit and encyclopedic mind mainly on third-year students unless, of course, we sought him out. I did so rather casually one afternoon toward the end of my fourth year. I was finishing my work in obstetrics and, with no delivery scheduled, I joined the rounds with Dr. Loeb, his string of third-year students, and a group of foreign dignitaries. Most students avoided him after their third year, but I had always done well in his classes, and unfortunately I wasn't afraid. As we stopped at the bed of a patient with inflammation of the kidney (acute glomerulonephritis), Loeb asked one student after another for the incubation period of the disease. As each confessed ignorance, Loeb's anger mounted. Finally, wheeling to me, he said, "Vagelos, tell these third-year students what *every* P&S student should know!" I had to admit I didn't remember either. Loeb turned to the visitors and berated me. To illuminate just how disappointed he was, he told the group that he had selected me as one of the two P&S students to receive a choice internship at Boston's Massachusetts General Hospital. I was stunned – stunned to learn about my internship, stunned by the manner in which I was told, and stunned at my foolishness in putting myself on Loeb's firing line so casually. Later that day, I walked past Dr. Loeb and his wife and heard him telling her how disappointed he was in me: "This is the person I was telling you about," he said.

* * *

Despite the stressful training at P&S, I managed to have an active social life in New York City. I dated several student nurses and a chorus girl from the Radio City Music Hall. None of my relationships became serious, however, until Christmas recess 1951. That's when I met Diana Touliatou at a party given by a friend from the University of Pennsylvania. Although I talked to practically everyone, the most interesting time I spent that evening was with Diana, a first-year student at Barnard, which was then the women's division of Columbia. As we chatted, it became clear that we had much in common. Her parents, Greek immigrants from the island of Kefallinia in the Ionian Sea, had settled in New York City in Washington Heights. She was a scholarship student who shared my interests in music and sports. I was immediately taken with her personality, intelligence, and striking good looks. It came very close to love at first sight.

She and I promised to see each other again, and I returned to medical school with a new view of my future. By the time I finished medical school, we had become familiar visitors to each other's families and knew that at some point soon we would marry. Before we could be married, however, she had to finish college and I had to come to grips with my year of internship at Mass General.

In 1954, there were only twelve internships in medicine at Massachusetts General Hospital (MGH), Harvard's premier teaching hospital (the other two being Beth Israel and Peter Bent Brigham). The intern-ships at Mass General were perhaps the most coveted positions in American medicine because of the extraordinary quality of the faculty and the other people in training. They were also probably the most trying. While I felt fortunate to be selected, I was unprepared for the startling transformation from the classroom and laboratory to the hos-pital. Along with one assistant resident (in his or her second year at MGH), I was now in charge of a ward with twenty acutely ill patients. The leap from solving abstract biochemistry problems in a test tube to the complex realities of patient care and healing pushed all twelve interns into a state of near shock. Suddenly bearing frightening respon-sibilities, we were all traumatized at first.

We drew together, quickly becoming a tight little community, which reminded me of how my family in Rahway always functioned. The clos-est bonding was between interns and assistant residents. Each intern formed a team with an assistant resident. They were together during the days but on duty alone on alternate nights and weekends. The team cooperated closely, sharing all their patients, eating together, and ex-changing vital information. We depended on each other, as well as on the nurses (who were unfailingly experienced and supportive) and on the more senior doctors, to care for our patients properly. I found that caring for an acutely ill patient brought out the best possible qualities in a person, and the assistant residents with whom I worked were, I believe, among the finest doctors in the world. We became close friends and met socially after finishing our rotations. I have remained close to some of these colleagues for forty-five years.

Our group of interns hardly lacked talent. One (Gerald Edelman) later became a Nobel laureate, and others outstanding medical re-searchers, department chairs, and leading physicians. Nevertheless, all of us leaned heavily on the assistant residents, especially in the begin-ning. We had diagnostic problems to solve involving patients whom we came to know – sometimes very well. New at making diagnoses, and always with an underlying fear of making mistakes, we interns needed to bounce our conclusions off our more experienced colleagues to get their insights and reassurances.

The fact that I was no longer in medical school came crashing home to me during one of my first solo evenings in charge of my ward. A comatose patient was rushed into the hospital. The emergency room physician told me the patient, who was being sent to my ward, was thought to be suffering from acute diabetic acidosis, a condition that occurs when a person requiring insulin to regulate blood sugar slips out of control because of a lapse in insulin treatment or an acute condition such as an infection or trauma that increases the insulin requirement. This can be fatal if not treated promptly. I knew from Dr. Loeb's dogma exactly how to diagnose and treat such cases. Having confirmed the diagnosis, I administered insulin and various intravenous salt solutions. I was very relieved when the patient slowly responded, awoke, and began speaking.

I was pleased, but the next morning my medical career suddenly became more complicated. When the assistant resident, Dr. Howard Rassmussen, arrived, the patient was sitting up in bed. After I described what I had done, Rassmussen said my treatment was quite all right, but he would have done it somewhat differently. I was stunned. The Loeb bible had been questioned, as it was again that same morning. When the visiting physician, Dr. Edward Bland, arrived, he said his procedure would have been somewhat different from either mine or Rasmussen's. Medicine, I suddenly realized, is not an exact science. It could not be learned and applied by rote, even from a body of knowledge as comprehensive as Loeb's. Once the disease state was understood, the physician could treat the patient in a variety of ways, using similar drugs and solutions on the basis of the blood sugar level, the amount of dehydration, the concentration of certain salts in the patient's blood, and so forth. Harvard medicine was different from Columbia medicine in that it was more flexible and left more to be determined by a thoughtful physician. It required more intellectual input. I was free to think, to use my understanding of the basic disease process, and to explore the "art" of medicine. I was no longer tied to the Loeb bible.

The physician who set the pattern of practice in clinical medicine at Mass General was Dr. Walter Bauer, Chief of Internal Medicine, Professor of Medicine at Harvard, and the antithesis of Dr. Loeb. Bauer was informal, friendly, sympathetic, and completely supportive of the young people in his service. He led by example – a very successful method I would try to emulate. He would question and examine the patient. He would then ask leading questions of the intern that led to the correct diagnosis and treatment. Trauma was not a component of the Bauer approach to teaching.

Although we were working long hours under intense pressure, I became deeply attached to clinical medicine. The hook, for me at least, was the opportunity to work closely with patients and to help them through their crises. Once again, Vagelos family traditions came into play. Healing offered an opportunity "to do things for others." Since patients in the 1950s normally stayed in the hospital longer than they do today, I came to know many of them extremely well. A patient with a heart attack, for example, might stay in the hospital for several weeks and be seen daily by his or her physician. After discharge, he would see his doctor weekly for months. This personal, helping aspect of clinical practice had great appeal for me.

Bear in mind that what we could do therapeutically was relatively limited in those days, no matter how much contact we had. One of my patients was a woman about fifty years old with chronic liver disease. She came into the hospital vomiting blood that was hemorrhaging from swollen blood vessels in her esophagus and stomach. At that stage of the disease, the only way we could treat her was by inserting a tube into her esophagus, inflating it, and stopping the bleeding by putting pressure on the ruptured blood vessels. Once the bleeding stopped, the tube was removed. If this procedure sounds gross, it was. The most common cause of such bleeding is alcoholic cirrhosis of the liver, and, indeed, my patient was a very serious alcoholic.

The next day and over the next six weeks, we placed her on a special diet to help resuscitate what little functioning liver she had left. Liver regeneration in such patients is minimal, and thus the only hope for recovery and no future bleeding is for the patient to avoid further liver damage by avoiding alcohol. I talked to this patient daily about the potential problems from continued alcohol abuse. She was a nice woman with a very solicitous family who visited her daily. She and her children were obviously close. She told me she had at last learned her lesson and would never drink again. But six months later I was crushed to learn that she had returned to alcohol, bled again, and died at home. I could not believe I had failed so completely. Over the years, I learned more about the frustrations of dealing with addiction to alcohol and cigarettes. This first failure in Boston impressed upon me the limited ability we have as individuals to solve these problems and the necessity we have as a society to confront them.

As recently as 1954, physicians still understood very little about the fundamental nature of most diseases and even less about the precise manner in which the accepted treatments worked. Take, for example, a heart attack due to a clot in one of the arteries supplying oxygen-carrying blood to the heart. Current drugs can now help reduce the probability of heart attack. Both high blood pressure and high blood cholesterol, for example, are risk factors associated with heart attack. New drugs can normalize both. Heart attacks, the result of clot formation, can also be relieved by newly developed procedures such as coronary angioplasty in which an instrument is threaded into the heart blood vessel to open the blocked artery and restore blood flow. If the blockage is very severe or involves more than one artery, new vessels can now be grafted onto the heart through a coronary bypass to lead the blood flow around the blocked area and reestablish normal flow to the muscle. If these medicines and surgical procedures don't cure the deficiency, then the heart can actually be replaced by transplanting a heart from a donor. As I write about all this, I am struck anew by how far we have come in less than a half century. Neither these drugs, surgical procedures, nor transplants were available when I was an intern. Medicine has certainly been revolutionized.

During the 1930s and 1940s, medical researchers had developed sulfa drugs, penicillin, and streptomycin, and we were able to use those antibiotics against bacterial infections. But we had no drugs to treat viral infections; we gave patients with rheumatoid arthritis massive doses of aspirin and wet hot packs. We could do even less for those with neurological problems such as Parkinson's disease or psychiatric problems such as depression or schizophrenia. Many in our wards had suffered heart attacks (for which we used anticoagulation), bleeding peptic ulcers (treated with special diets and, when that failed, surgery), or strokes (for which there was no effective therapy).

We frequently struggled with problems that were far beyond our knowledge and that stretched the hospital's resources. In the summer and fall of 1955, Boston suffered a poliomyelitis epidemic. It was heartbreaking to see hundreds of children and adults stricken. The city divided the acute polio cases by age group, sending most of the children to the Boston City Hospital and most of the adults to MGH. Many of those brought into our wards were partially or completely paralyzed after the virus attacked their central nervous systems. There was almost nothing we could do except try to keep these patients alive while we waited for the worst effects of the polio to pass.

About this time, I began to become concerned about one of the financial aspects of medicine. Patients entering MGH had to document their ability to pay. Massachusetts General was extremely charitable and committed to its vision of public service. All its patients received excellent care, even if they were indigent and could pay nothing. But patients who were neither rich nor poor – who had struggled to own their home but had few other assets – were in jeopardy of losing their house if the medical expenses were too great. Few people had health insurance, and the infirm aged were particularly vulnerable. They were often in a position to lose their total savings and their homes when struck down by a devastating illness. My own family's economic difficulties in the 1930s probably left me especially sensitive to this problem – one for which we had no solutions in the 1950s and with which we are still struggling fifty years later.

After finishing my internship, I spent the late summer and early fall as the resident in charge of all the adult polio patients who had to be in tank respirators to continue breathing. With thirty to fifty respirators working at one time, we immediately went into an emergency program, eliminating all elective surgery and mustering our staff to provide the extra care that was needed. We brought in volunteers to help, and the interns and residents signed in for extra duty on top of the 100- to 110-hour weeks they were already working.

This was the kind of experience that stays in your mind long after the crisis has passed. Initially, the patients were in the acute paralytic phase of polio, and a few succumbed to complicating bacterial infections that we couldn't adequately treat. This was my first exposure as a physician to large numbers of people who were completely paralyzed and unable to do anything on their own. At first, I was profoundly depressed about their plight. There was a terrible feeling of helplessness because we could do nothing to cure their disease and very little to relieve their paralysis once the virus had struck. The sense of tragedy was heightened by our knowing that researchers in the United States – most prominently, Jonas Salk – were on the very edge of producing an effective vaccine for wide distribution throughout the country. In 1954, public health authorities had administered the Salk polio vaccine to over 650,000 children. Those well-publicized field trials were an impressive example of what could be accomplished when state and national public health authorities, private foundations, university scientists, and pharmaceutical companies worked together to achieve a common goal. In the spring of 1955, when I was completing my internship, the successful trials were front-page news in Boston and all over the United States. But the vaccine was not available in time to prevent the fall 1955 epidemic.

Over the following months, though, we were encouraged as we watched most of our polio patients get better and better. Some recovered completely. Many with the worst cases of paralysis were able to recover to a surprising extent. The great majority left the hospital either walking with braces or in wheelchairs. I was impressed by their ability to face this crisis without losing hope. That experience made me realize how important it is in clinical practice to keep trying to help patients recover even when the outlook seems terrible. Hope plays a role in healing that I would never underestimate.

It was not easy to exude hope during our worst crises. Several times that year, all we could do was barely cope with the pressures on the hospital – and on us. We all suffered numbing sleep deprivation, and too often we had to deal with diseases we could do little to treat. On the other hand, the faculty we worked with was the best in the nation, and we knew we were delivering the best possible care to patients who were very sick. We had the smartest people and the most sophisticated resources – the most modern medicines and instruments – available at that time. My residency at Mass General strengthened my commitment to clinical practice and to a life-long effort to improve healthcare.

*   *   *

Coping was easier for me because I was sharing that experience with Diana. During my internship, she visited Boston from time to time. Her accommodations were the morgue in the antique building next door to the hospital where there were rooms for the only woman intern in our program.* Diana wasn't fazed by the morgue, her antique accommodations, or my schedule, and she took a deep interest in what our little group of interns was experiencing. She always listened sympathetically to my complaints or worries and set up dinners with friends that took my mind off my patients temporarily. Occasionally, she arranged for

---

* The woman intern was Kathy Spreng, who married Tom Waldman, one year behind us as an MGH intern. Kathy went on to have a productive medical career, and Tom became an important immunologist at the National Institutes of Health.

us to attend the Boston Symphony on my nights off (where, alas, I usually slept through much of the concert). During that tense year, she and I were able to see each other about every four months, and by this time, we had both passed muster with our respective families. Mine would have loved and accepted Diana regardless of her background. But the fact that her parents were both Greek was decidedly a plus for my father and mother. I sensed the same kind of easy acceptance when I visited her family in Washington Heights at the corner of 189th Street and Wadsworth Avenue.

Our families were remarkably similar. Both spoke Greek at home and supported relatives staying in Greece or making the challenging transition to the United States. Both went to considerable lengths to educate their children as much as possible. Diana's father had manufactured candy for wholesale when he first came to this country, but the Great Depression wiped out that business. He finally got another small business going, this time wholesaling coffee to hotels and restaurants, including Estelle's Luncheonette in Rahway, New Jersey.

After our marriage, our families always celebrated the high holidays – Christmas and Easter – together, either in Rahway or Washington Heights. The cooking was always done by the mother of the house. Subtle differences between the families were probably noticeable only to other Greeks. Cooking was one example. My family made certain cakes – especially the New Year's pita – with a spice (*masticha*) made from the gum of a tree that grows on the island of Chios (near Turkey) and on the Turkish mainland. Of course no one in my family *ever* identified any part of their cuisine as Turkish. When Greeks think of Turks, they reflexively remember how the Turks had subjugated Greece for four hundred years (1453–1821) and later burned Smyrna in 1922. The relationship resembles that between Jews and Arabs. When I ate dinner at Diana's home, I understood the difference between food from the Ionian side of Greece and cooking touched by Turkish culture. And I loved them both.

So too with language. On occasion Diana, very much the Greek scholar, would laughingly ask me to explain the meaning of a "Greek" word I had used. As she knew, my conversation was sprinkled with Turkish words that my parents had acquired during their childhood in Smyrna or Mytilene.

There were other differences between Diana and me. My education was heavily weighted toward science and was relatively narrow. Hers was extremely broad. She majored in economics and history at Barnard and was politically active. A campus leader (something foreign to me), she was elected a class officer every year and student body president as a senior. She invited me to my first Broadway play – I would never have splurged like that – and also gave me an informal art appreciation course, starting at the Met and the Museum of Modern Art. We loved the French Impressionists, but my all-time favorite was and is Van Gogh. I just love the light and color of his paintings. We also enjoyed the idiosyncratic sculptures of Calder, Henry Moore, and Giacometti.

We liked the way we complemented each other in those regards while sharing many enthusiasms. We were both intellectually inquisitive and extremely competitive. We competed in every sport we tried – especially swimming and tennis – without any hard feelings when the contest was over. By the time we learned all these things about each other, we were deeply in love, and our families doubtless had their fingers crossed hoping for a future together.

Actually, they had nothing to worry about. After Diana finished her degree at Barnard and I had survived my year of internship, we were married in the St. Spyridon Greek Orthodox Church in Washington Heights, where several P&S classmates and MGH assistant residents and residents attended their first Greek wedding. We had no settled future. I had a year of an assistant residency at Mass General to complete, but after that our destination was unknown. During the Korean War, I had been deferred from service to complete my medical training, and now I owed the U.S. government two years of military medicine. Indeterminacy notwithstanding, we were very much in love, energetic, and unbelievably optimistic about what life held for us. We were ready to start what we knew would be a lifetime partnership.

From the beginning, it was a type of partnership that has become less common in America since the 1950s. Diana took a position as a grader at the Harvard Business School, earning $3,000 a year, which was five times what I earned from my assistant residency at the hospital. This was the norm at this time, and we knew it would be temporary. Fortunately, the hospital supplied all of my meals (which I often shared with Diana), and we were able to rent a furnished apartment on Beacon Hill in Boston for $100 a month.

I concentrated on my career while Diana organized our home and family life and provided most of our income. I prepared for our future. We found great joy and comfort in our extended family. We also

Wedding of Roy and Diana.

shared important elements of my professional activity, including close friendships with my colleagues and their families. We had small dinner parties – usually with only one other couple since our apartment was so small – for my MGH colleagues or Diana's friends from the Business School. Diana would cook, we would listen to classical music, and we would all share a bottle of wine. Those were simple but wonderful times.

I never made a career choice without talking through the options carefully with Diana and our reaching a joint decision. We never disagreed on an important issue, which is probably why we are still married after forty-seven years. This style of life would, I think, have been uncomfortable for Diana if we had not shared so many values and interests. If we were starting out today, Diana's interests in political science, history, and economics, combined with her college leadership experience, would almost certainly have led her to law school and eventually politics. But back in the 1950s, the combination of Greek and American traditional values, as well as her personal priorities, kept her focused on our family.

* * *

Soon after our marriage, we faced an important decision. In 1955, while I was completing my assistant residency, we had to decide what to do about my military service. The war had ended, but the draft had not. I was unenthusiastic about practicing clinical medicine in the peacetime army, but I owed time to Uncle Sam so I enrolled as a medical officer in the U.S. Army.

When the chief nurse on my ward at MGH learned of my plans, she said, "You ought to consider going to the National Institutes of Health (NIH). That's where my boyfriend is doing his service." Her boyfriend, Daniel Federman, was doing research on diseases of the thyroid and caring for patients with endocrinological problems. Dan had been one of my favorite assistant residents when I was an intern, and thus it was a treat to go visit him in Bethesda, Maryland.

Because I could squeeze out only a twenty-four-hour break from my schedule, I flew to Washington, DC – the first time I had been on an airplane. The ticket cost $25, half my monthly salary at the hospital, but it was worth it. I was able to stay overnight in Dan's apartment and had a successful visit at the National Heart Institute. The Institute was able to arrange my transfer from the Army to the U.S. Public

Health Service so that I could work as an NIH research physician to fulfill my service obligations. I was to spend half my time over the next two years taking care of heart disease patients. As I explained to Diana on returning to Boston, the rest of my time would be spent doing research, which was not quite what I had anticipated when I flew to Washington. But I told her I had met a remarkable man who was doing some unusually exciting projects. As it turned out, Earl Stadtman's research was so exciting that it would change our lives and many other lives as well.

2 | *Hot Science in Big Government*

One of the important factors in the improvement in human health across the globe during the last half-century was the growth of basic research at the National Institutes of Health (NIH), a large government-funded organization headquartered in Bethesda, Maryland, just outside of Washington, DC. My assignment at NIH included the care of heart disease patients – a task for which my experience at Massachusetts General Hospital had prepared me very well. But I was also going to engage in basic research, and the search for fundamental scientific knowledge was another thing entirely. I was curious but a bit uncertain about what I could accomplish. My new mentor was also uncertain.

"I've never taken on an M.D. as a postdoctoral fellow," Earl Stadtman said during my interview at the National Heart Institute. All the scientists working with him had completed graduate training in biochemistry and, like Earl, they had Ph.D.'s. I was just a novice in biochemistry, having had only a single course in medical school. Up to this point in my career, my experiences with pure research hadn't particularly excited me. Stadtman let me know at our first meeting that he had some serious doubts about my interest in the kind of research he was doing. Nevertheless, he took the time to explain carefully and quietly the several projects under way in his laboratories at the National Heart Institute (one of NIH's eight institutes). He was so soft-spoken that I found myself leaning forward, trying to catch every word.

Stadtman had committed his life to understanding the biochemical processes that enable life forms to convert nutrients into energy, to grow, and to reproduce – in short, to perform all of the functions we associate with life. Everything we do, from reading a page in a book, to fighting off a cold, to converting our breakfast cereal into energy, results from biochemical reactions in our cells. Each reaction is instigated and regulated by a specific enzyme. These chemical processes occur in all living cells – whether plant, animal, microbial, or human. Stadtman's work was focused on microbial metabolism – the details of how microorganisms create and store energy and how their growth is regulated chemically by enzymes. He didn't think I would stay interested enough to make the same kind of commitment since I was a physician trained to take care of patients.

The longer he talked, however, the more excited I became. Like other catalysts, enzymes speed up a chemical reaction. Cellular enzymes are marvelously efficient catalysts; even tiny amounts produce astonishingly high reaction rates. Just a few molecules of enzyme can cause the rapid conversion of large amounts of sugar to fat within a cell. In addition, enzymes are highly specific: the ones that can break down fats to produce energy are entirely different from those that can produce a fat molecule for storage.

In the 1950s, Stadtman's work on enzymes put his lab on the cutting edge of biomedical discovery. Nineteenth-century studies of digestion had involved yeast, and the word *enzyme* is Greek for "in" (*en*) "yeast" (*zyme*). In the twentieth century, new developments in biochemical purification revolutionized what had become a sleepy corner of science. For the first time, biochemists discovered that enzymes are all proteins with complex molecular structures. Unlike other organic molecules (fats or sugars), proteins are uniquely able to function as catalysts. Protein molecules are large enough to contain different kinds of sites: sites that interact with substances being altered in the chemical reactions and sites that interact with substances that modify the rates of these chemical reactions. In the 1950s, scientists were just beginning to understand the three-dimensional structure of proteins and to chart with precision, using radioactive isotopes, where and how they function in the cell.

The human body has about one hundred trillion cells (that's 100,000,000,000,000, or fourteen zeroes); thus, instead of studying humans, scientists like Stadtman were analyzing bacteria – simple, single-celled organisms used for many years in research laboratories. Although a relatively simple life form, bacteria nonetheless contain from three to six thousand different kinds of molecules and synthesize as many as three thousand different proteins. Because they reproduce rapidly, bacteria can be studied to determine the impact of environmental changes (e.g., alteration of nutrients or temperature) on their biochemical reactions, and scientists can trace changes through several generations with considerable precision. Even working on simple cells, researchers can analyze some biochemical sequences that are universal; that is, they take place in all living animals and plants as well as bacteria.

By determining the biochemical sequences at the molecular level and then characterizing the controlling enzymes, biochemists were taking a giant step toward understanding life. Learning how to analyze normal, that is, healthy, activities of the cell, researchers could also provide a new understanding of how disease altered these biochemical reactions. Stadtman seemed completely unconcerned about the practical medical implications of what he was doing. His dedication was to basic science. I was intrigued by the basic research, but I was also attracted to the potential applications of enzymology in medicine.

I could see that Earl's microbial experiments had the potential to build a new biochemical foundation for modern medicine. That was something I had thought about in a vague, rudimentary way at medical school, where I had become interested in the body's ability to make and break down fats and sugars. Little was understood about these processes in the early 1950s, but it was obvious that the body could do this very efficiently. It was also evident that, with the new technology (spectrophotometers, radioisotopes, etc.) being introduced in laboratories, it was only a matter of time before someone would break open these fields.

Now I could see it was happening, and this was incredibly exciting. That first visit convinced me that a two-year stint at the National Heart Institute would satisfy two major passions I had developed. The first was clinical practice. For half of my service, I would be treating patients with heart disease and following them as their treatments progressed. The second passion was for intense intellectual experiences in problem solving. Enzymology, one of the hot sciences of the 1950s, was attracting a swarm of brilliant biochemists in addition to Earl Stadtman. They were lured by the opportunity to solve problems on the cutting edge of basic biochemical research. During that first visit, Stadtman convinced me I should try to join them.

Stadtman's doubts about my commitment to research were, I knew, perfectly reasonable. I would be starting from square one. But I was willing to take that risk, and so was Diana. With her interest in political science and history, she was also enthusiastic about spending the next two years in Bethesda, a short drive from Washington, DC.

* * *

The NIH is part of the Department of Health and Human Services, and its physicians and nurses are under the direction of the Surgeon General of the United States. Technically, I was in the Public Health Service during my two years at NIH, and that became important unexpectedly when I was threatened with a court-martial for insubordination. My problems arose over a tough diagnosis.

The case involved a patient who came into the National Heart Institute over the weekend when I was off duty. On Monday, I examined him and looked at the write-up by the admitting physician. The diagnosis was grand mal seizures (a severe epileptic attack) and a heart condition, but I couldn't find any serious problems with his heart. Besides, I didn't think a heart condition could be causing the seizures described in the patient's chart. I was puzzled. According to the report, he periodically suffered these intense attacks at night, wetting the bed and biting his tongue. Examining the X rays of his head, I saw no evidence of neurological damage. After examining him further to be sure I hadn't missed anything, I wrote a report saying that I couldn't find evidence either of heart disease or neurological damage. Still puzzled, I asked for a consultation with a neurologist.

That's where my trouble started. One of the top neurologists at NIH, a senior physician in the National Institute of Neurological Diseases and Blindness, swept in trailed by an entourage of foreign visitors. After examining my patient and the head X rays, he loudly announced, "There's *obviously* something wrong with his brain." He pointed to an "abnormal" area in the films, something I actually couldn't see. Then he demanded, "Who wrote this report?" When I claimed authorship, he said, "You could be guilty of malpractice for missing this diagnosis!" The correct diagnosis, he announced to his audience, was a brain lesion. When I again said I couldn't see any lesion in the X rays, he proclaimed to the foreign visitors that I was new on the case and inept.

That evening I made a serious mistake. Furious, I wrote him the kind of note that young people write when they are furious. I said that I didn't believe his diagnosis and that he had insulted me. I may have added a few stronger words – at any rate, the note sent him directly to the National Heart Institute's director demanding that I be court-martialed.

Even more incensed by this threat, I decided to do everything possible to confirm my conclusions about the patient. First, I needed to observe one of the seizures, which always occurred at night. The patient's room was just across from the nurses' station, and I arranged to leave the door slightly ajar so I could see what happened. I sat up all night at the nurses' desk, peering in through the cracked door. The patient experienced periodic pain, had a "seizure," and asked for morphine. Once the nurses administered the drug, the "seizure" stopped.

The morphine was a tip-off. People having seizures do not request morphine, a potent but addictive analgesic. They usually have no pain. Now I thought I knew what the problem was. Not only that, I knew how to confirm my diagnosis, and I didn't need a neurologist to help me. I called several city hospitals in downtown Washington, describing my patient. At one, the person I spoke to immediately recognized him: "Oh, you've got Charlie!" Surprised, he continued, "Charlie's up at the National Heart Institute? How'd he get in there?" Charlie, I learned, was a drug addict, and they were familiar with him and his "seizures" all too well at their hospital, where Charlie had mastered his routine.

I was furious with Charlie as well as the self-righteous neurologist. Our patient was faking these seizures to get doses of morphine, and the Institute had fallen for his scam. Confronting Charlie, I told him what the city hospital had reported and gave him five dollars. "Get yourself a cab," I said, "and get the hell out of here!" Charlie said, "OK, Doc," and left quietly.

The medical literature calls this kind of feigning behavior Munchausen syndrome. Cases are so rare that the director of the National Heart Institute (NHI) asked me to discuss Charlie at a teaching session for all NHI physicians, something I did very happily. I didn't mention the involvement of the neurologist, who, of course, did not attend the session.

So I wasn't court-martialed, but I did learn a lesson. I never again wrote a note when I was angry. For the rest of my two-year stint, I carefully avoided the neurologist and did not discuss the case again. With Charlie gone my clinical work floated along on a storm-free course.

* * *

Confident in the ward, I was anything but sure of myself in Earl Stadtman's laboratory. Earl gave me, his first M.D. postdoctoral fellow, his own personal copy of his preferred biochemistry textbook. At his suggestion, I would read a chapter and then we would sit in the laboratory after a long day of experiments and discuss the chapter and how that aspect of science was changing. Earl was a wonderful teacher. As a member of the NIH staff, he had no teaching responsibilities. But he nevertheless taught a course at the University of Maryland as well as one at the NIH night school, where he covered advanced topics in microbial biochemistry. His lectures were clear, succinct, and very popular among biochemistry graduate students and M.D.'s like me.

His one-on-one sessions with me in the lab resembled British university tutorials in which the instructor meets regularly with each student to discuss either assigned literature or experimental results. I realized how very fortunate I was to have one of the country's leading scientists guiding me, step by step, along the frontiers of biochemistry. I could ask him about any material that was difficult to understand, and of course he always had a clear explanation.

My other gateway to the discipline was a journal club that met twice a week. This little group included Earl, his wife Dr. Theressa Stadtman (herself a distinguished biochemist), several other senior scientists, and me. I was included because Earl considered these sessions part of the education program. He wanted everyone to learn to discuss science in an open forum. At each session, one of us discussed and evaluated a current article from a scientific journal. At that time in my life, I was uncomfortable speaking to any group, even a small one, and I was miserable speaking to a group in which everyone knew more about the subject than I did. Naturally I hated making presentations.

But I did them. I used brute force. My technique was simple. First I read the article and tried to grasp what it was about. On that initial pass, I usually failed. Then I reread the first paragraph, which usually contained references to other, earlier articles, and I would find and read them. If I still didn't understand the first paragraph, I would do the same thing with the references in the other articles, following the trail these scientists had left through their publications. By the time I finished the entire lot of articles, I was usually ready for my presentation.

In the meetings of the journal club, Stadtman was transformed. Literally. He was bald, except for a fringe of reddish-brown hair, and when he became agitated about one of the articles, which happened not infrequently, his forehead would turn red and his veins would stand out. His outbursts were all the more memorable because he was usually so quiet. "This *can't* be this way!" he'd shout. "These people are all wrong! This *can't* be this way!" Earl would tell us in blunt terms where the authors had, he thought, misinterpreted the experimental results. He had an eagle's eye for internal inconsistencies, and he frequently pointed to publications by others who had refuted the results being discussed. He loved pointing out scientific blunders, and he was especially careful in his own work and publications to make few if any mistakes. He had a deep appreciation for high-quality scientific research, and he was always willing to hand out praise when we discussed scientists making significant contributions to the discipline. But he was so intense and so knowledgeable about the science that I was initially intimidated and afraid to argue with him.

Gradually, as we worked our way through many of the major questions modern biochemists were trying to answer, I became more sure of myself. I got to the point where I could speak up and offer possible explanations when Earl raised a question. I even tried to defend some of the authors against the Stadtman attacks. In the intense atmosphere of the journal club I learned how both to criticize and to defend a scientific proposition. I soon developed a feel for this branch of science and found myself captivated by the intellectual currents reshaping the discipline.

* * *

Biochemistry, which essentially seeks to explain life on a molecular level, was making considerable progress in analyzing all three of the basic classes of organic molecules: carbohydrates, proteins, and fats (or lipids). Carbohydrates, which include sugars and starches, are a source of energy and can also be stored in the liver or muscle for later use. They can function as structural parts of cells, or they can line the surface of a cell, where they govern whether or not the cells react with antibodies. During the 1950s and 1960s, scientists were discovering how sugars are oxidized to derive energy and how the energy is utilized for muscle contraction – the basis of all motion. Similar progress was being made in the study of proteins, some of which are components of cell structure, some of which are antibodies that defend cells from outside attackers. Other proteins are hormones that control cell metabolism or enzymes. Proteins are large complex molecules built up of twenty-four amino acids in various sequences, and NIH scientists at that time were leading the work of determining the complete amino acid sequence of certain proteins and of showing that this sequence dictates the three-dimensional shape of the molecule. This was groundbreaking science, and NIH scientist Christian Anfinsen later received the Nobel Prize for this achievement.

I became obsessed with the advances being made in the study of fat, the most concentrated source of energy for cells and a depository for excess calories.* Several universities, funded by NIH, were investigating the process of how fat is converted to energy or forms cell membranes. Fat molecules (specifically phospholipid molecules) are one of the most important components of the cell membrane because they form a layer through which water, nutrients, and signals must pass to reach the interior of the cell. Cholesterol, a form of fat, is a structural component of all cell membranes, and it also circulates in the bloodstream where, when its concentration is too high, it can form plaques that cause heart attacks.

Guided by Stadtman, I began to explore fatty acid metabolism. It was clear to me that this would be some of the most exciting work I could imagine if I could hang on to what was happening in the laboratory – learn it and do it – while trying to master biochemistry. As I progressed, I began at some point to sense that this new science might lead to the ability to modify biochemical reactions – the basis for most drug discovery.

These were the glory days of NIH research, and frequently the scientists whose work I read for the journal club visited Bethesda. Their lectures helped me to understand the best research being done in the life sciences – in enzymology and other disciplines – everywhere in the world.

In the laboratory, I at first had to be shown how to take every step in running the reactions – from making simple solutions, to extracting enzymes from bacteria, to measuring enzyme reactions by following the conversion of one substance to another. I also had to be shown how

---

* Fats (lipids) come in three types: the triglycerides that make up body fat, phospholipids that are important components of the outer lining of all cells – called the cell membrane, and sterols such as cholesterol. Triglycerides contain three molecules of fatty acids (chains of carbon and hydrogen with oxygen at one end). The breakdown of triglycerides and fatty acids, which are released from the fat, yields energy.

to use every piece of equipment, from a Beckman spectrophotometer, which measures the characteristic ultraviolet spectrum of biochemicals, to radioactive-isotope-counting equipment. Stadtman, a hands-on researcher, walked me through some of the basic research techniques himself, and others in the laboratory – including a technician – were also good teachers.

* * *

I quickly became intrigued by the complexities of fatty acid metabolism – the process by which cells break down or synthesize these acids. I could just as easily have chosen to study sugars such as glucose, which undergo entirely different reactions and serve different functions (such as muscle contraction) in the cell. But nudged gently by Stadtman, I made an initial choice that would dramatically shape my life for the next thirty years and would ultimately touch the lives of millions of persons around the world. Stadtman had done considerable groundwork on this issue, and the subject was already becoming very productive. Like most hot niches, fatty acid and lipid metabolism were also being explored by other scientists, and I quickly found myself in an anxious race to understand how the cells synthesize the fatty acids that are building blocks for lipids.

The lab tutorials with Stadtman, the lectures by distinguished scientists, and the journal club combined to form a powerful whirlpool, pulling me deeper, emotionally and intellectually, toward basic research and away from clinical medicine. My obsession with the art of healing didn't disappear, but more and more of my hours were filled with problems issuing from Stadtman, whose research style required that lab work be done using two different experimental approaches. Stadtman was unusually meticulous, and I was strongly influenced by his cautious approach to experimentation. I was being transformed into a research scientist, and this second epiphany resembled my first. In each case, I had a mentor: in Rahway, Miss Brokaw; at NIH, Earl Stadtman. Both transformations were gradual and partial. In both instances I was gaining knowledge, experience, and confidence. But at NIH, the intensity of my work and my persistence in pursuing new knowledge were at a more mature level.

* * *

My first publication with Stadtman dealt with only one step in the oxidation pathway by which cells convert fatty acids into energy. Working in the methodical Stadtman style, we were able to characterize this one biochemical reaction by studying the enzyme's activity under different experimental conditions so that we could predict how it would react when the microorganism was in various growth phases. Several years earlier Fritz Lipmann, with whom Earl had worked as a postdoctoral fellow in Boston, had discovered coenzyme A (CoA), a molecule critical in the metabolism of fatty acids. Then Feodor Lynen, Earl's friend in Munich, studied the reactions involved in fatty acid breakdown and showed exactly how CoA is involved. This work on CoA was so new that it had not yet reached any textbooks, and thus I had heard nothing about it in my biochemistry course in medical school.[†]

As we pushed ahead, the scientific competition became ever more intense. Further work led us to study how cells build up long-chain fatty acids.[‡] A diet rich in carbohydrates and fats gives rise to the synthesis of fatty acids, which can be converted to storage fat (each fat molecule contains three fatty acid molecules). This fat can be converted to energy when the body exerts itself. So the best way to lose weight is to exercise and to diet. It is simple biochemistry. Other scientists were on the same trail, tracking the process of fatty acid synthesis. This cluster of explorers included Lynen, who later won a Nobel Prize for a combination of his work in explaining the pathway for cholesterol synthesis, his research on fatty acid synthesis, and his determination of the chemical structure of acetyl coenzyme A (acetyl-CoA). The other

---

[†] Fatty acid breakdown, which was understood when I began my work, occurs in a series of four enzyme-catalyzed reactions. A typical fatty acid contains sixteen carbon atoms. In the first cycle of oxidation, a two-carbon piece is split off as acetyl-CoA, leaving a fourteen-carbon fatty acid CoA. The fourteen-carbon fatty acid CoA undergoes the same sequence to yield another acetyl CoA and a twelve-carbon acid, and so on until the sixteen-carbon fatty acid has yielded eight acetyl-CoA molecules. This series of reactions yields adenosinetriphosphate (ATP), a form of biological energy. Additional ATP energy is derived from further oxidation of acetyl-CoA in the citric acid cycle – another complex of enzymatic reactions.

[‡] Long-chain fatty acids (containing sixteen carbon atoms) are built from two-carbon units. These two-carbon units (acetyl groups) are linked to coenzyme A, forming acetyl coenzyme A (usually abbreviated as acetyl-CoA). When the fatty acid synthetic enzyme system has an adequate supply of acetyl-CoA and energy (ATP), it launches the process of fatty acid synthesis. This acetyl-CoA comes largely from the metabolism of carbohydrates and fat in the diet.

main competitors included Professor Konrad Bloch at Harvard, who shared the Nobel Prize with Lynen for work on cholesterol synthesis, and Professor Salih Wakil at Duke, an excellent biochemist and a relentless competitor. This august group now included Roy Vagelos, M.D., who had only recently finished reading a biochemistry textbook. My experiments had landed me in the center of a very competitive field.

I was a squirt among giants, and I knew it. Lynen, the mightiest of the giants, was a close friend of Stadtman's, and he visited our laboratory one day. He sat down at my desk and did what scientists always do: "I'd like to know what you're doing," he said with a heavy German accent. Extremely nervous, I managed to explain the aspects of fatty acid metabolism that I was working on then. (The experiment involved incubating the enzyme with a fatty acyl-CoA, malonyl-CoA, and radioactive bicarbonate. At the end of the experiment the radioactive products were separated and identified.) Although I believed the reaction I was studying represented the first step in fatty acid biosynthesis, I was not sure at that time. I was nervous discussing the reaction with Lynen because I knew he was trying to identify a similar reaction in yeast.

The next year, Lynen came to visit again. The newer postdoc fellows, knowing I had spoken to the great man on his previous visit, turned to me for a briefing before they were introduced to this hero. "What's he like?" they asked, and I launched into an enthusiastic description. "This guy is an amazing scientist," I said. "He's a big guy. He's a skier. He limps a little bit because he's broken his leg several times skiing," and I carefully described a rugged, hulking six-foot-four athlete. When Lynen arrived in the laboratory, the postdocs were astonished, and I could hardly believe his appearance. The scientific giant was short, about five feet eight inches tall. My awe of his mental stature had added an extra eight inches to his height.

Surrounded as I was by scientists of the intellectual caliber of Lynen, Bloch, and Wakil, I didn't need anyone telling me that I had to run very fast to keep pace. My major limitation now was finding time to keep building on the results of my last experiments. During these first two years, I was still performing my regular clinical services on the wards at the National Heart Institute, and I found myself logging in eighteen-hour days and seven-day weeks. Nonetheless, I was still nervous about falling behind.

Anxious about what the titans and their teams of postdoctoral researchers were doing, I always raced to read the latest issue of the *Proceedings of the National Academy of Sciences* and the *Journal of Biological Chemistry*. Opening each issue quickly, I would skim through the table of contents. Early in any scientific study, the ideas for research often come from results published by another laboratory. As momentum builds in a good laboratory, most of the ideas for future experiments are generated internally. As we moved ahead, I no longer had to read the journal articles for ideas because my ideas all came directly out of my research, which I knew was on the front edge in the exploration of fatty acid synthesis. But right at that edge, there was a thin little strip of reality that couldn't yet be known because competing scientists didn't discuss their scientific results until they were published. There was a blind period between the time we understood the results of experiments and publication, which could come four to six months later. Thus, no one ever really knew who was in the lead in any field, and that helped to keep my adrenalin pumping and kept me checking the titles of the latest journal articles.

As I approached the end of my second year at NIH, Walter Bauer asked me to return to Harvard to join the junior faculty. I was a bit surprised because Walter, a traditionalist and unwavering nationalist, had been displeased when I opted for the National Heart Institute instead of the U.S. Army. After first visiting NIH, I had gone in to tell him what I intended to do. He didn't disguise his opinion: "Roy," he said, "is *that* what you call serving your nation?" But two years had apparently tempered his disapproval, and he now invited me to return.

Stadtman encouraged me to stay at NIH. In what for him was a great burst of enthusiasm, he said, "I think you're *pretty good* in biochemistry." "Pretty good" were among the most complimentary words he ever spoke to me during my first few years at NIH. I answered, "Well, I'm *very good* at medicine." But he countered with a proposal: "If you'll stay a third year," he said, "you'll be entirely independent." Being independent meant that I would be responsible for planning and interpreting my own experiments – with no help from him. Any publication generated by the research would be written without a senior coauthor. This would establish me as a biochemist and was an appealing prospect. Besides, I was absolutely hooked on biochemical research and our efforts to characterize the vital enzymes and coenzymes in lipid metabolism. I knew I would return to a department of medicine at some point, and I convinced myself that when I did return, I would need to be as capable and independent as possible in biochemistry and enzymology. Diana agreed, and we decided to stay at NIH another year.

The next day, I discovered what Stadtman meant when he said I would be independent. He stopped talking to me. He abruptly cut off our conversations even though we continued to work in the same small laboratory. About that time, I began to get some results I couldn't explain – ultraviolet spectra different from anything I had seen before. I suggested to Stadtman that I must have found a new compound in the biochemical sequence I was studying.

EARL: Oh fine.
ROY (persistent): What do you think it is?
EARL: I don't know. You'll have to find out.

From that moment on I had to make my own decisions. Stadtman forced me to work out these puzzles myself.

* * *

Stadtman stopped solving my problems, but he certainly didn't stop supporting me. He decided it was time I had a research assistant, and he put me in touch with an unusual man who would play a decisive role in my career and become a lifelong friend.

Al Alberts, two years my junior, was doing graduate work in cell biology at the University of Maryland while, as he put it, "I tried to find myself in science." By the time we met in 1959, he had learned three important things about himself: he hated teaching, he loved laboratory research, and he was electrified by Earl Stadtman's course in microbial biochemistry at the University of Maryland.

Besides sharing Stadtman as a mentor, we had several other things in common, including immigrant parents. Al had grown up in a Jewish neighborhood in Brooklyn, where the work ethic was as important to his family and neighbors as it had been to mine. In high school, he drifted naturally toward the sciences even without the benefit of a compassionate teacher like Miss Brokaw. (He once described his high school teachers as ranging from "excellent to sadistic.")

At about this point in our careers, we took different paths. Al ventured only a trolley ride away to Brooklyn College, where he was a good student in the sciences without fully tapping his potential.

Always a bit of a dreamer, he was less obsessive about his academic work than I was. After graduation and the standard confrontation with his draft board, Al spent two years in the Army before becoming a graduate student, first in Kansas and then at Maryland. In the meantime, he married his high school sweetheart, and he and Sandy had their first child, Heather, in 1957.

Al Alberts the family man needed a full-time job, and he and I quickly agreed to work together. We recognized our differences. I was more theoretical than Al. He was the great bench scientist with a green thumb in research and bulldog determination about getting results. In our early days together I would prepare the chemicals to be used in the experiments because I had a stronger background in chemical synthesis, and I would instruct Al in the preparation of enzymes and the running of enzymatic reactions. At the beginning we worked together, but soon we worked on different aspects of the same experiment – our skills complementing each other's. In the morning I would explain what we would do, and at the end of the day we would compare results. Al learned very quickly, and soon we were close research colleagues.

Our different ways of loving science showed in our reading habits. I was compulsively focused on covering the literature directly related to my current projects. Al would pop out of the lab on a break, quickly read an article translated from a Russian journal in an unrelated field, and come back to chat about its implications. His wide-ranging enthusiasm was infectious. My role was that of "pusher," making certain neither of us wandered too far from the biochemistry of lipid metabolism and fatty acid synthesis.

My pushing paid off in every way but one. Although I was able to keep Al operating on a schedule similar to my seven-day week (with only minimal bullying), I totally failed in getting him to write up his own work. I understood his reluctance because I, too, had disliked reporting my research results during my first two years at NIH. I was not initially convinced that publication was worth the effort since I was planning to return to a career in medicine. But Stadtman had convinced me that the only way to establish priority in a scientific discovery is to publish. If after great effort you make a discovery, you should get credit for it; otherwise, someone else will. In time I realized it was prudent to document what had been accomplished, and I made writing a regular part of my schedule.

Al, however, preferred to do the research and leave the writing to me. Since I did not want our work to be beaten at the publication stage, I wrote the initial drafts on everything we were doing. Al was happy to edit them. While we were pushing ahead with our joint research, I asked him to take time off to complete his doctoral dissertation at Maryland. He disappeared from the lab for a few weeks but then returned and said he wanted to do research, not write papers. That was the last I heard about the dissertation. I began to worry that he would finish his scientific career as an "ABD" (All But Dissertation). If so, he would be underselling himself because he was a superb research scientist.

With four hands instead of two, we accelerated our analysis of the intricate biochemical transformations we and our formidable competitors were studying. In 1959, Al helped me complete my first independent research paper nailing down one of the early steps in this pathway. We were not much closer to a complete understanding of the controlling enzyme(s) in the synthesis of fatty acids, but our project now began to develop its own momentum. Each successful experiment generated ideas for the next step in a sequence of studies that mirrored the chemical cycles we were trying to chart.

About this time, I started thinking more and more about the links between the process we were studying in bacteria and what goes on in the human body as it synthesizes fat. Stadtman was a purist concerned only with microbial science. But I was again feeling the tug of medicine. I believed that our work would explain fatty acid synthesis in humans as well as bacteria, and, as a well-trained physician, I wanted to relate my work to human biology. Cholesterol was already in the back of my mind as a potential target for our research when Stadtman gently redirected my life once again.

"Look," Earl said in 1959, "why don't you stay another year while Terry and I take a sabbatical leave?" He wanted to go to Munich for six months to work with Feodor Lynen in the enzymology of a system that converted methyl malonyl-CoA to succinyl-CoA. (During the course of this study, Stadtman and Lynen identified a vitamin B_{12} coenzyme, a very important discovery.) He and his wife planned to spend the rest of their sabbatical year with Georges Cohen in Paris, where some interesting research in regulation of enzyme activity was being done. "While I'm gone," he said, "you can oversee the laboratory and the postdocs."

By this time, Stadtman's crew had grown, but running this little operation would be no burden. My clinical responsibilities – I was now a Senior Surgeon at the Heart Institute – had been reduced. Moreover, I felt a strong sense of obligation to Earl Stadtman, as I still do today, and I was also completely immersed in a research project that was producing exciting results. We believed we had a bacterial enzyme system that could make long-chain fatty acids (sixteen carbons) from acetyl-CoA and malonyl-CoA. The enzyme system was complex, but we believed we could dissect it and work out all the intermediate reactions. This was new and exciting. After Diana and I had our usual career discussion, we decided once again to stay at NIH. Clever Stadtman. Once he had me on board, he dropped a bombshell. "By the way," he asked casually, "would you also teach my course in microbial biochemistry?"

ROY (amazed): "Earl, I *just* took that course myself. I don't even have a complete set of notes because I couldn't go to all the lectures."
EARL (musing): "You can use my notes."

So of course I did teach this advanced course – two years after I had finished reading the textbook.

Lecturing at NIH in those years was a traumatic adventure because my audience consisted of unusually talented professionals. The cream of the crop of American M.D.'s had come to NIH to fulfill their military service. I was still acutely aware that I was learning by doing, mastering with my students the fundamentals of this red-hot, rapidly changing science. I was literally one chapter ahead of the class.

* * *

Teaching Stadtman's evening course added another few hours to a day that had already become inhumanly long. I have never needed much sleep, but the combined teaching, research, and clinical consultations pushed me very close to my physical and emotional limits. No longer able to exercise as I had at Penn and Columbia, I was living off of the physical capital I had built up in those early years. It would have been impossible to maintain this pace without Diana's enthusiastic support. She somehow kept all of us going because she fully understood the importance of my work to me as well as the critical nature of the competition. We functioned as a team then and throughout our lives.

Our family was growing. Randall, our first child, was almost two years old, and his sister Cynthia was born in February 1959. Fortunately, we had found a house within walking distance of NIH so I could pop home quickly. I *never* missed our family dinner, which was a special time for us to be together with the children.

But after dinner, I normally headed back to the laboratory. This was the kind of schedule that breaks up many marriages, but ours survived. Being sincerely in love helped. But that probably would not have sufficed if Diana were not a remarkably accomplished person able to sustain all of us through those tense times. She was also a wonderful cook, picking up her expertise from her mother – Greek cuisine – and from a neighbor who was a French master chef trained in Paris. We ate very well. No matter how tough the day was, dinner was relaxed and left time to play with the children. Then we washed the dishes and bathed the children, and Diana would read to them as I slipped out to return to the laboratory to finish an experiment or prepare for the next day.

Despite the demands of my various jobs, we insisted on two weeks of vacation every summer, usually near some large body of water. Diana's parents and mine joined us each time, making it a true family vacation. At least once a year our parents had two solid weeks to spoil their grandchildren – a custom practiced equally by both sides of the family. The grandparents told stories, played hide-and-seek with the children, and took them to a local park to play on the swings and feed the ducks. Best of all, they would visit a local toyshop to pick up a few little trinkets that the children would cherish. On occasion the grandparents would come with a small tricycle or roller skates – just in time for whatever level of dexterity had recently been achieved. They also stayed with the children when Diana and I needed a day or two on our own. When we returned, the children would have new shoes or clothes that were just perfect. Our children were Diana's parents' first grandchildren, whereas my parents already had three grandchildren before Randy appeared. No matter where they stood in the sequence, each grandchild was very special for all four grandparents.

* * *

Even at the beach, I sometimes couldn't completely switch my mind off the laboratory work. Al and I were continuing to make exciting progress in determining the biosynthesis of fatty acids. Every experiment was producing new insights into how the cell produces long chains of these important acids – insights we confirmed Stadtman-style by doing each experiment two different ways.

Stadtman enlarged our team to support my research as it gained momentum in what had become a very hot, competitive field. We were joined by Donald Martin, a Fellow of the Boston Medical Foundation, and later by Peter Goldman, who came to NIH from Columbia Presbyterian Hospital. Pushed by Martin's interest in mammals, we launched a study of the regulation of fatty acid biosynthesis in the cells of rat tissues. Whereas Stadtman, ever the purist, was still dedicated to conducting his own experiments exclusively with bacteria, we now inched a bit closer to the study of human biosynthesis.

In some of our early experiments, Don and I were able to edge ahead of Salih Wakil at Duke. At this point, we were following the trail of acetyl-CoA, the starting substance for fatty acid synthesis, analyzing its relationship to the citrate cycle, a crucial sequence in energy generation. Citrate, formed from acetyl-CoA and another substance, is critical for energy production and fatty acid synthesis. When energy is needed, citrate is metabolized to form energy. When the cell has excess acetyl-CoA and energy, citrate will activate the enzyme acetyl-CoA carboxylase to form malonyl-CoA, which is the first reaction of fatty acid synthesis. (For more on the citrate effect, see the appendix to Chapter 4.)

It turns out that the enzyme acetyl-CoA carboxylase is the critical "switch" that controls the human body's rate of fatty acid synthesis because it catalyzes the rate-limiting reaction of the sequence. When the body has taken on excess calories in the form of carbohydrates and fat from the diet, it will store these calories by making fatty acids, which are converted to body fat.

This research kept pushing us clearly to an understanding of how the human body regulates the amount of fat it makes. Many human diseases are associated with excess fat. High blood pressure, diabetes, strokes, and heart attacks, to mention some of the most obvious problems, have a higher incidence in obese people. Since our bodies contain about three trillion cells of over two hundred types, I recognized that there is a substantial gulf between microbial research and clinical medicine. But I also knew that many of the chemical sequences are the same, and so I saw a light flicker on that part of the clinical horizon.

My research was all-consuming, and fortunately, I was in an institution, the Laboratory of Biochemistry at NIH, that built its program by developing the careers of people like me. Many other M.D.'s have come through the Stadtman laboratory since my arrival in 1956. Many were similarly infected by the scientific bug Earl spread and went on to pursue research careers after leaving NIH. Two of Stadtman's protégés were awarded Nobel Prizes: Michael Brown for his work on the regulation of cholesterol metabolism and Stanley Prusiner for his discovery of prions and their implication in diseases of the nervous system. In science and in medicine at Bethesda, we were all encouraged to operate independently, setting our own pace and developing our own goals and careers.

During my sixth year, for instance, I changed my career after I attended a lecture in New York by a distinguished French scientist, Jacques Monod. Stunned by the clarity of his thinking, I decided on the spot that I needed to learn more about Monod's research on the role of genetic information in shaping the life of microbes. He was working in two areas. He studied the way DNA (deoxyribonucleic acid) transmits genetic information to proteins. Nucleic acid was implicated in this information transfer, and that fascinated me. He also studied the regulation of enzyme activity and demonstrated that molecules can affect enzyme activity by binding to a site on the enzyme separate from the active site. He called this allosteric regulation. Both of these imaginative research fields were exploding in his laboratory. He was able to explain his complex experiments and hypotheses beautifully, and I decided that I wanted to learn much more about his research into microbial genetics. I thought I might use his techniques in my own experiments in the future.

Diana was excited by the prospect of a Parisian interlude, and we quickly agreed to explore this possibility. Without unreeling any red tape, the National Heart Institute agreed to provide me with a sabbatical year at the Pasteur Institute in Paris. Monod was interested in our work on enzymes, and so it was no problem to arrange the visit.

* * *

Looking back, almost all of my experiences at NIH were extremely positive. This was a government organization that was flexible, innovative, and highly productive. It was clearly serving the public interest. The secret of its success was its ability to attract and often hold people of the quality of Earl Stadtman and my other peers. None of us was getting rich at the National Institutes of Health, but we worked

Roy (left) in the lab at NIH, 1959.

incredibly tough schedules because we were dedicated to our projects and surrounded by other scientists who valued scientific discovery.

The momentum at NIH came from a fruitful combination of the scientific disciplines and a special kind of loose government organization that provided us with all the resources we needed as well as all the freedom necessary to use them creatively. Without these conditions, scientists like Earl Stadtman wouldn't have stayed for their entire careers. Although many of the brightest young researchers initially went to NIH as an alternative to U.S. military service (as I did), we stayed beyond the required two years because it was an environment in which we knew we could be productive.

We could pursue any area of science we chose, from the regulation of glutamine synthetase to the genetic code. There was no pressure to work on disease-related phenomena. The only demand was research excellence. This kind of researcher-led project selection was the basis for most of the important science coming out of NIH. As undisciplined as this appears to nonscientists, it is the most productive way to take maximal advantage of inventive scientists. Let them decide where they will invest their lives. Support them with modern laboratories, excellent equipment, and supplies. Challenge them to discover new knowledge that will change our world. Some of the knowledge may lead to a better understanding of disease; some may lead to new methods of treatment or prevention. Since we don't know in advance which knowledge is going to be most productive, it is important to promote work in numerous disciplines and subdisciplines in biology, biochemistry, molecular genetics, structural biology, and neurobiology. Only the government can afford such broad-ranging research, and during the 1950s and 1960s the most important government programs in the biomedical field were at NIH or at research universities funded by NIH. No country has devised a better way to stimulate scientific endeavor. None has been so productive.

3 | *The French Alternative*

W e went to France by ship in the summer of 1962 and immediately started looking for an apartment in Paris. Both Diana and I thought we knew enough French to figure out the Parisian real estate market on our own, and besides, we enjoyed feeling self-reliant. Since I had been spoiled by living within walking distance of the NIH laboratory, we concentrated on locations close to the Pasteur Institute. At first we were disturbed to learn that all apartments in Paris had two prices: the official, legal, taxable price, which was very low, and the unofficial, illegal, cash price, which was higher. But even the cash prices were reasonable, and we decided not to buck the system. If French apartment owners wanted to avoid taxes – apparently a national tradition – we would just have to play by their rules.

Once we made that decision, we were surprised at how easily we found just what we wanted: a modest apartment within reach of our very limited budget on the right bank of the River Seine near Montmartre. The location was attractive, close to the great museums and restaurants, and I would be only a short distance from the Institute.

The next day I went to the laboratory to meet Jacques Monod. Knocking, I heard him answer, "Entrez!" Primed to continue practicing my French, I walked into his tiny office and said, "Bonjour, Monsieur." Monod glanced up and said, "Hi, Roy." Monod was completely fluent in both languages. Everyone else in the laboratory also spoke English to me because they wanted to practice what had become the international language of science. Diana, who took courses at the Alliance Française, mastered the language, as did our children, who went to a public school. But it became clear on day one that my own French was not going to improve at the lab.

In that first meeting with Monod, I rather proudly described our real estate deal in Place Pigalle (found without troubling him). "Oh," he said, "Place Pigalle? Do you know anything about the neighborhood?"

I admitted knowing nothing. "It's the red-light district of Paris," he said, thus explaining why the rent was so reasonable.

With some guidance from colleagues at the Pasteur Institute, we quickly located another, more suitable apartment in Porte Saint-Cloud, in the west end of the city, just off the river. Here we were within easy walking distance of the excellent subway system, the Métro, which I regularly took to work.

* * *

At the Institute, I started my second crash course in modern science, this time in microbial genetics, one of the three revolutionary developments taking place in the medical sciences in the middle of the twentieth century. One of these developments involved a new understanding of viruses and how they cause disease. Another, the one I had been exploring at NIH, focused on the biochemical sequences that take place in all living organisms. The third was providing new knowledge of how genes control organisms, which is the subject matter of molecular genetics. Monod and his colleagues were analyzing, in microbes, the manner in which genes trigger the responses the cells make to changes in their environments.

At NIH, our work in Stadtman's group had been tightly focused on the biochemical sequences that take place in the cells. We had not been studying the DNA command structure that controls those sequences. If, however, we could now put these two molecular fields – genetics and biochemical sequencing – together, we would have the first full understanding of how and why life forms develop as they do, how and why they respond to changes in their environments as they do, and how and why they malfunction when diseased. Traditional medical science, based to a considerable extent on physical observation of the body, or on organic chemistry, physiology, and pathology, could not provide this level of understanding either of life forms or of disease.

My new mentor in microbial genetics, Jacques Monod, was an unusual scientist. When I first heard him speak in the United States, I had been tremendously impressed by the quality of his mind and by how far ahead of the rest of the scientific community he appeared to be. He didn't use traditional descriptive terms when discussing phenomena, and he challenged older observations by proposing direct experiments based on current molecular thinking. It had been less than a decade since J. D. Watson and Francis Crick had discovered the molecular structure of DNA, for which they were awarded a Nobel Prize. Their discovery opened the way for analysis at the molecular level of the mechanisms of inheritance. Every cell in our body has a nucleus containing chromosomes composed of multiple strands of DNA. Each molecule of DNA is paired with another DNA molecule in the familiar double-helix pattern, and groupings of these pairs make up the genes that control the characteristics of our cells – and to a great extent, of us. Whether we are tall or short, are able to compose music at an early age, and are able to make good use of the food we eat, are all controlled by our genes.

In the early 1960s, what was only beginning to be understood was how DNA exercises its control. Monod's group was analyzing the chemical reactions that take place when the genes send messages to the cytoplasm (the part of the cell where metabolism takes place) to start or stop a particular activity. Since every action of the body involves these biochemical sequences and every sequence involves a gene message, Monod's work was of great importance. The opportunity to stay with him for a year gave me a chance to broaden my knowledge and my command of the connection between biochemistry and molecular genetics.

Monod, like Earl Stadtman, studied bacterial rather than human cells. In these cells proteins enable a bacterium like *Escherichia coli* to perform essential functions. Some of these are normal, ongoing housekeeping functions of the cell, such as building up the cell wall. Others are performed only when the cell needs them – when, for instance, it is necessary to digest or metabolize lactose or the fatty acids I had been researching. In each case, the DNA sends signals to the cell by way of ribonucleic acid (RNA) to synthesize or to stop synthesizing the necessary enzymes.

That was where the work that Stadtman and I had been doing linked up with molecular genetics. That was why Monod had wanted me to visit the Pasteur Institute. He and his colleague François Jacob were brilliant geneticists, but no one at the Pasteur Institute had the command of enzymology we had acquired at NIH. Monod and Jacob needed research that would follow the DNA signals past the RNA messenger, into the process of enzyme biosynthesis, and then on to the resulting biochemical activity controlled by the enzyme. They had shown that clusters of genes – called operons – control entire biochemical sequences such as the metabolism of sugar. These clusters work together to signal the cell to produce a series of enzymes that control the biochemical processes of metabolism.

Their theory was impeccable: if there was something that started a cell's digestion of sugar, transforming it into energy and thus stimulating growth, there had to be a switch that turned off the process, suppressing particular enzymes and thus halting the chemical reactions essential to metabolism. But no evidence as yet indicated whether these sets of genes functioned as a cluster, nor were the biochemical pathways of the metabolism fully specified. In effect, Monod and Jacob were researching on two frontiers at the same time. Neither the molecular genetics nor the enzymology had been worked out. Thus, the experiments to substantiate the theory were complex and difficult to perform successfully – especially for a novice.

* * *

I was not alone in recognizing the importance of Monod and Jacob's explorations. Exciting ideas like these were attracting some of the world's best scientists to Paris and Monod's laboratory. The Pasteur Institute – like NIH – stood at one of the crucial scientific crossroads of the twentieth century, and I was able to learn what was happening from the stream of visitors passing through that establishment.

I was also able to learn from Monod, who was even more brilliant than I'd thought when I heard him speak in New York. Most evenings he'd drop into my lab around 6:30 or 7:00 to sip cognac and talk science. I knew he liked cognac, so I kept a bottle in my locker. As I quickly discovered, Monod, who turned fifty that year, had an incredibly broad range of knowledge – and not just about science. This versatile scientist had been a high-ranking officer in the French underground and was a war hero. His education and family background in music and literature had made him an intellectual as well as an academician. He organized a string quartet that on one occasion included his twin sons and me, on my violin, in an informal concert for Diana and his wife at their home – a true honor. In France, much more than in the United States, a man's home really is his castle.

My new teacher had a rare ability to talk about any field in science. I was especially impressed by his willingness to discuss seriously ideas that seemed off-the-wall or heretical in terms of current scientific thinking. Monod was quick to propose explanations of important biological phenomena based on early, even minimal data. Such forward thinking had led him to sketch in the proposed steps of information transfer leading from the information coded in a gene to the formation of a protein. His ideas came fast and early, and experimental evidence supporting his hypotheses often followed from various laboratories. For instance, Monod correctly postulated the existence of messenger RNA when there was as yet virtually no data to support this hypothesis. To some other scientists, his ideas seemed merely to be lucky guesses. To me, it was apparent that those ideas were the insights of a truly brilliant scientist.

Most U.S. scientists I knew were more tightly focused and contemptuous of scientific heresy. They were also more constrained by their reliance on what they considered to be hard evidence. Monod was always willing to float an intellectual trial balloon, but both he and Earl Stadtman were critical of scientific work they thought did not represent progress in their field of research. Both men had very strong opinions about what was happening in the world of science, and they seldom understated their evaluations. As Monod and I reviewed what was happening in X's laboratory in Germany or Y's in the United States, he would frequently exclaim: "Their approach is wrong! I think we can do some experiments that will challenge their conclusions!" Monod was passionate about molecular genetics and its ability to explain fundamental biological processes.

Equally passionate about this field was his colleague François Jacob, with whom I usually started my day in the Institute laboratories. He and I would talk about what I was trying to accomplish with that day's research. Like Monod, Jacob, who was in his forties, was a well-decorated World War II hero as a result of his service with the Free French. When we first met, he had been exploring genes and biosynthesis since the late 1950s, and I was indeed fortunate to have him guiding my initial efforts to master the research techniques I needed to study microbial genetics.

For the second time in my short career, I felt like an idiot in the laboratory. Although I had survived the experience at NIH and become an accomplished biochemist and enzymologist, I now had to learn how to conduct experiments on the process by which bacteria control the expression of their genes. Using novel genetic techniques involving mutations, Jacob and Monod had already postulated that certain genes suppress metabolism. But they had not been able to work out the biochemical system that performs this function. My job was to help them elucidate that system within the cell by identifying mutants of a suppressor gene.

Bacteria, which reproduce every twenty minutes or so, frequently produce spontaneous mutations. Some mutant forms are resistant to antibiotics, and when the bacteria are dangerous, the resistant microbes have created major health problems in humans (such as resistant forms of tuberculosis, staph infections, and many other infectious diseases). We are, in fact, constantly racing against the development of resistance to discover new antibiotics that will eliminate or control infections involving mutant bacteria. These problems will never completely disappear because the process of mutation goes on endlessly and at a remarkable pace.

In our case, bacterial mutation was a friend, not an enemy. We guided the process using X-ray irradiation to control and increase the incidence of mutation, hoping to isolate mutant *E. coli* cells containing genes suppressing the metabolism of sugar. By comparing these mutated forms with normal cells, we reasoned, we would be able to study the functions of this particular gene. I spent months irradiating cells in an effort to change the activity of the suppressor gene. Although we learned a great deal about bacterial mutations, we were never able to identify a suitable mutant suppressor gene.

I found it difficult to separate potential errors in the theory from problems in the experimental system we were using. I was learning entirely new laboratory techniques: I had no previous experience in the mutation of bacteria or the identification of particular mutants. These techniques would be extremely useful in my own research on fatty acids back in the United States, but while in Paris, I shed little light on the function of the suppressor gene. I found this incredibly frustrating.

In addition to Jacob, I was fortunately paired with a researcher who had the laboratory experience I lacked. Dr. Agnes Ullmann and her husband had escaped from Hungary in 1956, when Hungary revolted against Soviet control. This attractive, volatile Hungarian scientist and our laboratory assistant patiently walked me through our repeated efforts to isolate the elusive suppressor gene capable of switching off sugar metabolism. We seldom read about this aspect of science: the failures. When we do hear about them, they are usually used to highlight the heroic successes that followed. But in my case, there was no triumphant conclusion.

* * *

Learning by doing was in this instance frustrating, but I gradually acquired an understanding of microbial genetics and of laboratory techniques using microbial mutants. Because it was obvious to me that the work that Jacob and Monod were doing was of immense importance, I was surprised to discover that the French university system held them and their colleague, Andre Lwoff, in little regard. These three pioneers in molecular genetics were considered mavericks – nicknamed the Three Musketeers by their friends – and thus they were at the Institute, which encouraged fresh approaches to science and attracted brilliant iconoclasts, instead of at the tradition-bound universities. France has a magnificent tradition of creativity in the arts and sciences, but it was France that introduced me to a rigid, centralized government–university bureaucracy that blocked change. This bureaucracy was reinforcing traditional approaches to life sciences at a time when revolutionary developments were taking place. And many of these developments were taking place at the Pasteur Institute in Paris.

In 1965, when the Three Musketeers shared the Nobel Prize in medicine and physiology, the honor was accorded to the Institute as well as to the brilliance of these scientists. The award also implicitly disparaged a government-dominated university system that had not produced a single French Nobel laureate in science in the previous thirty years. It was hard for me to ignore the marked contrast with NIH – a public institution that encouraged and sustained creativity.

* * *

Not all of my time in France was spent learning genetics. My work schedule was much less demanding in Paris than in Washington. In Paris no one showed up until about 9:30 A.M. They worked until about 6:30 or 7:00 in the evening, but no one returned after dinner. On holidays there was no reason to come to the laboratory – it was locked.

Easily adapting to our new environment, Diana and I explored the art, music, food, and wine of Paris. Each month, we spent every last franc we had eating out. Quite taken with French wine, we tried drinking it, as my Institute colleagues did, with every evening meal. But soon we decided that our genes permitted us to enjoy this treat only on weekends if we were to maintain our normal pace of life.

That now included a Paris museum at least once or twice a week, accompanied by our children. We were close to Versailles, and the Tuileries became one of our favorite "parks." As soon as we were settled, we bought a Peugeot, and on the weekends all four of us set out for the Loire Valley determined to visit every castle in that part of France. If we missed any, it was by accident. We also explored the Normandy beaches the Allies landed on in World War II. Some of our relatives and friends had been wounded there. We read to our children passages from our guidebook describing the battles and mentally recreated one of the epic experiences of the Second World War.

* * *

On returning from summer vacation, which occupied the entire month of August, all of our French friends immediately began discussing their plans for a winter sports vacation. We joined in, and along with our children, we all learned to ski. This was a joy because both Diana and I prefer sports that are active, and skiing combined the physical thrill of sliding rapidly down a steep mountain with the enjoyment of a glorious alpine environment.

We spent a wonderful vacation in Zermatt, but about a week after returning to Paris, I developed a fever and headaches. As an experienced clinician, I recommended bed rest for myself and went home to recover. After a couple of days, however, my temperature shot up and the headaches intensified. I decided to go to the American Hospital in Paris. There, the attending physician (recently qualified in internal medicine) told me I had hepatitis.

ROY: But I don't have any of the symptoms of hepatitis.
DOCTOR (refusing to give ground): Well, that's because it's *French hepatitis.*

French hepatitis, he explained, is not accompanied by the loss of appetite that occurs in hepatitis elsewhere. This explanation seemed to be more a tribute to the glory of French cuisine than to diagnostic precision.

I stayed home a couple more days, but since I was clearly not recovering, I next decided to check into the hospital. Although I didn't think I had "French hepatitis," whatever that was, I didn't know what I did have. I just knew that I was very sick and that Diana was concerned about me. Two Americans doing research at the Institute had been trained in medicine, and they both visited me in the hospital. One tried to be reassuring. "Roy," he said, "there's one thing I don't want you to worry about."

"What's that?" I asked.

"You shouldn't worry that you might have Hodgkin's disease."

He was right. I didn't have Hodgkin's disease, a form of cancer that often presents as a fever of unknown origin, but his distressing bedside manner made it apparent that this well-meaning young man was better suited to research than to clinical care. I, of course, continued to worry about an illness that wasn't improving and still wasn't diagnosed to my satisfaction.

As luck would have it, friends brought me a small portable radio for my bedside. I was in isolation because the hospital still thought I might have French hepatitis. The radio kept me company and also reported news of a typhoid fever epidemic in Zermatt. Apparently, local innkeepers there had removed signs warning that the tap water was contaminated. Although many people were becoming ill, the innkeepers said the signs were bad for business.

"That's it!" I decided. "I don't have the typical symptoms, but that's what I *must* have." I called the attending doctor and told him about the news from Switzerland.

DOCTOR: No, you've got French hepatitis.

ROY: I need to have blood cultures to settle this matter.

DOCTOR (not about to bend on his diagnosis): They won't do any good. You have a form of hepatitis, a viral disease, and virus doesn't grow out of blood cultures.

He flatly refused to do a culture.

Fortunately, I was able to call on another friend for help. Dr. Irving London, a professor of medicine from the Albert Einstein School of Medicine, was on sabbatical at the Pasteur Institute. He came and took cultures. Salmonella – the cause of typhoid fever – grew out of every body fluid he tested. Knowing at last that I had neither Hodgkin's disease nor French hepatitis, the hospital successfully cured my typhoid fever with an antibiotic.

After a month of typhoid, I was quite weak and needed many weeks to convalesce. Monod, who once had contracted polio and still walked with a slight limp, told me that as part of his recovery he had walked along the "elephant rocks" at Fontainebleau, just south of Paris, and he directed us there to help me regain my strength. We took his advice, and every few days, Diana, the children, and I walked along this beautiful trail up and down the great rocks. Alternating climbing and resting, it took me about a year to get completely back to normal.

In the family, Diana bore the brunt of my hospitalization by herself because we never told our parents about it. Throughout our marriage, she always protected them from any upsetting news. When Randy contracted a viral infection as an infant and became dehydrated from diarrhea and fever, we drove him from Bethesda (we were at NIH at the time) to Johns Hopkins in Baltimore, where we had confidence in the pediatric care. We spent two days there while he was rehydrated with injected fluids. Our parents had never learned about that either.

* * *

My illness cut deeply into my research on microbial genetics. Whereas at NIH I had hit a rich, well-defined line of research so that each of our experiments was productive and we turned out important research papers at a blinding pace, in Paris, Agnes Ullmann and I completed only one research report that entire year. That publication, which drew heavily on my NIH research, explored the control of the enzyme that catalyzes the conversion of glucose into a chemical (glycogen) that can be stored in the liver and muscles for future use. This particular metabolic pathway had long been the special turf of Professor Carl Cori at Washington University. Cori and the university would play an important role in my life a few years later, but in the early 1960s I considered him one of the distant giants of biochemistry. Although our paper was solidly grounded, it barely carried us over the threshold of Cori's complex scientific domain.

I was still on the steep part of my learning curve in genetics, and I believe a major problem was my divided commitment. At NIH, I had been totally immersed in my enzymology experiments, and during my sabbatical year, Al Alberts, a postdoctoral researcher (Peter Goldman, who joined our team just before I left for France), and a technician were pushing ahead with our joint projects. I stayed in close contact with them by mail throughout the year. I know that while I was in Paris, an important part of my mind was still focused on our search for the enzymes controlling fatty acid synthesis. The moral of this episode is, I believe, that you can't do hot science without a total, undivided commitment to a single line of research. That was the kind of commitment Earl Stadtman had and the kind of tight focus he expected in all of us who worked with him. It was the sort of commitment our entire NIH team had as we raced against the giants.

Stadtman nevertheless also understood the importance of acquiring a broad knowledge of the medical sciences and establishing an international reputation. That was why he had encouraged me to go to Paris, an important research center. Statdman himself had spent a year abroad developing similar contacts with important work being done in Germany and France. Going abroad was a common experience among ambitious scientists who wanted to achieve breadth as well as depth in their research.

Although I was unhappy with my productivity at the Institute, Jacques Monod was sufficiently pleased to invite me to stay in Paris and carry forward the research Ullmann and I had started. I explained that I couldn't afford to because I would no longer receive a salary from the United States if I stayed another year. He offered Institute funding for my work. Because at that time American scientists received much higher salaries than their French counterparts, this meant he would pay me – seventeen years his junior – a salary roughly equivalent to his own. I was profoundly honored by his proposal since I knew it reflected his belief in my potential as a scientist, and I agreed to consider the offer.

* * *

Diana and I carefully compared the two situations. Both of us loved France, and we knew it would take at least two years to become completely acclimated to a new society. We were already accustomed to the flow of life in Paris – shopping for vegetables and fruits in the open market, picking up fresh bread daily at the bakery, buying oysters on the half shell at the corner just in time for dinner on the weekend, and walking in the numerous parks and gardens. We were also strongly influenced by our new French friends, who had intense interests and strong conclusions about contemporary and classical music as well as modern art. We liked the strong family orientation among our colleagues (an orientation tempered, we knew, by some interesting liaisons outside the family). We appreciated the fact that they worked very hard in the laboratory during the days, but in the evenings and on weekends they were equally dedicated to seeing the new play or movie that would then be discussed critically in great detail. I saw myself as rather narrow, single-minded, and uninteresting in comparison with my French friends.

We were all learning the language. Diana's French had improved enormously through the classes she diligently attended. Even my French improved and was quite passable because of our immersion in Parisian life. Parties were still hard work because we had to concentrate so intensely on speaking and listening in French. But, as my comfort level rose, I no longer left a French film with a headache. This new facility with the language and comfort with the pace of my contemporaries set me up for business dealings I would have many years later in France.

Our children were adjusted to their school and friends, astonishingly bilingual (after entering school speaking not a word of French), and happy in Porte Saint-Cloud. When we toured the countryside, hotelkeepers would from time to time ask the children why they were traveling with an American couple.

In primary and secondary education, unlike the universities, France appeared to be significantly ahead of the United States in several regards. The French schools were more demanding, required more instruction in foreign languages, and had generally higher standards than many American schools at that time. Students had to pass long and difficult examinations before entering a lycée (a high-school-level prep school). Failure meant they would not be eligible to enter a French university.

Although both children had caught every infection that passed through the school, we knew that situation would improve during the following year as they developed immunity to this new pool of bacteria and viruses. Meanwhile, they had acquired an appreciation for how differently other societies do even the smallest things. In France, children were more rigidly regimented in clothing and behavior, and they were pushed hard academically. Fortunately, Randy and Cynthia did very well once they had learned the language. Some of their best friends were Danish, and thus our children had now encountered two new cultures in a friendly neighborhood setting.

The science being done at the Institute was also exciting – at a world-class, Nobel Prize level. The opportunity to collaborate with a scientist of Monod's caliber and breadth was also attractive. I recognized the power of molecular genetics and was certain that in the years ahead it would dramatically reshape our thinking about human diseases and their treatment. The knowledge base of this new science was still relatively narrow, and much empirical work remained to be done. But it was already obvious in 1962 and 1963 that the explanations derived from Monod's research would blend with the findings in enzymology and provide us with a greatly improved understanding of the cell.

After Diana and I had totaled up that side of the ledger, we did the same for the Bethesda option. There we had a familiar, comfortable setting for our family. Maryland had the additional draw of being close to our parents in New Jersey and New York – an important consideration for both of us, even though trans-Atlantic visits were always possible. With all due respect to the Washington, DC, area, Paris was incredibly interesting. Washington was a political rather than artistic center. Washingtonians at that time had little interest in cuisine, and our capital was essentially a one-company town. Washington was not urbane; Paris was. Washington was national; Paris was international. Washington was oriented to the present; Paris was oriented to a deep, rich past as well as a complex, interesting present.

What tipped the scales decisively was the science, and Diana was willing to sacrifice her delight in Paris for my work. Arrayed against the promising explorations of microbial genetics were the exciting biochemical analyses that were bubbling in Bethesda. Our laboratory at NIH was, I was certain, on the brink of a major breakthrough in understanding the active intermediates in fatty acid biosynthesis. We had already attracted considerable attention and were receiving applications from outstanding postdoctoral researchers. So the pull of Bethesda was powerful in 1963.

Two national styles were also at stake: a looser, more imaginative Monod style versus Earl Stadtman's more cautious, more rigorous scientific approach. This style of research had a deep appeal for me, and besides, I was still drawn toward medicine. Genetics offered powerful ideas and exciting research opportunities, but enzymology promised faster results in medical research. For me that was a crucial consideration. I had drifted away from clinical practice, but I knew I would soon find my way back to medicine through science. So I was pulled back to NIH by my confidence that Al Alberts and I were developing a line of research that could yield new insight into human diseases in the next few years. I wanted to take the shortest road to that destination – a destination I could still only perceive in the most general terms.

So we declined Monod's generous offer and prepared to return to NIH. Monod, always a gentleman and by then a good friend, promised we would remain close through science.

* * *

Before returning home, we decided to mount one last European adventure. We drove across the Continent to Greece, where we immersed our children in Greek culture and their Greek roots. Good fortune was on our side. We barely missed a devastating earthquake in Yugoslavia, and our little Peugeot made it to Athens in good shape. Settling comfortably in a pensione-hotel outside of the city, we organized a two-week tour that blended the ordinary and the extraordinary in a ratio of about one to three.

The ordinary part was our venture through the cultural landmarks. We followed the guidebook from the Parthenon, to the Erechtheum, and on to the Propylaea and the Agora, doing what millions of visitors have been doing for years. So too with the beaches, where the children enjoyed a respite from temple gazing and our tireless marches through the ruins of ancient Greece. In 1963, the waters of the Aegean Sea were still clear and inviting. We took day trips to Mycenae, Nauplion, ancient Corinth, and Delphi, and we sailed to Mikonos and Delos. Greece was stunningly beautiful, and there were still very few tourists or tourist accommodations.

The extraordinary touches arose from our being the second generation of our family in America. We spoke the language, we followed the Greek news, and in Greece we ate in neighborhood rather than tourist restaurants. Because of our facility with the language and because our parents had honored their heritage instead of hiding it, the Athenians treated us as Greeks. Although both children had learned some Greek from their grandparents, neither was fluent. We found to our delight, however, that they could converse with both sides of our extended family in their new language, French, and they learned popular Greek children's games from their relatives. We left Greece determined to return many times.

I was struck by the contrast between the hard-driving Greeks I knew in the United States (including my own family) and the easygoing pace of some of our Greek relatives and friends. That pace made Greece a wonderful country for a vacation. But I began to suspect that many of the Greeks with drive and initiative had emigrated to the United States, where an intensely competitive environment had encouraged them to become the achievement-oriented immigrants I knew so well. I, who could hardly wait to get back to my work, clearly identified with the intense Greek-Americans of my childhood.

* * *

The whole family returned to Bethesda in August 1963, but our French interlude continued to have an impact on our lives and, in particular, on my career. In later years, we had many opportunities to return to Paris, and every time, Diana and I jumped on the Métro as soon as possible and headed toward the neighborhood open-air market we had frequented during our sabbatical year. At NIH, my research gradually extended from fatty acids to complex lipids, and in the work on lipid metabolism, we made excellent use of genetic mutations. Much of that research was done through various postdoctoral researchers, and one (David Silbert) specialized in microbial genetics. We also had several interesting French visitors to our NIH laboratory, including Gerard Ailhaud, whose elegant research on the cell's use of the acyl carrier protein (ACP) in complex lipid synthesis would make an important contribution to our studies of ACP.

Long after I had completed my personal explorations in the genetics and biochemistry of the cell, Jacques Monod continued to influence my life. Although I had opted for the more rigorous U.S. style of science, I would stay open to the ideas of mavericks who were operating outside the comfortable boundaries of accepted practice and were following up ideas that were not based on solid evidence. My interest in mavericks would become particularly important years later at Merck, when I became involved in drug research.

The highest-risk drug research targets an enzyme or cellular receptor that has never been used as a target for drug discovery. These enzymes or receptors are understood at the biochemical level and known to be involved in certain body functions. Results are nevertheless much less predictable because no one knows whether blocking that particular enzyme or receptor will in fact be therapeutic or if interfering with that function will produce unacceptable side effects. It is these high-risk projects that distinguish scientific leaders and result in major breakthroughs. At Merck Research Laboratories, prudence led me to support some lower-risk projects to assure the company a steady flow of products, but I pressed hard to direct a significant part of our research toward the discovery of the breakthrough products without which medical science can make no genuine advances.

Greater risk taking had become part of my research and lifestyle. That was Monod's greatest gift to me, and I still treasure it.

4 | *The Research*
University – American Style

ack on a familiar path at NIH, I quickly settled in with my growing team as we pressed on with the research on biosynthesis. Al
Alberts and Peter Goldman were now joined by Phil Majerus, a
scientist of enormous intellectual capacity. Phil, who was one of the
smartest people I had ever met, was able to understand new concepts
and master new techniques faster than almost everyone else. When he
joined our laboratory, we had determined some of the characteristics of
the acyl carrier protein (ACP), which is linked to various biochemical
intermediates in fatty acid synthesis. Phil, Al, and I were now able to
isolate a pure form of ACP and to establish that all the intermediates
involved in fatty acid synthesis are bound to this single protein.

Majerus next wrestled with defining the structure of ACP, which
would give us additional clues as to how it functions in fatty acid
synthesis. We knew we had a protein to which all of the biosynthetic
intermediates were attached, but we couldn't be certain of its function
until we clearly established its composition and structure. All the while
we were looking nervously over our shoulders, fearful that Harvard's
Konrad Bloch or some other giant was going to beat us to the solution.

For a time, second best seemed a likely outcome after Phil, Al, and I
embarrassed ourselves in front of what seemed like a million talented
scientists. I had initially resisted making reports to professional meetings, which seemed a hundred times worse than reporting to the journal club at NIH. At the professional conventions, all of your talented
competitors – giants and near giants – are in the audience alongside
hundreds of other scientists you don't know. But Earl Stadtman had
gently persuaded me that these appearances, like publications, were
essential to a career in research, and I had begun to present regularly
at the major scientific meetings. I had gained some confidence as I
went along, but now my worst fears were realized. After we had identified ACP, our crucial protein, we made a major effort to determine
its amino acid composition. Working under tremendous pressure and

doing a series of experiments in protein chemistry that were new to us, we raced across the finish line, beating the giants.

Or so we thought. Feeling rather proud of ourselves, we published the results at once and went off to report to the first International Congress of Biochemistry meeting in New York City. Phil and I gave our report followed by Salih Wakil. Both reports described the amino acid composition of ACP, but they differed in one residue – a crucial one containing a sulfhydryl group. Wakil's team included one of the world's foremost chemists in the field of protein analysis (Robert L. Hill), and he of course was not doing these kinds of experiments for the first time. He and Wakil got it right. Speechless, Phil, Al, and I were mortified.

When you're young, however, you can quickly work the dents out of your pride. We returned to Bethesda somewhat humbled, but we knew we were still slightly ahead of the competition. We quickly identified the active site of ACP (phosphopantetheine) – a finding soon corroborated in all biological systems that synthesize fatty acids. We were then back in the race, writing papers about once a month as we refined our analysis of ACP, the intermediates, and the sequence of fatty acid synthesis.

At about this time, one of the largest giants in our field confirmed our sense that we were in front of the pack. At a convention in Atlantic City, our team (Al, Peter, and I) met with Konrad Bloch and part of his team in a bar. "Oh Roy," Bloch said in a friendly way, "we seem to be working in similar places." I still felt like a young squirt, but by this time I had a great deal of confidence in our research. In an equally friendly manner I countered, "We are, Konrad, but I believe we're ahead in our work with ACP." He didn't argue with my assessment and proposed that we divide the research. He would focus on the synthesis of unsaturated fatty acids, leaving us the ACP on which we were already concentrating. I quickly accepted his offer. One major scientist had dropped out of our race.

But plenty of other giants were still competing, and I remembered what one of them had been able to do at the International Congress in New York. A worrier by nature, I had become confident in the laboratory even though I still had major doubts about my ability to be a successful scientist. I would have a rush of great confidence, when I had just finished a significant project, but soon I would begin wondering if my success was a fluke. Could we do it again? Science and medicine are different in this regard. In medicine, most patient encounters are repeats of earlier patient experiences. In science, when you are breaking new ground with every experiment, there are greater risks of making errors. Your reputation is on the line with every publication. It seemed as if every week or so I would tell Diana, "If I don't make it in science, we can always go back to clinical medicine." She understood. She knew that I was confident in my ability to practice medicine, and she would happily take either career path with me. And she also sensed that it was important that both of us keep that emotional back door open so we could, if necessary, make a graceful retreat.

At one point, my self-doubt welled up, and I started exploring the possibility of going into either dermatology or ophthalmology, two specialties in which I thought I could continue some research while maintaining an active practice. Phil Majerus reacted to this idea with his typical restraint: "You're crazy!" he said. "You're one of the best biochemists in the country. Why do you want to spend your time looking at skin rashes?" Although Phil was clearly short on tact, Diana and I decided his evaluation of my work was probably sounder than ours. So once again I swallowed my doubts.

By this time, my research team and I found ourselves very close to working out the entire sequence of fatty acid synthesis and its related enzymes. Now we avoided our previous mistakes with protein chemistry. Along with several other scientists, we were able to establish that ACP plays a crucial role in this process because all the intermediates starting with acetyl-CoA and malonyl-CoA are transferred and bound to ACP in the building of long-chain fatty acids. In addition, an ACP-like protein was identified as the central actor not only in microorganisms but also in plants and animals, including humans. Learning that this crucial protein is a universal component of all biological systems made this the most exciting series of events in my entire career.*

* * *

When you do good work in hot science, you receive many attractive job offers. That was especially true in the 1960s, the go-go years for big

---

* Readers wanting to know more about the biochemical sequence we were researching can turn to the appendix to this chapter. It includes a diagram of all seven steps in the biosynthesis and a brief explanation of how the process is regulated by the cell.

science. The government was pouring billions of dollars into American research. Universities were expanding and enlarging their faculties. Industry was recruiting for its laboratories. The NIH and other public organizations were thriving.

By 1965, I had received several attractive offers to teach and do research at medical schools, but each time Diana and I decided not to bite. We were both happy and busy living close to Washington. Our children, Randy and Cynthia, were settled at their schools and with their friends. We were able to visit their grandparents regularly, and we were near enough to large bodies of water to take the kind of vacations we liked: with plenty of children, as many relatives as could make it, some close friends and their children, and lots of sports and swimming followed by long, talk-filled dinners. Despite nagging doubts about my career in science, the Vagelos "five-year plan" for NIH had been successful and gradually became a "ten-year plan," almost by default. At NIH, Al Alberts, Phil Majerus, and I knew we were moving our research ahead as fast as possible. By then, I was heading the National Heart Institute's Section of Comparative Biochemistry, and our laboratory was attracting outstanding young postdoctoral researchers who enabled us to accelerate our work on fatty acid biosynthesis.

Despite all those blessings, however, I was becoming restless. Most of the reasons were apparent to me at the time. Before my first day in Bethesda I knew I would return to a medical school at some point. Medicine was not a high priority at NIH. The people who mattered were the scientists doing basic research. The clinicians took good care of the patients, and after finishing my two years of required service, I continued to work on the wards for some time. But then our research in the laboratory intensified, moving so fast that I found it impossible to give even a few hours a day to medicine.

Isolation from medicine left me uneasy and wondering if all my training and early ideas about working with people were for naught. I was already considering medical applications of the biochemistry we were doing and had thus guided our research toward laboratory animals (mostly rats). But I began to sense that wasn't enough for me. I needed to get closer to medicine, so I was ready to listen when the dean of Washington University's School of Medicine, Dr. M. Kenton King, called in early 1965 and invited me to lecture at their campus in St. Louis.

Washington University's Department of Biological Chemistry had for years been chaired by Nobel laureate Carl Cori, one of the giants of biochemistry. Appreciating how important he had been to the development of my style of science, I was honored to lecture on the work we were doing at NIH. I was even more honored when the university asked me to be Cori's successor. Ken King later told me that, when he initially spoke to me, he had been in his first year as dean and needed to fill the chair in biochemistry to prove to himself that he could do the job. Since he stayed in the deanship for about twenty-five more years, I figure he was satisfied with the outcome.

After Diana and I had a thorough discussion of this new offer, we decided to accept it and move on. Much later, I saw that this was part of a clear pattern in our lives. We changed our lives decisively about every ten years. Each time the move came when we began to feel we'd accomplished most of what we'd set out to do. When that happened, a new challenge became appealing. In this case, Washington University would enable me to practice my science in a setting in which I'd be directly involved with medicine, teaching medical students while I continued to conduct biochemical research.

Being part of Washington University's first-rate medical school was important, but the hook was really the challenge of rebuilding the school's biochemistry department. Carl Cori had trained many outstanding scientists who went on to lead biochemistry departments all around the United States. As he approached retirement, however, he had let the department lose its momentum and level off. I was convinced I could have a major positive impact on the university's biochemistry program and get that momentum back.

Although my income would increase, neither Diana nor I was particularly interested in money. Our lifestyle didn't change when we moved from NIH to the university. Much later, we would have more money than I ever imagined, but even then, we never really changed the way we lived. We did move into a bigger house to accommodate our larger family, but we never made a significant career move in order to increase our income.

* * *

Phil Majerus flew into orbit when he heard the news. A graduate of Washington University's School of Medicine, Phil proclaimed that I had just been offered the best job in the country – maybe even the world. A native of the Midwest, he considered St. Louis the center of the universe. Phil knew he would be coming too because he was able to secure a primary faculty position in the Department of Internal Medicine. At the same time he would retain a joint appointment in our biochemistry department. He was overjoyed to move back to the school and the city of his dreams. Of course, Phil continued to tease me about my flirtation with dermatology, but I now denied that I had ever been *that* doubtful about my future in science.

For Al Alberts, St. Louis and Washington University were also a dream – a bad dream. Al still hadn't finished his Ph.D., and we both knew the importance of an advanced degree in a research university. At NIH, he had already risen as high as he could go on the pay scale without a doctorate. "It might not be wise to go to St. Louis," I warned him, "because you'd be stuck at a very low level in the university hierarchy."

But Al yet again ignored my advice, took the risk, and ventured off with the rest of us. In fact, he left first, heading out to set up our laboratory before our research group moved so that we would lose no precious time on our experiments. I was touched by his loyalty and impressed by his willingness to risk so much. Certainly I was pleased to know Al would still be working beside me, but my warning had been heartfelt. I didn't know what would happen if the faculty members were stuffy and status-conscious about Instructor Al Alberts.

Earl Stadtman didn't want us to leave. He and his wife Terry had practically adopted Diana and me, spending a great deal of time with us on the job and off. For several years now, Earl had been throwing my name in the hat every time a good university asked him to recommend a chair for its biochemistry department. But once I decided to accept an offer, he and others at NIH tried in a very flattering way to persuade me to stay by offering a blank check: "Tell us what you want," they said. "How much space do you need? How many people do you want?"

Diana and I, however, had already made up our minds. So we left Terry and Earl, a man who had as much impact on my career as any-one outside of my immediate family. I'd continue to learn from those around me, some of whom would help me master new skills. But I knew when I left NIH that Earl was my last true mentor and that I had reached the point where I would now become a mentor to others.

* * *

We went to St. Louis in 1966 bearing gifts that eased the transition into our new life. Before leaving Bethesda, I had received a large grant from NIH to renovate the department at Washington University. In addition, I received a very large grant from NIH and the National Science Foundation (NSF) to support my research team for seven years. The first year of this grant provided over a quarter of a million dollars (well over a million dollars a year in today's currency) – a comfortable level of support for a large biochemistry research group.

Here's how this worked in the go-go years. When I applied for the NIH research grant, NSF asked to share in the project and provide part of the money. Of course NIH and I accepted their generosity. Today that wouldn't happen. Congress cut back significantly on support for basic research, and thus getting funding has become much more complicated – and painful – because each research agency has been forced to protect its own interests. But in the mid-1960s, science was on the government's front burner, and biochemistry was one of the hottest sciences in the country.

Diana and I felt like pioneers as we headed into the heartland, a new country for both of us. Diana had grown up in New York City. I was no big city boy, but she and I shared an East Coast orientation and an attraction to urban entertainments. Visiting St. Louis in the spring of 1966, when the weather was great and flowers were in bloom, we found a newly built house we could afford about twenty minutes from campus in suburban Ladue. But when we drove to St. Louis early that summer, knowing very little about the Midwest, we made an important discovery: it is *very* hot in Missouri in July.

Then we made a second discovery: our new neighborhood was deserted because everyone who could leave had gone on vacation looking for someplace cooler and taking their children with them. That summer a very pregnant Diana mastered Monopoly, playing what seemed to be ten hours a day to keep Randy and Cynthia occupied in childless Ladue. Seeking relief from both heat and boredom, we found the Lake of the Ozarks in central Missouri, but the water was warm and the heat still oppressive. Back in our new home, as we looked out over our hot, treeless two acres of clay, we pondered the remarks of those friends in Bethesda who had asked in dismay, "*Why* are you going to Missouri?"

* * *

The answer, of course, was the university, where I was scrabbling up the steep part of a new learning curve. Carl Cori had retired unhappily – a situation I wouldn't fully understand until 1994 when I had to retire myself – but to his credit, he left behind a department with almost no deadwood. There were only a couple of scientists whose work wasn't going anywhere. As I walked the halls and talked science with each member of the department, it was obvious whose work had momentum and whose research had plateaued. A few of my new colleagues soon realized that, as the euphemism has it, "they would be happier elsewhere."

At many universities, efforts to rebuild are thwarted by a heavily tenured collection of sluggish faculty members. On occasion, tenure protects professors whose views need protecting, which works to the long-run advantage of the university and society. But usually it simply protects weak faculty members who have lost their intensity, let their research projects sag, and become tired, out-of-date teachers. This problem is particularly acute in the sciences, where a world-class research organization cannot afford to carry much deadwood. In the humanities, careers peak at a later point, and first-class work can be expected from scholars well advanced in age. But generally this is not true in the sciences. I think abolishing tenure entirely – perhaps using three-to-five-year contracts instead – would strengthen academic departments in the sciences and in the humanities as well.

Fortunately, the nucleus of my new department was solidly productive, so my job was essentially one of addition, not subtraction. We already had several outstanding biochemists – names anyone in the field would recognize. I was pleased to share enzymology with Carl Frieden, who led the biochemistry Ph.D. program, and George Drysdale, a meticulous researcher and fine teacher who later headed up our affirmative action tutorial program. Luis Glaser was a brilliant carbohydrate biochemist. After we applied for and received a grant from NIH to train M.D.–Ph.D. students in medical sciences, Luis took over the leadership of this program. Students from all of the graduate departments in the medical school were able to receive joint degrees under this plan.

Within a short time, graduate education at the medical school was blossoming. We added Robert Roeder, a marvelous molecular biologist who was trying to figure out how proteins are put together. He was focusing on the transfer of information from the gene to the cellular protein-building apparatus, doing research that may someday win him a Nobel Prize. We recruited Ralph Bradshaw, who had just finished a postdoctoral fellowship with Hans Neurath, the leading protein chemist at that time. Craig Jackson came in to do blood coagulation research, and David Silbert gave us strength in microbial genetics. Robert Thach joined the department from Harvard. Phil Majerus's primary appointment was in the Department of Internal Medicine, but he held a joint appointment in biochemistry. Phil set up an independent research project that quickly demonstrated he was now as remarkable a researcher as he had been a medical student at Washington University.

When we put these outstanding scientists together with the productive nucleus of scientists who had moved with me from NIH, Washington University was soon on the cutting edge of biochemistry and enzymology in the United States. Normally, a turnaround of this sort would take five to ten years because academic positions in a major university generally open only when people retire. Our department was, by contrast, rebuilt in a staggeringly short two to three years. We were lucky to have positions to fill from the beginning of my chairmanship. Our newcomers were just beginning their careers, helped along by the excellent senior members of the department. We were delighted with the performance of the youngsters, who were already recognized in their fields based on their postdoctoral work and who began publishing from our department almost immediately.

We all did part of our business over lunch. When I arrived, I found that my new departmental colleagues ate lunch almost every day in a tiny room resembling a large, walk-in closet. In fact, it was an empty storage area with no windows. So we were close in more ways than one. The brown-bag lunches were a great time to talk about science, about what was happening in the university, and about what we needed to do to improve our department. We talked about potential recruits, hot developments in other areas of medical science, and about university appointments or problems being tackled by the administration (such as trying to recruit African American students). This kind of collegiality is important to science, whether it is being done at NIH, in a university, or in an industrial laboratory. All the productive laboratories I have been a part of have shared an informal social life over lunches, dinners, basketball games, and picnics. That was certainly the case in St. Louis as we rolled forward with our new appointments. Soon we were getting positive feedback: In the hallways at scientific conventions, the word was that Washington University Biochemistry was again a "hot department."

Roy teaching at Washington University Medical School, where he served as Chairman of the Department of Biochemistry from 1966 to 1975 and Director of the University's Division of Biology and Biomedical Sciences.

Once we established that identity, we attracted a wave of outstanding postdoctoral fellows. Our regular faculty members quickly generated new research grants, providing "soft money"* to support the postdocs, who in effect become our additional hands and a source of great enthusiasm. The money came pouring in, and the department sprouted like mushrooms in the rainy season.

Once a year, I visited with the dean of the medical school, M. Kenton King, to "negotiate" our departmental budget. King, who'd worked on infectious diseases before becoming an administrator, was soft-spoken and smart. He had the thorny task of presiding over the various chairs, who were a bunch of prima donnas all determined to protect their own departmental turf. But my department's turf was not in play. The dean

---

* Soft money comes from specific government or foundation grants. Hard money is income from endowments or tuition, and you can more or less count on having it available. Hard money pays for faculty and administration salaries. In a medical school, research grants also provide a portion of faculty salaries, thus stretching the hard money budget.

understood that biochemistry was thriving, bringing in new grants, and adding terrific research scientists to an already high-powered faculty. Every year our budget talks lasted about twenty minutes and ended when Dean King said, "OK."

Having the support of Bill Danforth, who was first vice chancellor for medical affairs and then chancellor of the university, didn't hurt. Bill understood exactly what we were trying to accomplish – in part because he'd been trained as a biochemist during the Cori epoch and for some years had been active in research, working with Ernst Helmreich in the department. Bill and I agreed about means as well as ends. We were both elitists. Neither of us was interested in rewarding average performance by spreading resources around equally to all. We were determined to create and then hold together an elite department that would keep the medical school at the nation's forefront. This meant a department full of first-class scientists doing innovative work. All leading scientists in a hot subdiscipline know the other leading scientists, many of them personally, and know their projects. They also know which departments or research institutes are producing the best work. Keeping up with the field and who's who is just part of the job.

Danforth's backing was all the more powerful because he was chairman of the Danforth Foundation. Established by his grandfather, the foundation had long been generous with grants to Washington University and would be even more generous in future years. The chancellor's stature in the university was high, so he was an admirable and effective guide when I started to work my way through some of the thickets of academic politics.

* * *

University politics are often described as intense – even vicious – because so little is at stake. But in one of the first thickets I had to scramble through, a great deal was at stake. The problem was racial. St. Louis has a large African American population, but at that time, Washington University had almost no African American medical students. This was not unusual for a U.S. research university during those years. It reflected the lack of educational opportunities for African Americans and a center-city society and culture uninterested in the kind of science that took me from a restaurant in Rahway to a department chairmanship at a major university.

Almost all the faculty and students in the medical school were main-line liberals. They deeply believed that African Americans had been discriminated against throughout their lives – denied access at all levels of education – but for many years issues of race had not been a high priority for them. Mainline liberalism had been focused instead on class and economic issues. Thus, the New Deal of the 1930s attempted to solve the "farm problem" by cutting production under the Agriculture Adjustment Administration (AAA) even though this put many African American sharecroppers out of work. Liberals supported unionization but did not protest union discrimination against African American workers. The faculty members were working hard to meet all of their teaching and research commitments. The students were struggling to digest the tons of scientific–medical information that we were jamming into them during their four-year curriculum. All of us were meanwhile ignoring social problems other than those dealing with health.

Like most white Americans, I hadn't given much thought to those problems until urban riots erupted during 1966 and 1967. St. Louis was spared the worst kind of looting and burning, but emotions ran high, students at Washington University became deeply concerned, and Bill Danforth decided the medical school should do something creative about our enrollments. He asked me to head a program to increase African American participation. I accepted even though at that time I was still feeling my way around the university.

Bill asked me because, in my first year at the university, the biochemistry department had begun sending faculty members into primarily African American colleges in Missouri and other southern states in an effort to recruit premedical students. These visits with science faculty and students elicited more African American applicants than the school had ever had. The medical school made scholarships available since most of these students could not afford a private medical education. We also quickly recognized that few of the students willing to come to the medical school were prepared to handle our science courses. George Drysdale volunteered to run a summer tutorial, and this helped most of our candidates bridge the gap between their previous work and our rigorous biochemistry curriculum.

Although the tutorial program was initiated in biochemistry, it was quickly extended to the entire medical school as the affirmative action program got under way. Faculty from all the basic science departments became involved in recruitment as well as tutorials offered in each course during the first two years. The new program quickly boosted minority enrollment throughout the school; however, as the biochemistry department had discovered earlier, recruitment was easy but retention difficult. Summer tutorials helped, but many students continued to struggle through the first two years of the program, which was concentrated on the basic biomedical sciences.*

These early years of affirmative action were rough and often frustrating. On at least one occasion, we were publicly charged with racism for failing a minority student on a biochemistry exam. I explained that the exam paper in question was identified only by a number, not by name. The questioner, unconvinced, asked that I meet with members of the African American community, which I did, along with some of my faculty colleagues. The concerned African Americans were skeptical and accusatory. They demanded scholarship support (which we were providing), an African American dean for the African American students, additional assurance that students would pass our courses, and more. But we didn't back down; the failing grade stood. Happily, the student repeated the course and passed, and most of our students did fine with the aid of the tutorials we had set up. As we discovered, once the African American students cleared the hurdle of the first two years, most did very well in the third- and fourth-year clinical courses having to do with patient care.

The medical school enthusiastically supported our recruitment efforts and tutorials and soon appointed an African American associate dean. Although we frequently stumbled, we were gradually able to bring up the minority representation in the medical school. We were pleased to see Harvard's medical school and other universities introducing similar programs, and we thought of ourselves as leaders, constantly experimenting and pressing on with a social movement of great importance to our institution and to the United States.

---

* The four-year medical school curriculum begins with two years largely devoted to basic science courses (anatomy, neuroscience, biochemistry, microbiology, physiology, pathology, pharmacology). The final two years are spent in clinical courses and working with patients either in a hospital or as outpatients. The coursework for these later years includes internal medicine, surgery, pediatrics, neurology, ophthalmology, dermatology, psychiatry, obstetrics, and gynecology. After successfully completing these courses, the candidate earns an M.D. degree and goes on to a hospital internship and residency.

We failed miserably, however, when we tried to achieve the same goal in our graduate program for students seeking to become science researchers, that is, Ph.D.'s rather than M.D.'s. They generally took basic courses along with the medical students but then concentrated on advanced science courses, specific for each discipline, and, of course, took none of the clinical courses of the last two years of medical school. A major component of their program was a research project leading to a dissertation. After graduating with a Ph.D., they worked as postdoctoral fellows in the laboratory of a prominent scientist for two to four years.

Our problem resulted from a common failing of white liberals during those years and today as well. We assumed that African American students would want the same things we did. But as we learned, they were interested in becoming doctors in order to practice medicine, not to do research in science. They had some role models in medicine but very few in the biomedical sciences. We found it extraordinarily difficult to recruit African American students for our Ph.D. program, and at the time, I was enormously disappointed because we wanted to enlarge the pool of scientists capable of doing basic research and making discoveries that would ultimately change the practice of medicine. Some years later, at Merck, I would have an opportunity to return to this issue and would again try to get African American students as excited as I am about the biomedical sciences.

* * *

As I became more familiar with the workings of the university, I began to see other possibilities for creative change. At one point, I spent a short period as a visiting professor at Harvard, where I taught at three levels: undergraduate, graduate, and medical students. I was startled to discover that I had a better time and was most interested when teaching the undergrads. They were bright and lively, still excited about ideas. They had not yet learned to be "cool" and "professional." When I visited Johns Hopkins, I found that many faculty members in biology, who also taught medical students, had reached the same conclusion: they were usually happier teaching the brightest undergrads. I realized that medical school faculty were missing out on something important.

After I returned to St. Louis, Bill Danforth and I agreed that I would reorganize the university's undergraduate biology and all of its biomedical graduate programs. Under the new plan, the medical school science faculty would be involved in teaching the biology and biomedical science courses for both undergraduates and graduate students. This would raise the level of science education for the undergraduates, extend high-quality graduate work through more departments, and spread the high academic standards now established at the medical school. This plan would also help recruit top graduate students to both of Washington University's campuses. The medical school had its own campus, whereas the rest of the university was on the Hilltop Campus. The two campuses were separated by Forest Park and a considerable amount of history. Reorganization meant that faculty members would have to change their routines – a difficult transition in any university and one that needs to be carefully managed.

The merging of the faculty was a bit tricky because the medical school was one of the best in the country, but in the 1960s several of the Hilltop undergraduate and graduate programs in the biological sciences were mediocre. Our medical school hotshots looked down on most of their counterparts in biology across the park. There were two outstanding biologists at Hilltop: Rita Levi-Montalcini, who would later win a well-deserved Nobel Prize for her work in nerve growth factor, and Victor Hamburger, her mentor, who deserved to share the prize but was passed over. Most other members of the department were not, however, up to the standard of the medical school.

With the goal of developing a unified teaching organization representing a shared set of values, I, along with several colleagues from the medical school and the biology faculty, set out to create a combined Division of Biology and Biomedical Sciences. The new division would encompass the formerly separate medical school basic science faculties and the Hilltop graduate and undergraduate biology faculty. There were, of course, some hard feelings about this innovation. There almost always are when change takes place. The Hilltop biologists had heavier teaching loads than those of us in the medical school, and that fanned their resentment. At our first joint meeting to discuss the merger, some of the Hilltop faculty were skeptical. "Well," they said, "if you guys want to come over here, will you teach these undergraduate courses?" We shocked them by simply saying yes. I told them I would be happy to kick off the new combined operation by teaching part of the introductory biochemistry course to undergrads. And I did, much to my own enjoyment.

We also made the entire graduate operation a joint divisional responsibility. I stood at a blackboard before the combined faculty and asked, "OK now, we're going to have these eight graduate courses. Who wants to teach biochemistry?" As hands went up, I listed the faculty for that field and went on to the next one. "Who wants to teach molecular biology?" Hands went up again, as they did for immunology, cell biology, microbiology, and neuroscience, while we ticked off the basic courses that would now be taught for all the graduate students of Washington University. By enlisting the best people in the university to teach core material, we made our program deeper and broader. In effect, we created a new faculty for the graduate school that afternoon as well as long-term prospects for improving the quality of the undergraduate faculty. The process, called "averaging up," put pressure on the mediocre faculty in the short term and ensured that promotions and appointments would be of the highest quality in the long term.

These innovations had a striking, almost immediate impact. We didn't just change the structure of the organization. That alone would not have made much difference. What we changed were the internal values and expectations about performance as well as the external perception of what we were doing at the university. The gaps between departments at the school of medicine and on the Hilltop campus began to close, in part, because now all vital decisions on recruitment, promotion, and tenure were made at the divisional level, where standards were very high.

When prospective students visited, Ralph Bradshaw, head of the combined graduate program, shepherded them through the entire division and introduced them to the best professors in each field. "If you join our graduate program," he told them, "you won't even have to decide which department you'll be in until you've been with us for a year." For many bright students, that was an attractive part of our offer. Very quickly we began to draw better students, adding to the momentum we had already achieved by improving our faculty and creating a combined M.D.–Ph.D. program.

Most students enter medical school either as medical students or as graduate students. However, a small proportion of the medical school class enters a combined program that leads to an M.D.–Ph.D. degree, usually at the end of six years. I started the combined degree program at Washington University, but Luis Glaser soon took it over and ran this program for the entire medical school. Students completing this program were trained to work in biomedical research either at a university or in industry. Their clinical training gave them particular insight when defining and solving research problems important to human health. With Glaser's leadership, our medical science program became one of the largest and most outstanding in the United States.

Our next goal was to raise the general level of the undergraduate program throughout the university by recruiting top students. One step was to guarantee admission to the medical school to a few outstanding high school students who were considering entering Washington University as undergraduates. So long as they continued to perform at a high level, they knew they would be admitted to our medical school. In effect, we used the high visibility of the medical program to upgrade the quality of the undergraduate class by eliminating a major source of anxiety for premeds. Along the way, we also recruited the cream of the undergraduates for our medical school. Some years later, when the undergraduate profile had become truly outstanding, the university was able to discontinue this program. But for a time, it helped improve the quality of the student body on the Hilltop campus.

This was my first major experience with reorganization as a vehicle for upgrading personnel, improving performance, and strengthening an institution's commitment to innovation. In the years ahead, I would have many opportunities to broaden my knowledge of this process and of the pain as well as the promise of organizational change. Organizations that don't change don't last unless they are in some very isolated, unchallenging environment. Organizations, whether university departments or businesses, need to be revitalized periodically if only because people tend to settle into routines and drop out of touch with their changing environments. One role of a leader is to convince people, before the fact, that they should change.

* * *

All of these academic innovations involved many individuals. Within the department and then the division, we were constantly recruiting and interviewing candidates for academic appointments and postdoctoral research positions. As head of the division, one of my primary responsibilities was recruiting department chairs. Thanks to Diana, our house on Rolling Rock Lane became a center for recruitment as well as general entertainment. We were close to our colleagues and their families, most of whom lived within a short distance. Our children, who in some cases attended the same schools, played together, and the neighboring kids frequently joined us on expeditions to the zoo or gardens. The children pulled us together, as did our efforts to build a stronger department and university.

Because of these multiple connections, my colleagues and I were all powerfully aware of our being involved in a common enterprise. In this regard, the contrast between Washington University and the National Institutes of Health was dramatic. Both institutions were extremely good at what they did, but they had entirely different cultures. At NIH, when a colleague said he was leaving, the first thing most scientists thought about was whether they could take over his vacated laboratory space. At the university, scientists reacted to the departure of a colleague by first thinking about the hole in the program, the weakening of the department, and the loss to the community of a good friend and a productive colleague. We had socialized at NIH, but mostly with our immediate colleagues. Our circle in St. Louis was extensive and our commitment to the institution much deeper. We were collegial in the best sense of that word, meaning that we shared a strong sense of common purpose. At NIH, where most of us were just passing through, the scientists had a strong sense of their individual purpose. At Washington, most of us planned to stay for a substantial time – most until retirement. It was thus natural to spend a great deal of time with our colleagues, the staff, and their respective families, developing strong personal ties.

I found this sense of community immensely pleasing, as did Diana. If she hadn't, she might have rebelled after the thirtieth or fortieth university dinner party over which she presided at our home. She was always the hostess and chief cook; her favored party offerings were moussaka, paella, and beef tenderloin. I was the kitchen assistant, which is a role I had mastered years earlier in Rahway. I chopped, cleaned, and did whatever the chief cook told me to do. I grilled outdoors when weather permitted, and I certainly washed many dishes after the parties.

Not long after moving to St. Louis, I decided we should have an annual pig roast for the biochemistry department. I had never roasted a pig before and had no idea how to do it. But I thought that with some help, we could bring it off successfully. My secretary, Diana, and I reviewed all the barbeque pits in public parks within fifteen miles of campus, and luckily, the largest pit in the city was at Tilles Park, close to our home. Through the Yellow Pages we found a local smokehouse that provided us with an appropriately sized porker, about 125 pounds – large enough to feed the crowd but still, we hoped, tender enough to eat. It turned out that roasting an entire pig is not as simple as I first thought it would be. First, we had it split down the middle, seasoned it with salt and pepper, and then laid it over hot coals on the huge grill at 7 A.M. to have it ready to eat by 2 P.M. (during the last hour we brushed on homemade marinade). The pig had to be turned about every fifteen minutes, and the whole biochemistry faculty roster shared in this task, two at a time, wearing asbestos gloves, one holding the two front feet, the other the two hind feet. We kept cool by drinking beer from a keg we tapped early in the morning.

Everyone in and around the department came to the roast, from me, head of the department, to the cleaning staff, to administrative assistants, to the faculty, and all our families. Over the years, the crowd kept growing until finally we had too many mouths for one pig, which would feed about 100 people. We began to buy green (fresh) hams at the smokehouse and cook them along with the porker. One year we graduated to a side of beef. We set up games for the children and staff – everything from baseball to sack races to raw-egg-catching. Everyone played. We got to know each other's children at these affairs, and the kids couldn't wait for the annual biochemistry picnic.

The pig roast, the dinner parties, and the departmental lunches in our tiny room all made us feel part of a common enterprise. Linked at first only by science and a job, we were soon tied together by our spouses, children, ailments, and even the weather in St. Louis. As we became more Midwestern, the weather turned into a subject of conversation rather than one of concern.

Unlike some easterners who just never felt at home in the Midwest, we were happily settled in St. Louis after a couple of years. Our family was growing: Andrew Spyros was born in the fall of 1966, just as the vacationers returned, school started, and Diana could finally stop playing Monopoly. Ellen Thetis came along two years later. By that time, departmental and neighborhood socializing had taken hold, and our family had good answers to the question "*Why* are you going to Missouri?" We appreciated the way easygoing, friendly people spoke to us, whether they knew us or not. We loved the public schools, as did Randy and Cynthia. For easterners, life and the people in the heartland seem different. In the Midwest, people are less aggressive, more personable, slower to move through the grocery store, and faster to make friends. Organized religion is stronger, and divisions between groups (ethnic, economic, and otherwise) are less distinct. We now understood why Phil Majerus had longed to return to St. Louis.

As we explored the city, the family found plenty of things to enjoy together. Our favorite family weekend activity was the city's remarkable zoo, and we also spent hours strolling through Shaw's Garden, a child-friendly horticultural center. One Ladue neighbor was concertmaster for the St. Louis Symphony, which Diana and I regularly attended.

In St. Louis, Diana and I became sports maniacs, regularly playing tennis and canoeing together. We had played tennis together since getting married, but now we became more heavily involved with this and other sports. Diana played women's mixed doubles with a neighborhood group. At that time Jimmy Connors (a local tennis urchin) was rising to fame, and Diana and her buddies took group lessons from his mother at one of the tennis clubs. I played men's doubles on public courts with friends from the medical school and neighbors.

We shared our love of athletics and competition with our children. Randy, a strong athlete, competed in cross-country, tennis, and wrestling in high school. Watching Randy run in junior high prodded me to begin jogging myself. I started at one mile and then steadily increased the distance over the years. Because of Randy, I still jog fifteen to thirty miles each week, even after passing my seventy-third birthday (October 2002). Insufficiently challenged by shorter distances, Randy ran his first marathon while in high school in St. Louis and has run many since then, including several in New York City. Cynthia, another good athlete, pursued tennis, which she played in high school after we moved to New Jersey. Andrew began soccer as a youngster in St. Louis, and in New Jersey he became an excellent player for his high school. Ellen, our youngest, began with soccer and then switched to field hockey in New Jersey. We had enormous fun watching her play both in high school and college, where she became an All-American. Both Andrew and Ellen also became excellent tennis players in New Jersey. As it turned out, tennis is the one game everyone in the family plays. We play at home and on every vacation. Swimming is another favorite family sport. The children all learned to swim early in their lives, often competing at their schools. I like to think it is deeply genetic, since both Diana's and my family originated on Greek islands.

It was very Midwestern to be this enthusiastic about sports. The region offers many more opportunities to get into the countryside and participate than do most eastern urban areas. It is less of a hassle to find open public facilities or to belong to a club or make reservations for a court, and people take advantage of those conditions. Since Diana and I generally wanted to participate directly in whatever was going on, we were not wild about spectator sports when we moved to the Midwest. But we quickly changed. Everyone in St. Louis seems to love baseball, football, basketball, and ice hockey. Randy and Cynthia's school friends infected them with their passion for these spectator sports, and they passed on the contagion to Diana and me – at least for baseball and ice hockey. The baseball stadium and the ice arena were both a short drive from our home, and getting tickets was easy. Watching the St. Louis Cardinals and being vocal fans of the St. Louis Blues, we shared the local madness, which we loved.

At home we had an outdoor court that hosted what Phil Majerus dubbed "Death Basketball," a game in which only visible wounds warranted a foul call. Many of these games took place after dinner parties at which a great deal of beer had been consumed. The beer lowered our accuracy, but it made the fouls more tolerable.

When not engrossed in weekend sports, I obsessed about my newest passion: trees. I had always had all the trees I wanted (except at Columbia P&S), and so I hadn't paid much attention to them. But in St. Louis, our property was two acres of grass-covered clay that included only a few dying American elms. Very quickly, Randy and I started a reforestation experiment. Many years later, he told me he had envied the "normal" kids who were doing sports on Saturdays, but he was a loyal hand until he left for college. Diana and I would visit the local tree farm, pile the top of our old station wagon with bags of peat moss, and load the back with tiny pine trees or taller hardwoods. Randy and I would then spend the rest of the weekend digging holes and planting. Some years later – after a good deal of water and fertilizer – we had a little forest on Rolling Rock Lane. Even Randy seemed pleased with it.

To his relief, we didn't work every weekend in the summer. Sometimes we took family float trips on the many streams that cut through the Ozarks. My personal favorite was the Black River because it passes through such beautiful countryside. Although these trips could be done in a day, we often spent two or three days on the river relaxing and just being together. We would meet the Friedens, the Helmreichs, or the families of postdoctoral fellows Mike Glaser, John Elovson, or

Osamu Doi, and pack our food, tents, sodas, wine, and beer into rented canoes and take off without any preplanned campsites. Sometimes we rented the canoes from Treehouse Brown, who indeed lived in a tree house alongside the Huzzah River with his wife and two daughters.

We would navigate the moderate whitewater rapids and then stop for a swim in clear, clean, rushing water. Late in the afternoon, we would set up camp on a gravel bar, one of the great piles of small white stones that line these rivers. At the campsite, I always shared the jobs of pitching tents and cooking. But as night fell and the Ozarks turned dark and quiet, I would perform the task that was mine alone: telling spooky stories to the children. It didn't take too much acting ability to make a ghost seem real as our fire burned down and the country darkness closed in around our campsite.

The next morning we would break camp, pack the canoes, and float on down the river. From time to time, we turned over a fully loaded canoe or bumped into a tree and knocked a snake off a branch. It was not clear whether the snake or our children were more shocked when a copperhead landed in the canoe. Less dangerous but more irritating were swarming attacks of deer flies. It was easy to float off course when you were swatting flies.

When we felt the need for a large cool body of water, we drove north to Lake Michigan. These two-week vacations continued to be full family affairs attended by grandparents and siblings whenever possible. For thirty years we always had at least one grandparent on our vacations. My parents flew out from Rahway, and Diana's came by train from New York City. At this time, my younger sister Helen and her family lived near Detroit, and so we spent some vacations together at Crystal Lake, near Lake Michigan.

Our children loved being with their grandparents (and vice versa) and were thus exposed to Greek culture, especially the language, which our parents used when they were together. Our children also got to know their cousins very well during these holidays. The closest friendship was between our daughter Ellen and my sister Helen's younger daughter, Jonie. They were of similar age and disposition, and they loved being together from the time they were three. Both are married now. Ellen has one child, and Jonie has two children. Even today they phone each other almost daily, often eat together in New York City on weekends, and regularly vacation together along with their husbands and children. Diana and I both find it very gratifying that our family members are so compatible.

***

By the early 1970s, our family was completely Midwesternized, settled in, and feeling very much at home in our wooded corner of Ladue, Missouri. Neither Diana nor I could imagine a better place to raise a family. Although teaching and administration in particular consumed more and more of my days, I was never far from science and no longer insecure about my future. When we first arrived in St. Louis, one thing I did very quickly was to get my laboratory up and running. It helped immensely to have the core of our NIH research team together, including Gerard Ailhaud (our visitor from France) and David Silbert, both of whom had moved with us from Bethesda. The laboratories had been completely renovated, allowing us a quick restart of the work in lipid synthesis in general and ACP (the acyl carrier protein) in particular. During the renovation, we had the carpenters cut a door from my office directly into the laboratory. I was determined to continue as a hands-on researcher, rubbing elbows and talking science daily with the postdocs and Al Alberts.

My fears about Al's position in this high-powered research university were quickly dissipated. In a short time he was interacting with the senior faculty, making important contributions to the seminars, and teaching the laboratory section of our medical student course in biochemistry. His interest in the work of others, the high quality of his comments in seminars, and his great enthusiasm for, and experience with, laboratory research made him an important member of the faculty. He became indispensable not only to the department but also to me personally, since we still worked closely together in our research. While I was occupied with department administration, Al guided the research of some of my newer postdoctoral fellows as they began their studies in my lab. The faculty responded by unanimously recommending his promotion, first to assistant professor and then to associate professor *with tenure*! Rarely do institutions like Washington University even consider candidates for tenure who have not completed their doctorates. But his colleagues recognized Al as a rare man and lobbied me to recommend him for promotion because of his contributions to biochemistry, to our department, and to the students.

Our research during these years followed three interrelated pathways. One was to understand more fully the structure and function of ACP. We had established ACP's central role as the protein carrier that guides the construction of a cell's fatty acids. Now we pressed forward to analyze with greater precision each enzyme involved in this process, seeking to learn the source of ACP's high degree of specificity. Although we could explain how the cell builds up long-chain fatty acids, we still didn't know why and how it stops after reaching a certain chain length. We were certain the off-switch would prove to be an enzyme, but it took our team and others several years to determine the exact mechanism of this reaction.

Each enzyme in the process of biosynthesis had to be isolated, its mechanism analyzed, and the source of its specificity determined. In every case, we had to discover the subunits of the enzyme as well as their binding sites. By 1971, we knew we were much closer to our goal of achieving a full biochemical understanding of this vital process.

Thanks to my training from Jacques Monod and his colleagues at the Pasteur Institute, we regularly made use of mutant bacteria in our lipid research. David Silbert initially led this work while still a postdoctoral fellow. The procedures were painstaking, but the principle was relatively simple. By developing a mutant form of *E. coli* that did not perform a normal cell function under certain conditions, we could determine which particular enzyme is involved in the process and thus analyze its function.

We also employed the bacterial mutants as we launched a new line of research on the role of complex lipids in building and maintaining the membrane of the cell. The fatty acids that the cell uses to make these lipids, including phospholipids, are important constituent elements in the envelope of the cell. By identifying and studying enzyme activities in cell extracts, we were gradually able to extend our analysis of the cell's membrane-building biochemical processes.

This work carried us into research involving cholesterol, another lipid receiving a great deal of attention from clinicians as well as scientists in the 1970s. Since the early 1900s, researchers had suspected a link between atherosclerosis – thickening and hardening of the arteries – and a high-fat diet. Over the years, scientists had gradually determined the structure and multiple functions of the cholesterol molecule, winning several Nobel Prizes along the way. In the 1960s, they made substantial progress in delineating cholesterol's biosynthetic pathway, that is, in determining exactly how the body makes cholesterol.

Meanwhile, interesting epidemiological findings – based on studies of large populations around the world – had linked cholesterol with coronary heart disease, the cause of heart attacks. One study found that the incidence of death from heart attack was extremely low among the Japanese, who also had very low blood cholesterol levels. In striking contrast, people in Finland had unusually high cholesterol levels and were fourteen times more likely than the Japanese to die from heart attacks. These and many other epidemiological studies implicated high blood cholesterol as an important causal factor in coronary heart disease.

In 1972, a Stockholm clinical study developed a statistical link between a low-cholesterol diet and reduced risk of heart attack. Since only about 25 percent of the body's cholesterol is derived from diet, these findings provoked intense debate in the medical community. But I never doubted for a moment a causal relationship between heart disease and cholesterol because I found the epidemiological evidence overwhelming. No matter how strong the statistical relationship, however, I knew that direct proof could come only from an experiment showing that reducing the cholesterol level would stop the advance of disease in a patient with progressive coronary heart disease and high blood cholesterol. In the 1970s, that crucial experiment could not be performed because researchers did not have drugs that would adequately reduce the cholesterol level.

Although I was thinking about these questions in the early 1970s, our research was directed at different problems. We were exploring the positive contribution cholesterol makes to the life of the cell. One of the things we learned (using mammalian cells grown in cultures) is that this lipid is essential to the development of cell membranes. Cells deprived of all cholesterol are unable to maintain their membranes and die. Thus, a certain amount of cholesterol is critical for normal cellular structure and function.* Meanwhile, our studies on enzyme activity in

---

* This was beautifully demonstrated by T. Y. Chang in our laboratory. Chang mutagenized mammalian cells and selected a mutant clone that would not grow normally unless cholesterol was added to the culture medium. These cells were not capable of synthesizing their own cholesterol but could utilize cholesterol added to the growth medium. With the added cholesterol, the

mammalian fat and liver cells were taking us closer and closer to the study of human diseases.

Drs. Michael Brown and Joseph Goldstein, two brilliant researchers at the University of Texas, were already studying human patients who were born with enormously high blood cholesterol levels (familial hypercholesterolemia). As Brown and Goldstein reported in 1973, these patients had inherited a defective gene. As a result, their livers lacked the receptors that normally remove low-density lipoprotein (LDL) from the bloodstream. This accounted for their abnormally high levels of LDL and for their early deaths from coronary heart disease and heart attacks. These researchers also demonstrated that one particular enzyme in the cholesterol biosynthetic sequence, HMG-CoA reductase, regulates how much cholesterol the cells will synthesize. For this work, Mike and Joe won a well-deserved Nobel Prize in 1985. I felt a close attachment to them and to their research. Mike and I were both graduates of the University of Pennsylvania with majors in chemistry. He and I also shared a mentor. Earl Stadtman had launched both of us on studies that had produced a body of knowledge that was clearly relevant to medical practice.

At Washington University we now began studying molecules that inhibit enzyme action in the cells. Having identified enzyme-binding sites associated with the function of fatty acid synthesis, we were able to analyze substances that could lock into one of the binding sites and stop a particular cell function. This was wonderfully demonstrated in Konrad Bloch's laboratory at Harvard by Satoshi Omura, who showed that cerulenin, a natural antibiotic isolated from a fungus, stops the growth of fungi, bacteria, and yeast. It does this by direct inhibition of a single enzyme.** Omura collaborated with our laboratory in identifying the molecular mechanism that enabled this substance to inhibit cell growth by blocking fatty acid synthesis.

cells appeared entirely normal. He also demonstrated that the cells' need for cholesterol from outside was due to a single damaged (mutated) enzyme that under normal circumstances is involved in the synthesis of cholesterol. In addition to showing the absolute requirement of cholesterol for normal cell growth, this elegant experiment also established that, when any one of the fifteen or so enzymes required to synthesize cholesterol is knocked out (by mutation), the entire biosynthetic sequence stops.

** Cerulenin inhibits the enzyme that catalyzes the condensation of acetyl-ACP with malonyl-ACP in fatty acid synthesis.

Now my goal of taking my science back to people appeared to be almost within reach. The gap between bacteria and a complex mammal was still awesome, but many of the biochemical processes we were analyzing are universal to all life forms, and that encouraged me to believe the gap between medicine and enzymology was closing.

Although I was getting closer to medicine, I had actually moved further and further away from bench science. I had become a senior scientist – a role marked by our laboratory refrigerator. In 1972, I was elected into the American Academy of Arts and Sciences and the National Academy of Sciences. But it was the refrigerator that really told the story of my new status. In 1966, when first arriving at Washington University, I was a hands-on bench scientist doing at least part of my own experiments in the Stadtman style. But as our operation got larger and my responsibilities more complex, I began to do less and less of my own research. I still directed the experiments, but I no longer performed them.

All of my lab work was now being done by the hands of others: a growing team of energetic, very smart postdoc scientists, a few graduate students, and some dedicated, skillful technicians. When Al Alberts and the postdocs needed a place to put a refrigerator, they shoved it in front of my door to the lab. There it stood, an eloquent signal of the price of progress in a scientific career. Al and the others neither needed nor wanted me in the lab. We met frequently to plan experiments and discuss strategy, but I no longer had any bench space.

Our laboratory was now attracting talented researchers from all over the world – from Argentina, the Netherlands, New Zealand, Canada, Italy, Japan, and many first-class biochemistry programs in the United States. We were getting the cream of the crop – the kind of young people determined to make their mark in science. The kind who assumed the normal working day to be sixteen hours or so. Now I was the mentor. Like Earl Stadtman, I took substantial pride in their accomplishments and followed their careers with interest.

One lab alumnus was Osamu Doi from Tokyo University, who worked along with his wife, Fumiko, in our laboratory studying the phospholipids of bacterial membranes. Years later I encountered Doi back in Japan. You could say we experienced a role reversal. No longer the striving young postdoc, Doi was now an important figure in the Koseisho, the Japanese regulatory agency responsible for approving drugs. He was judge and jury for a product Merck had submitted for approval to be introduced in the Japanese market. Fortunately, our product met the high Japanese standards, and so we never really tested the limits of friendship. Diana and I enjoyed his success, and in the years that followed, we had many similar experiences as our various graduates and postdocs spread throughout a worldwide biochemistry network of public and private institutions.

By the mid-1970s, our research efforts had carried us rather far into the analysis of the form and function of lipids, including cholesterol. Twenty years of scientific investigation in a global network of labs had greatly improved our understanding of lipid biochemistry and, in particular, of the role of enzymes, coenzymes, and carrier proteins such as ACP in the normal and pathological functioning of cells. Studying enzymes, I could see, was the best way to understand disease states in all animals, including humans. My early interest in cardiology made the role of cholesterol in heart disease particularly intriguing for me as did the potential to find enzyme inhibitors that might actually alter disease states.

* * *

I was thinking along these lines when I received an invitation to consult with a prestigious pharmaceutical company that was already well known to me. During medical school, I had spent one unexciting summer working in the Rahway laboratories of Merck (but now I could spell the name correctly). Since then, even when practicing medicine, I had had very little to do with the pharmaceutical industry or its sales representatives. I just didn't have the time and didn't think they had information I needed. But in the early 1970s, I was willing to return to Merck's laboratories in Rahway to help their scientists better understand what was going on at the cutting edge of biochemistry and enzymology.

Besides, I had a good friend at Merck, Dr. Harry Robinson. He had gone to Merck directly out of high school, and the company, which was very paternalistic, had helped him complete an undergraduate degree, a Ph.D., *and* an M.D. After completing this arduous route to professional standing, he had gone on to become one of the firm's important scientists and a vice president of research. It was his lab in which I had worked during my summer research stint in 1951, even though I had seldom seen him there. Some years afterward, he had begun to visit with me at various professional conferences. He would call and say,

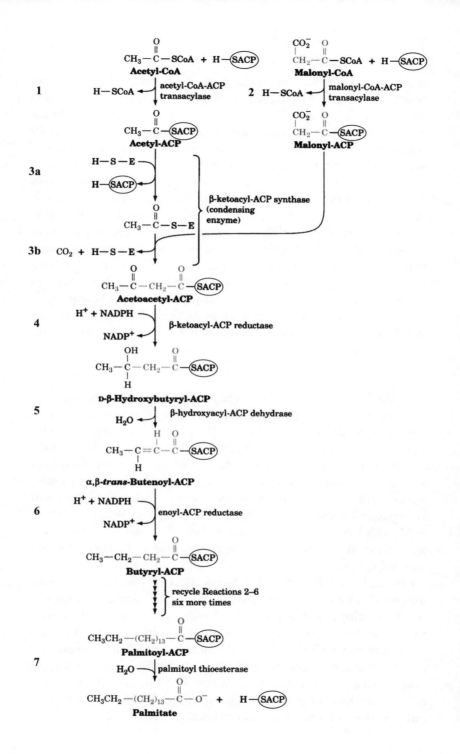

"Roy, you're going to the biochemistry meetings, aren't you? Want to meet for lunch?" I liked and respected him, and so I was always pleased to get together for a casual chat – or so the lunches had seemed to me at the time.

Then in the early 1970s, another Merck vice president of research, David Jacobus, invited me to consult with the company's scientists, and I quickly discovered I had plenty to tell them. Merck had a long record of superb accomplishments in organic and fermentation chemistry. Organic synthesis had yielded important vitamins, and research in soil samples had produced significant antibiotics, including streptomycin, the first effective treatment for tuberculosis. But by the 1970s, chemistry was no longer providing adequate targets for drug discovery. Perhaps, I thought, biochemistry could help.

When I visited Rahway, it was apparent that the company's laboratories had fallen behind the front edge of the field. I gave as much advice as I could, but I came away with the strong impression that their scientists were not really prepared to listen to an outsider. Particularly an outsider with no experience in drug discovery. I was rather disappointed with this reception, but Harry Robinson had been following my visits and was interested enough to invite me back the next year. When I returned, I of course found that the Merck labs had not begun to make the changes needed to deploy modern biomedical research for drug discovery. But, paradoxically, that left them ideally positioned to land a hook in the Vagelos family.

Appendix

More about the Biosynthesis of Fatty Acids

The first committed reaction in fatty acid biosynthesis is the conversion of acetyl-CoA to malonyl-CoA, a reaction catalyzed by the enzyme acetyl-CoA carboxylase:

$$\text{Acetyl-CoA Carboxylase}$$
$$\text{Acetyl-CoA + Bicarbonate + ATP} \rightarrow \text{Malonyl-CoA + ADP + Pi}$$

The seven reactions (numbered to the left) in the biosynthesis of palmitate, with the ACP of the intermediates circled. Figure courtesy of Donald and Judith G. Voet, *Biochemistry* (John Wiley & Sons, Inc., 1995), p. 683. We have added the numbers and circles.

When a person overeats, the metabolism of carbohydrates and fats creates an excess of acetyl-CoA and energy. Acetyl-CoA is converted to citrate in the citrate cycle and to fatty acids by the fatty acid biosynthetic enzymes. Acetyl-CoA carboxylase (the critical first enzyme for fatty acid synthesis) is stimulated by citrate, which is an allosteric activator of the enzyme. Malonyl-CoA, the product of the acetyl-CoA carboxylase, is quickly and efficiently converted to fatty acids that end up as adipose tissue fat. The citrate stimulation of acetyl-CoA carboxylase was discovered by Donald Martin, who joined our laboratory and turned our attention toward mammalian as well as bacterial enzymes. Acetyl-CoA carboxylase is also regulated by several hormones such as epinephrine, glucagon, and insulin.

Under conditions of dieting and exercise, acetyl-CoA carboxylase, and therefore fatty acid synthesis, is shut down while, reciprocally, fatty acid breakdown by oxidation is increased to produce energy for the body. Body stores of fat are reduced. This reciprocal regulation of synthesis and breakdown, controlled by effects on acetyl-CoA carboxylase, accounts for a majority of the effects of overeating versus dieting and exercise. This work, explaining the critical role of acetyl-CoA carboxylase, was done in numerous laboratories over many years.

Most fatty acids end up as fat, the major energy reservoir of an animal or human. Small amounts are converted to phospholipids, which are components of the membranes that envelop all cells – those in animals as well as plants. When the cell has plenty of fatty acids, palmitate, the long-chain fatty acid that is produced, inactivates acetyl-CoA carboxylase by feedback inhibition; that is, the ultimate product of fatty acid synthesis, palmitate, can inhibit the first step of biosynthesis. The regulation of fat synthesis is thus quite complex, but it largely turns upon acetyl-CoA carboxylase, the rate-limiting enzyme of the entire series. In Chapter 5, I will discuss the same mechanism for another rate-limiting enzyme in relation to the regulation of cholesterol formation.

Readers interested in understanding the details of the biosynthesis of fatty acids may find the diagram (provided courtesy of Donald and Judith G. Voet, *Biochemistry*, John Wiley & Sons, Inc., 1995, p. 683) on p. 102 helpful. I have numbered the seven enzymatic reactions involved in transforming acetyl-CoA and malonyl-CoA (derived from acetyl-CoA) into palmitate. This figure demonstrates the central role of ACP, since this molecule (circled in each case) is involved as a carrier of every substrate in the seven enzymatic reactions illustrated.

Fatty acid synthesis begins with a 2-carbon unit of acetyl-CoA, which is transferred to ACP in Reaction 1, and a malonyl group of malonyl-CoA, which is also transferred to ACP (Reaction 2). Acetyl-ACP and malonyl-ACP undergo a series of reactions (3–6) yielding an ACP intermediate (2 carbons longer each cycle) that can substitute for acetyl-ACP in Reaction 3, each time picking up an additional malonyl group. Thus, after six more cycles, palmitoyl-ACP is formed and gives rise to palmitate (16-carbon fatty acid) in Reaction 7 with the release of ACP. The ACP then becomes available for another biosynthetic sequence. These long-chain fatty acids are the building blocks of both triglycerides (storage fat, the body's main source of energy) and phospholipids (the lipids of biological membranes which, along with certain proteins, form the selective permeability barriers of all cells). Thus, fatty acids are important for both energy storage and biological membrane integrity.

5 | *Turning the Corner at Merck*

"**R**oy, don't you know you'll be selling toothbrushes and combs?" Phil Majerus crowed. I played it straight: "Phil, I don't think Merck sells those products." But the truth was, when I accepted the company's offer to head basic research for a year and then become president of the Merck Research Laboratories, I didn't know everything Merck was doing.* In 1975 the company had several subsidiaries, and so it was possible that one of them did make toothbrushes or combs. But if so, I would never admit it to Phil.

What I did know about Merck & Co., Inc., consisted of an impressionistic blend of Rahway memories, family lore, and recent personal encounters. From my days jerking sodas at Estelle's Luncheonette, I had a good feeling about the technical people who worked for the company. Not only were they smart and excited about their work, but they were also fun. They played tennis and touch football, they read interesting books, they were on top of current events. I wanted to be like them. I also knew many Rahway families in which two or three people were employed at Merck. I thought of it as a benevolent, paternalistic organization that took good care of its employees. My sister's husband, Robert Currie, had been a process chemist in Merck Research for years, and so stories about the company, mostly positive, had always floated around our family gatherings.

My consulting visits had given me a very focused view of what was going on in the research laboratories. One program I had looked at involved research on cholesterol, an area of basic science that was both familiar and intriguing to me. Through screening, MRL researchers had found halofenate, a product candidate that lowered blood cholesterol,

---

* At that time, the R&D organization was named Merck Sharp & Dohme Research Laboratories (MSDRL). The name was later shortened to Merck Research Laboratories (MRL). We have used Merck Research Laboratories throughout to avoid confusion.

106

and had advanced it to clinical testing in patients even though they didn't know the mechanism of action at the molecular level. They didn't know which enzymes, if any, the compound inhibited.

On that visit, I gave an informal lecture on the cholesterol biosynthetic sequence, explaining how the body produces and controls blood levels of cholesterol. I described the experiments that Feodor Lynen's and Konrad Bloch's groups had done as they worked out this complex biochemical pathway. Researchers in several laboratories (those of Lynen and Rodwell, as well as Brown and Goldstein) had identified the particular enzyme, HMG-CoA reductase, that controls the slowest reaction in the synthetic sequence. That enzyme, I said, should be the target for inhibition because it is the slowest step – hence the rate-limiting step – in the entire complex process. If a pathway involves fifteen sequential steps, as this one does, it seemed only logical to work on the rate-limiting reaction that would control the rate of the entire sequence.

Controlling synthesis was important because most of the body's cholesterol – about two-thirds to three-quarters – is produced internally. The rest comes from the food we eat and drink. Abnormally high blood cholesterol (hypercholesterolemia) can result in a circulatory system clogged with fatty deposits that cause coronary artery disease and strokes. Although physicians were, and still are, promoting proper diet as a means of lowering the level of blood cholesterol (especially LDL, the "bad" low-density form), it is hard to make a significant dent in cholesterol level through diet alone. That is why physicians and their patients needed an effective means of impeding the body's ability to produce cholesterol. I thought Merck could probably find a molecule that would inhibit the crucial enzyme.

Historically, most drugs had been discovered the way Merck found halofenate. The process of discovery was empirical, whether it was conducted in a laboratory or by simple folk observation of what happened when people ingested a substance. This is how aspirin, morphine, digitalis, and vitamin C came into use. The empirical process works, but it depends on luck and takes an enormous amount of time to bear results. Starting around the 1940s, scientists sped up the discovery process by testing drugs on animals. They produced "animal models" of human disease, usually in a mouse or rat, and then treated the animal with various chemicals to see which was the most effective. The most promising candidates were then refined or modified to increase potency and reduce side effects and were subsequently tested on humans. For example, a rat could be made hypertensive by causing damage to the kidney and then fed small amounts of chemicals to see if they reduced the blood pressure. This was the method used to discover the first drugs for treating hypertension, arthritis, and infections.

Cell culture screens were a more modern approach to drug discovery. Mammalian cells could be grown in test tubes or on plates in the laboratory so that many chemicals could be tested simultaneously. With cell culture screens, scientists could study the ability of cells to make cholesterol and determine whether certain chemicals slow cholesterol production through synthesis. An advantage of cell culture over live animal screening is that very small quantities of chemicals can be tested. Live animals require much greater quantities. The disadvantage to both of these approaches is that the target molecule (an enzyme, cellular receptor, or ion channel) is not assessed directly.

When the age of enzymology was dawning, Merck, as well as the entire pharmaceutical industry, was still discovering drugs using blind screening experiments. Its researchers were either treating cell cultures with broths isolated from soil microorganisms from different parts of the world or with chemicals drawn from the chemical "library" Merck scientists had built up over the years. The library consisted of compounds that had demonstrated pharmacological activity in an animal or cell culture screen. An active chemical constituted a "lead." It was then the job of Merck chemists to tinker methodically with the molecule's atoms to eliminate undesirable properties that caused side effects. This classical pharmaceutical industry method, based on synthetic organic chemistry, was far more efficient than working with animal models. Using animals, a researcher could run perhaps twelve experiments a day. Using cell cultures, he or she could run 100 in a single day. Nonetheless, even with cell cultures, the process was random and slow because there was no understanding of the actual chemical functions at the molecular level.

Having been mentored by Earl Stadtman at NIH, I believed that targeting specific enzymes offered a much more efficient method for developing drugs. All enzymes have active sites, and biochemists use the metaphor of a lock and key to describe the start of the chemical transformation that takes place in these sites. The substance to be acted upon (the key) must fit the active site (the lock) exactly or nothing happens. When a chemical interferes with the precise fit, the interaction doesn't take place, and a whole chain of sequential steps is interrupted. This sequence could be one that produced cholesterol or it could be a disease process such as an infection. By isolating and understanding the structure of a crucial enzyme, researchers could greatly increase the odds of discovering a chemical agent that would block the reaction and stop the sequence.

Another efficient approach to drug discovery might involve the targeting of receptors on the membranes of cells. These membrane receptors receive chemical signals (such as hormones) released from other cells that cause them to carry out certain biological functions critical to the human body. Some of these functions were certain to be involved in disease processes. But our understanding of the interactions of membrane receptors with the substances that activate them was still very rudimentary in the 1960s and 1970s, and so I focused on enzyme inhibition as the best approach to drug discovery. That's what I told them when I consulted at Merck.

* * *

Merck Research Laboratories had responded to the changes taking place in the medical sciences by hiring several biochemists – including Lew Mandel and Mike Greenspan, one of my former postdocs – but they had had little impact on the basic strategy of drug discovery in the laboratories. The organic chemists were still kings of the hill at Merck. They were optimistic about halofenate.

I wasn't. The compound didn't seem to inhibit any of the specific enzymes I'd mentioned in my lecture on the control of cholesterol synthesis. Worse, as the clinical trials progressed, the company's researchers found that, besides lowering blood cholesterol, halofenate also lowered triglycerides and blood sugar. Some of the researchers were delighted with so many potentially beneficial effects. But I was stunned that they were continuing with a product candidate that did so many things. As a physician, I considered the "perfect" drug a compound that does only one very specific thing. As a biochemist, of course I knew that a perfect drug with no side effects at all would probably never be discovered. But halofenate caused such a broad range of poorly understood responses in the body that I was convinced it couldn't possibly become a useful therapy. Even though I had no practical experience in drug discovery, I knew there had to be a better way to do things.

That's what I told Chief Executive Officer (CEO) Henry Gadsden when Merck started to recruit me. Henry was a tough bread-and-butter executive with a photographic memory and an immense appetite for numbers. On one of my visits, I said to him, "If I become head of the laboratories, I'll want to make dramatic changes in the way they try to find new drugs." I also told him what he already knew: "I've never discovered a drug, Henry, but I want to go about it in what I think is a more scientifically rational way." Gadsden replied, "If we didn't want big changes, we wouldn't be talking to you."

He also reassured me about the support for MRL. "What happens," I asked, "if your sales are not what you think they should be?" Gadsden said, "Roy, we'd cut back in every part of the company. We'd cut back in sales and promotion. We'd tighten up our production. We'd do everything we could to hold down costs. But we'd try very hard not to cut back on research because that's our future." I liked that answer very much.

Merck's second-in-command, Dr. Tonie Knoppers, expressed similar sentiments. Like his boss, Knoppers was smart and knowledgeable about pharmaceuticals. Unlike Gadsden, Knoppers was an urbane, worldly sort who knew more about music and art than anyone, academic or otherwise, I'd ever met. Educated as a physician and pharmacologist in Holland, he would land in a European capital for a business conference and go to the opera or a museum first, keeping the business people waiting while he checked out some special exhibit. It was Tonie who flew out to St. Louis to offer me the position of research director of Merck and who wrote assuring me that, after one year in charge of basic research, I would become president of the laboratories. Merck also promised me a new biochemistry building.

* * *

When Merck made that offer, in November 1974, I was convinced of two things: First, discovering new drugs could help millions of people live healthier, more productive lives. Second, although I couldn't be absolutely certain I could lead MRL to a medicine that would help millions, I knew that if the company improved the quality of its research and MRL's strategy for drug discovery, we would have a much better chance of someday developing new therapies that would really make a difference. That was the hook for me – knowing I could have a major, positive impact on the company's ability to reach that goal. Over the

Christmas holiday in 1974, Diana and I had to decide whether to bite.

We discussed the move through the vacation, which we shared with Diana's mother, who was known as Nona to the grandchildren. After Diana's father died in 1972, Nona had begun to spend a month with us at Christmas in addition to our summer vacations together. In the manner well understood in Greek families, she expressed her affection by cooking. She prepared special Greek dinners, usually with lamb, as well as baking *yaourtopsomo*, *galatobureko*, and baklava, the traditional Greek desserts. We usually spoke Greek with her, and Diana arranged for many of our St. Louis friends to visit us over the holidays. Our children never became fluent in the language, but they also never had any problems communicating with Nona.

Diana and I talked a great deal about the children as we labored over our decision. It was not easy for any of us to leave Rolling Rock Lane. Along with the trees that now covered our two acres, we'd all put down deep roots in Ladue and at Washington University. We especially worried about Cynthia, who was fifteen and would be vulnerable on a major move to the East. Ellen's best school friend was moving to Texas, so she was not torn up by the thought of leaving Missouri. She and Andrew could still see any move as an adventure, and Randy, who was finishing high school, was headed to college the following year.

He'd applied to all eight Ivy League schools and was far more relaxed about the admissions process than either of his parents. After Christmas he visited eastern campuses with some St. Louis friends, and he interviewed at several. Princeton was on a break when he went east, and he arranged to have his Princeton interview in St. Louis, with one of my friends at the medical school, Dr. Lew Aveoli. A few weeks later, Lew assured me and Diana that the interview had gone very well, and we finally relaxed. In April, however, when the acceptances rolled in, Randy was admitted to every school he had applied to except Princeton. "So much," I said to Diana, "for insider information."

We decided the children would be fine with the move. Randy would be away at the university (he picked Harvard), Andrew and Ellen were so young that the move would affect them only minimally, and we believed Cynthia could tolerate the change in schools. So Diana and I settled on our next five-year/ten-year plan. She understood that I was considering leaving Washington University only because I thought we'd accomplished what we'd set out to do in 1966. Biochemistry was thriving. The new division was a success. The faculties from the various departments of the medical school and the undergraduate school had embraced the idea of joint teaching, joint graduate programs, and joint recruitment of graduate students. Recruitment of new faculty was very successful as newer candidates recognized expanded opportunities at the university. Our graduate and postdoctoral programs were in excellent shape by virtue of being able to attract greater federal funding based on the new jointly taught curriculum and joint research programs. This permitted the recruitment of even better graduate students and postdoctoral fellows.

As the reputation of the Division of Biology and Biomedical Sciences spread, I had begun to receive unsolicited invitations from search committees recruiting for a medical school deanship. I asked myself: "Do you want to be a dean? Do you want to spend your days parceling out resources to the prima donna chairs in some other medical school?" The answer was obvious. I never looked at a deanship. Deanships are administrative jobs devoid of real scientific content. I didn't think I could contribute much to the world by listening to departmental chairs explain why they absolutely had to have an additional appointment or an extra ten thousand dollars. I saw myself as a contributing scientist with the potential to make new discoveries and to organize and run a research organization even bigger than the one I had at Washington University. I couldn't stand the idea of being separated from my science, from a direct role in scientific discovery. I still feel that way today.

Our lives had become very comfortable in St. Louis, but I think Diana realized for the first time that I would never be held by that kind of comfort. Just the opposite. Professional comfort made me reach out for a new challenge. The series of job inquiries and the Merck job offer made me realize that I wanted to continue to lead the kinds of changes I had brought about at Washington University. Biochemistry at the university had reached a plateau of excellence that left little room for dramatic improvement. The opportunity to lead an enormous laboratory whose mission was the discovery of important new medicines was, although I had not thought about it before, right up my alley. Now both Diana and I could see the need for a new setting in which I could really make a difference. And we had a vague understanding that this compulsion would probably take hold again some time in the future.

Once we made our decision, I immediately told Bill Danforth, who understood why I had to go. Dean King was stunned and perturbed but also understanding. Then I had to confront one of my best friends, Phil Majerus, who promptly accused me of giving up a life in science to make money selling toothbrushes and combs. Phil later denied saying that, but in 1975, I was still so uncertain about my future in a pharmaceutical company that the words, however affectionately motivated, stuck very deeply in my mind.

* * *

This time we were going home – back to New Jersey, in the shadow of New York, where Diana's family still lived. Back to Rahway, where I had sold milkshakes and where my parents still lived. Back to Merck, where I knew that I had a great deal of organizational repair work to do. The business was in good shape, paying regular dividends and continuing to increase its sales. The problems that concerned me, however, were internal to the Merck Research Laboratories, where I knew I had lots of walking and talking to do.

That's how scientists find out what is going on in any laboratory. That's what Feodor Lynen had done when he came into my laboratory at NIH and what Jacques Monod did in Paris. I knew that introducing changes in this kind of well-established scientific organization would take a long time; thus, I carefully studied the internal memos and then scheduled a review of every research group at Merck, starting with those I thought would benefit from a new direction. With every group I stayed as long as necessary – at least half a day and often more – to understand each project. It was a very intense study. Merck Research Laboratories was a large operation, much larger than anything I had worked with at the university. That year's budget was $125 million, and there were 1,800 people in research and development. Many of the researchers were in Rahway, but there was also a large laboratory complex in West Point, Pennsylvania, as well as a small contingent in Montreal.

I quickly discovered that Rahway and West Point were two different worlds. The Pennsylvania organization had belonged to Sharp & Dohme (S&D), a pharmaceutical company acquired by Merck in 1953 for its marketing and sales capability. According to the original plan, Merck was to supply the research power and S&D the

Roy (right) and Maurice Hilleman discussing vaccine discovery strategy at Merck, 1977.

promotional know-how and distribution network, thus blending the two pharmaceutical organizations into one seamless, integrated operation. But twenty-two years later, the employees at West Point still said "I work for Sharp & Dohme." They looked on Merck's Rahway headquarters as the "Emerald City" and refused to identify with Merck even though outgoing CEO Henry Gadsden had come up through the West Point organization. The incoming president, John Horan, had worked in both Rahway and West Point, but he was no more successful than Gadsden had been in dissolving the powerful sense of separateness that persisted at West Point. Both organizations felt great local pride: Rahway in its research and chemical manufacturing; West Point (though it also housed a large research group) in its finished product manufacturing (tablets, capsules, injectables), marketing, and sales to physicians. Neither group would accept the complementary nature of this very successful merger.

This alienation didn't make my job any easier. I was the new research boss on the block driving down from the Emerald City to tell the West Point pros how to improve the way they did their research. One West Point scientist with no need of improvement was the head of Virus and Cell Biology Research, Dr. Maurice R. Hilleman, one of the world's great immunologists. He had successfully developed some of the country's most important pediatric vaccines. Most of the country's children were being immunized with the company's combination vaccine (*M-M-R* and later *M-M-R II*) against measles, mumps, and rubella. The science of immunology and vaccine development is very different from the science involved in drug discovery. Hilleman's major contributions had been with live attenuated viral vaccines, which are made from viruses that have been modified to be incapable of causing disease although they retain the ability to stimulate an immune reaction. No chemicals are involved in vaccine development, and there was very little interaction between Hilleman's group and the rest of MRL.

Aside from Hilleman, the scientists at West Point were using the same dismaying research strategy as those at Rahway. Random screening of chemicals was followed by attempts to improve the molecule and then to test the potential drug candidate for safety and efficacy. Repeated failures didn't persuade them to change this technique: years of random screening had hardened them to expect failure with most "leads." From time to time there were successes, which made them unwilling to change a strategy that seemed as logical to them as it was illogical to me. I returned to Rahway pondering my options and looking for a new way to turn the operation around.

I had to convince them to adopt my approach, which involved targeting a particular enzyme involved in a disease process and identifying a medicine to react directly with that molecule. Once we identified our target enzyme, the medicinal chemists would search for inhibitors in the laboratory, and the microbiologists and natural product chemists would look for inhibitors in nature. The search for drugs that act as enzyme inhibitors would be faster since experiments would not involve animals or cells in the initial phase. Hundreds of experiments could be done each day. If we could find inhibitors that fitted tightly into the active site of the target enzyme, our drugs would also be likely to have fewer side effects. This approach, which relies on better scientific understanding, had already been used sporadically in the industry. I didn't invent this strategy. Beta-blocker drugs for treating high blood pressure were discovered by targeting specific receptor molecules. But no laboratory had adopted the new strategy as its primary mode of discovery, and when we started the transformation of MRL most of the industry was still almost exclusively using screening in animal models of disease.

* * *

I was not about to conduct a major housecleaning, firing all the scientists at West Point or Rahway who didn't recognize that a new day had dawned in biochemistry and enzymology. I didn't want a nickname like "Chainsaw" or "Axeman." Some of the MRL people left soon after I took over, including the vice president for basic research in Rahway. That helped. Some who left didn't understand the targeted molecule approach because they lacked the training. Others were unwilling to learn, especially since it was being promoted by a leader who had never discovered a drug. My style of biochemistry and enzymology was relatively new. Although all of the scientists trained earlier could have learned these new disciplines, some didn't make the effort. Most did.

I respected what Merck had accomplished using traditional techniques of discovery. That record included drugs like *Diuril* for congestive heart failure and high blood pressure, *Aldomet* another treatment for high blood pressure, and *Indocin* for arthritis. Soon after I joined the company (and without my involvement), the Food and Drug Administration (FDA) approved *Sinemet*, a treatment for Parkinson's disease that became the drug of choice almost overnight. I was deeply impressed by the impact *Sinemet* had on people, especially the elderly, suffering from this debilitating disease. So I erred on the side of tolerance and patience. My positive rather than negative approach worked to Merck's long-term advantage in some respects, although there was as usual a price tag for patience.

* * *

Besides coaxing and guiding, I wanted to prove by example that biochemical targeting was the best route to drug discovery. In this, I was once again indebted to Al Alberts, who decided to give up tenure at Washington University and help me move our laboratory to Rahway. Many of our postdocs – including Osamu Doi and Arnie Straus, who later became an important pediatric cardiologist – also came along. That gave us a core group familiar with the latest developments in lipid biosynthesis.

After a brief foray into vitamin research, Al and his group began to work on the inhibition of cholesterol synthesis. Following one of my earlier consultation visits, the Rahway scientists led by Lew Mandel had set up a cell culture assay to screen for a chemical that could stop cholesterol formation. Although the cell culture assay method is faster than live animal studies, it lacks the precision and speed of molecular targeting using enzymes and cellular receptors directly. The Mandel group's efforts hadn't produced any chemicals more promising than halofenate, which was still progressing through clinical trials and was MRL's product candidate. Al and his new co-worker, Julie S. Chen, ignored halofenate and focused their efforts on finding an inhibitor of the crucial rate-limiting enzyme (HMG-CoA reductase). By the time I took over the presidency of MRL in 1976, that work was well under way in Merck's new biochemistry building, the one they had promised me when I accepted the job.

While I was struggling to introduce a new research strategy at Merck, Diana and I were getting settled in our new home on Canterbury Lane in Watchung, New Jersey. We could make only one house-hunting trip that spring, and so we bought the house even though we knew it was a little small for our family of six. The location was its major attraction: the house was close to the children's schools and about twenty-five minutes from Rahway and ninety minutes from West Point, Pennsylvania. The lot was in a wooded area with enough space in the back for a pool. The pool, we decided, would make the move to New Jersey more palatable to the children. We checked on the local public schools, which were fine, swallowed our doubts, bought the house, and picked out wallpaper. Our lives were clearly in fast gear.

We knew the house wasn't perfect, but as we discovered it was plagued by problems we hadn't anticipated. The builder had just finished the house, which had a very modern design alternating flat roofs and cathedral ceilings. The outside cladding consisted of rough gray boards nailed onto the house. After one year, the boards began to warp and the nails began to pop out, and we learned that the contractor had used nails that were too short. Our first summer, Randy spent several weeks hammering in more nails to hold the house together. "Don't worry," I told Diana, "if I'm successful at Merck, in a year or two we can take more time and find a permanent home." Of course I had an escape hatch in mind: "If things don't work out," I said, "we can always return to a university and we won't have wasted all that time house hunting." But we stayed in that house for seventeen years before we finally decided to move to a permanent place.

***

We quickly made new friends at Merck and continued to entertain as we had in Ladue. But there were no more pig roasts. The powerful sense of unity and comradeship we had developed at Washington University didn't exist at Merck, where relationships were cordial but more formal – especially if you moved across divisional lines. The people in the research division, which was large in comparison with the Washington University groups, were similar in their total dedication to science. But they had very little in common with the people in the marketing and sales divisions or the central administration. Although these groups were friendly, their differences in training and interests kept them apart. Each acknowledged the importance of the other groups, but most of them understood only their own challenges. We all ate lunch in the same cafeteria, but the research people ate early and were leaving by the time "the suits" – the corporate types – came in.

None of the activities I participated in drew people from all the divisions together except tennis. I competed on the tennis ladder, making my way to the top rung for a very short time before being deposed. I also played with the "Merck Sharp & Dohme International Tennis Team," holding down the number three singles slot and teaming up with Hollis Williams, a friend in research, at number one doubles. The team was "International" because of its membership, not because of its competition. We played against other company teams, and one year we actually won the intercompany league. Proud of its accomplishment, the team apparently decided to buy jackets. A poor memory can be your friend, and I actually can't remember what happened next. But according to Hollis, I didn't buy one because I thought they were too expensive. If true, it must mean that, although I'd traveled a long distance since leaving the Westfield Sweet Shoppe, the hard times of the Great Depression had traveled with me. That makes sense because I remember quite clearly being appalled some years later by the idea of a corporate jet.

***

During my first year at MRL, I spent much of my time trying to climb the steep part of the learning curve. I had to develop a thorough understanding of each of the projects we had under way, evaluate each of the scientists, and rough out a strategy for improving our research operations. One of the first things I learned was that most of the research groups were trying to do too much, not too little. Instead of concentrating on one or two promising projects, they were conducting research on eight or nine. When I tried to get the endocrinologists to focus all their resources on their most promising lines of research, the head of that laboratory promptly left and joined the Yale Medical School faculty. That suited me. I didn't need research leaders who wanted to continue long-term projects that were going nowhere. After a period of floundering, a new leader emerged from the group. The endocrinologists began to prioritize their research, accelerating their work on a project to prevent enlargement of the prostate gland, a serious problem for many older men.

I tried a similar approach to "Management by Objectives" (MBO), a program used throughout Merck and many other American corporations. When I started with the company, I had never heard of MBO or any other technique for managing personnel. The way it worked at Merck was that each employee sat down periodically with his or her supervisor, the person to whom that employee "reported," to discuss goals for the coming year. The pair also regularly reviewed the employee's progress in achieving the previous year's goals. Since I had never "reported" to anyone in my career, at first I found the entire procedure crazy.

But Merck, which had been using MBO for two decades, wasn't about to change the plan, so I decided to take it seriously. I could see that most employees were simply reproducing their job descriptions, listing everything they were going to do during the next year. That could produce as many as twenty-five objectives. At the end of the year, they'd go over the list again, highlight what had been successful, and explain that someone else's shortcomings had prevented them from accomplishing the remainder. I decided to change that procedure. I announced that at MRL we would each have a maximum of five goals. At first they went bananas, but they soon calmed down after they'd actually tried the new procedure. We were always able to agree on their top five priorities, and by doing that, we made MBO something more than a bureaucratic game. I saw to it that people reporting to me set goals that they and I agreed were critical to the success of MRL – goals that were challenging but, in my estimation, achievable. I made a point of discussing the goals with our research people frequently, making suggestions I thought would help. In my way of running MRL, their goals were my goals. They quickly understood my way of working out the strategy in research. They recognized that we were in it together and appreciated that I was determined not to allow us to fail.

Making MBO work was important to me because basically I'm a people person, not a structure person. I don't believe you can turn a university or a business around just by changing the way it's organized. The key to making your operation more effective and innovative is to recruit and encourage talented risk-takers – the more the better. When I became president of the laboratories in 1976, I quickly set out to recruit more of these entrepreneurial types for MRL. I began to look over the files of all of our job candidates and to interview every senior scientist and physician who was going to be offered a position in Rahway or West Point.

Wherever our operation was weak, I was particularly attentive to the new hires. I thought, for instance, that neither our clinical research nor our engineering was as good as it should have been. I was just as much an elitist at Merck as I had been at Washington University. When I saw a second-rate résumé, I just said no. The key thing I looked at was performance in previous positions – either in training at a university or in a job. Had the applicant taken difficult courses? Carried a heavy course load? Was he or she involved in sports or in other extracurricular activities? Had he or she been a leader?

We were seeking outstanding people, and they are recognizable. Some department heads shy away from recruiting outstanding people because of fears they will not fit in well, will be too ambitious, or will become dissatisfied in the job and leave to move up in the organization. Those were the people I wanted to recruit, tigers anxious to show us all how to do it better. But that was not a popular position when I first went to Merck. In due time, the company changed. As department heads recognized what could be accomplished by outstanding new recruits, they shed their inhibitions and began seeking their own tigers.

In the case of clinical research, I rejected about a dozen candidates in a row, and finally the head of the operation came to see me. "Why are you turning down all of these good people?" he asked. I explained what I wanted to accomplish. Exasperated, he finally blurted out, "You wouldn't have hired me!" I just looked at him without saying anything because we both knew he was right.

Gradually, we began to upgrade our recruitment across the board. It couldn't be done quickly. You had to bring in top-grade people who were good learners and incrementally improve the operation. I asked everyone in charge of a department or research group to list the top eight or ten schools in their field. Then I told them I wanted to see applicants mostly from those schools. They groaned. "This is snobbish," some complained. Others were more upset. "My God!" they said, "I didn't graduate from one of those schools! What does that say about me?" But I told them, "You picked the best schools in your field, not me. We're just trying to be efficient." I said, "I can't see why we would recruit elsewhere. Of course there can be terrific people at any school, but let's play the odds." The truth was that most department heads had been recruiting at the schools from which *they* had graduated. That was OK in some cases, but if their alma maters were weak, the weaknesses in our program were being reinforced.

* * *

Part of the resistance to change came from outside of Merck. In the universities where we were trying to recruit, many of the best scientists thought that applied research (now called translational research) was inherently second-rate. Paradoxically, this mind-set was reinforced by the explosive growth in government support for basic science after World War II, the very setting in which I had built my career in biochemistry and enzymology. During this great expansion, many university scientists began to believe that what they did was the only thing to do. They guided their exceptional postdocs toward careers in the university system because, after all, anyone who was really bright would want to follow in the footsteps of the senior professors. Only the failures were recommended for industrial jobs. I called some of these scientists after they had sent us second-rate people to interview. "You son of a bitch!" I would say, "why are you sending me someone like that?" I could get away with this because of my standing in science, and usually the professors learned rather quickly that we had high standards at Merck.

The recruitment process was nevertheless slow, painful, and time-consuming. During my first year at Merck, I was invited to lecture in the Biochemistry and Molecular Biology Department at Princeton.

Afterwards, I met informally with the graduate students and postdocs. I asked how many would be interested in a position in an industrial laboratory like Merck after finishing their training. Out of about thirty young scientists, only one graduate student and one postdoctoral fellow admitted any interest. I was really depressed. I realized we had to get some of our exciting scientists to publish more of their work and to lecture at universities. We had to demonstrate that young scientists and engineers could have an exciting career at Merck. Besides doing good science, they would be involved in drug discovery – and what could be more fulfilling than creating new drugs that help people live healthier lives?

If recruitment had not been absolutely vital to the company, I wouldn't have done it. Fortunately, applied research became more fashionable as university growth leveled off and government funds for basic research got tighter. That transition, taking place in the late 1970s, began to have a decisive impact on our recruitment efforts by the end of the decade. Also, more young people became interested in research that was "relevant," and they liked the idea of improving health.

I discouraged our research department heads from hiring people from other companies unless we were starting work in an entirely new area of science or engineering. Then we needed a seasoned research person with industry experience in that field. But hiring from other pharmaceutical companies just seemed to be a way for headhunters to make money and to provide the lucky applicant with a raise he or she wouldn't otherwise have been given on the basis of performance. I wanted to build strength from within, gradually improving the organization until ideally we could promote most of our talented senior people out of our own ranks.

We were also able to improve MRL by making better use of the people who were already there. One of these was Dr. Arthur Patchett, who had joined MRL shortly after receiving his Ph.D. from Harvard and completing a postdoctoral fellowship at NIH. On the basis of his outstanding research talents, he'd quickly become head of the entire synthetic chemistry operation at Rahway at a very early age. A brilliant chemist, he was not a great manager in his early years. He flopped and was banished to an old dungeon-like laboratory building out of the mainstream. His boss there had him making random peptides, removing the solvent from the reaction mixture, and then diluting the leftover material and running portions of it through assays to see if it showed any signs of activity. He'd been doing this a couple of years when I arrived at Merck.

Art was in his laboratory every day, including Saturdays. I usually walked around the laboratories on Saturday mornings, stopping to chat with anyone who was there. Many researchers work on Saturdays – in part because some experiments run right through the weekend. Most of the scientists left before noon on Saturdays to run errands or get ready to go out with their wives or families or friends. But Art would always be there late in the day. I'd visit the others and then stop to talk to him. Or rather listen to him and watch him draw. As I quickly discovered, he was a genius in chemistry, and when we talked about any project, he would start to draw the chemical structures involved on the blackboard. This was an ideal chemical tutorial for me, and I would sit transfixed while Art free-associated in organic chemistry.

After several of these Saturday sessions, I could see that Art was an unusually talented scientist, and I thought he was probably the kind of risk-taker willing to tackle really difficult projects. Whether that was true or not, he was too talented to be cranking out random assortments of peptides. Finally I said: "Art, this can't be the way to discover drugs. It's not going to work. Wouldn't you like to target a molecule and try to make a drug that way?" He was ready for a change, and once we decided on a new project that he wanted to pursue, he became one of our most creative scientists. A few years down the road, he led his team of chemists in a successful project exploring a new treatment for high blood pressure. He also made vital contributions to the cholesterol research that Al Alberts was doing. Art Patchett was one of the most innovative chemists in MRL, but he had to be allowed to be productive – not told what to do.

A rescue of a different sort took place in regulatory affairs, the department responsible for Merck's applications for FDA approval of its new drugs and vaccines. For all pharmaceutical companies, getting FDA approval is a complex, expensive, time-consuming, life-or-death matter. If you become very good at it, you can actually use this capability as a bargaining chip in dealing with other firms in the industry. If you're not good at it, your company will lose a great deal of money, or even worse.

This is how it works. When a researcher discovers a novel substance that looks promising, the company files for a patent, which gives it exclusive marketing rights for twenty years. The company then invests an average of about $800 million to develop a new drug from this substance. The new medicine can be brought to market only after large-scale clinical studies demonstrate that it is effective and safe in humans, and the study results are then compiled by the research group and submitted to the FDA for approval. By the time a medicine receives FDA approval, about eight years of the patent have been used up – leaving about twelve years for sales of the patent-protected product. The faster the FDA grants approval, the faster the product can be launched and the sales begun. Any time lost because of delays in regulatory approval causes a loss of sales revenues during the patent-protected life of the product.

Every pharmaceutical company wants as perfect a regulatory filing as possible by the research group. Incomplete or ambiguous data will cause the FDA to request additional explanations or even additional experiments. Time and sales will be lost. Even worse, the FDA can decide the results are not convincing and turn down the application.

I learned that our head of regulatory affairs had long considered himself a glorified mailman – a significant job given that the paper alone for each New Drug Application (NDA) could literally fill a small truck. When I asked him, "What's your job?" he said, "I file the New Drug Application." I pressed harder: "What does that mean to you?" He replied, "I gather the information, put it in a book, and send it to the FDA." He was in effect orchestrating the applications without becoming engaged with the data being presented to the government.

One of our compounds – *Timoptic*, a beta-blocker to treat glaucoma – had produced some unexpected results in one of the studies in animals. Although one interpretation was that the drug could be dangerous in humans, a series of ingenious experiments (by Del Bokelman and his safety assessment team) demonstrated that the drug was safe, clearing the way for FDA approval.

When discussing *Timoptic* with the head of regulatory affairs, I found he didn't understand the experiments exonerating the beta-blocker and planned to ask our technical experts to explain the results to the FDA. I told him that the head of regulatory affairs is responsible for FDA strategy and that he and his colleagues must understand all of the data presented for approval well enough to explain them to the agency. I pointed out that the time to approval can be greatly affected by an optimal presentation and explanation of all the experimental results.

He was a very bright man who understood at once that he and his group were now expected to do a different job and that he would need a better class of professionals – scientists at least as good as those in clinical research – to get that job done. He began recruiting and found some good scientists willing to give up lab work, especially those not currently working on an exciting project, by making it clear that regulatory approvals are critical to the success of a pharmaceutical company. By enlisting people with better scientific training, the head of regulatory affairs began to turn this operation around, and instead of running away from the challenge, he became one of the architects of the new order.

* * *

Much of my time was spent talking to researchers about their work or listening to more formal presentations about their projects. In the pharmaceutical industry, a researcher can easily spend ten to fifteen years on a project before it produces an approved drug. I had no problem with such projects if they looked promising. The ones that worried me were those taking three to five years while producing no glimmer of success.

I tried to eliminate those projects in two ways. One was to keep talking and listening on a one-to-one basis with the scientists. My private conversations were far more useful than any of the regularly scheduled, formal show-and-tell presentations made to senior members of research management. There, the worst thing anyone could do was to embarrass a presenter in front of the entire organization by, say, pointing out that the experimental results were insufficient to support a conclusion or that proposed future experiments were not appropriate given what was already known. As a result, comments were hedged at these meetings. In general, I found that large public meetings of almost any sort were fine for disseminating information but very inefficient, even counterproductive, for making critical evaluations or decisions on strategic directions. When I talked science face-to-face, I got a more accurate picture of what was or wasn't working at the bench level of research. Often I heard the most important things while standing in the lunch line with the scientists, walking to a lecture, or waiting out in the hall before a presentation. "How are things going in the lab?" I'd ask. "Jesus Christ!" would be the answer: "We'll never get that done!" "Why?" "Because we're taking a ridiculous approach." "Why?" "Because so-and-so told me to do it that way."

The scientists leveled with me because I, a scientist myself, was one of them, and I understood their difficulties. They knew that, as head of the lab, I didn't hold grudges and took on each project with them, suggesting solutions to help them solve their problems. Some bosses were reluctant to change scientific projects because so much time had already been invested in the current effort. Some were unwilling to admit that an approach wasn't going to work. So they procrastinated – for months or years. I wanted definite objectives with a defined time and effort. If the goals could not be achieved, then I wanted to try something that was more likely to work.

If a problem was tough, I thought about it and often called our scientists at home at night. Or the next time I saw them, I would try to suggest something better than that "ridiculous approach." There's no substitute for that kind of involvement if you want a high-morale, high-intensity research organization. The best way to get a researcher to stop a bad project is to convince him or her to work on something much more exciting with the prospect of making an important contribution.

My second elimination tactic was to press all of the groups to prioritize their projects continually and shift resources toward the most promising areas of research. It worked much as it had with MBO. "Look," I'd say, "if you're going to make this kind of inhibitor this year, you'll never do it with only four chemists. So let's put ten chemists on that project." Often the reply I got was, "Aaach! Where are they going to come from?" Then I'd point out that they had chemists working on projects with very little prospect of succeeding for many years. If ever. "Yeah," they would say, "but these good old guys have been working on that for many years." We had to break through the "good old guy" barrier.

Breaking that barrier was a major function of our annual research conference. Every year we held a big meeting at Seaview, a resort on the southern New Jersey coast just north of Atlantic City. In the late 1970s we began to make considerable progress in Merck's laboratories by keeping the pressure on across all these fronts, including the whole spectrum of research activities: establishing new hypotheses, setting up new screens, judging productivity of older screens, identifying product leads, identifying product candidates, developing results of clinical studies, and updating the patenting potential to ensure exclusivity in product ownership. An annual strategic plan would ultimately evolve in which the costs of all the activities would be tallied. We discussed candidates evolving from our own research, possible product breakthroughs outside of Merck, and the possibility of Merck research entering a new field based on activities in other pharmaceutical or academic laboratories. If Merck research was not working in a new field, could we license a product candidate from another source? Discussions also covered the potential costs of our new product candidates as projected by our research chemical engineers and finance people. In addition to the annual review of strategy, some time was also given to an update on our five-year strategy. This was especially important because we needed to project the impact of future clinical studies – usually the most expensive stage of product development.

At Seaview all the project directors gave presentations on what their research teams had accomplished and what they expected in the year ahead. The MRL leaders decided which projects would continue into the new year and which would be killed. It was uncanny how much exciting information was generated just a few months before this meeting, and the new findings seemed always to make it more difficult to stop a project. Because it is very tough for project leaders to pull the plug on the losers, the Seaview sessions focused on sifting and analyzing all the information that would enable us to decide which way to turn with each of the projects. When projects had produced viable candidates, we pumped in enormous resources to develop the product. When projects had established proof of principle (that is, demonstrating that the product of their research had the desired effect and would work in human disease), we provided the support they needed to optimize a lead before selecting a product candidate. We also tried to identify projects in which the team had a promising hypothesis but had not yet been able to achieve proof of principle. Then, too, we sifted out proposals for new undertakings based on hypotheses generated by our scientists from their own research or results from either university or competing industrial laboratories. These sessions were long and tough. We spent most of our time on the long-term projects for which proof of principle had not been achieved, with everyone straining to devise an experiment that would either lead to a product candidate or kill the project. There were winners and losers every year.

* * *

These annual meetings ran Sunday through Thursday, and we broke the tension with tennis and golf matches on Wednesday afternoon. We also had a small group of people who jogged at dawn in the flat, quiet countryside of southern New Jersey. For me that was a time to clear my head for the next intense session. I've never picked up a golf club, but I always played in the tennis doubles. This was a great way to see our people outside of the laboratory. I am a great believer that sports reveal important insights into people. In tennis, for instance, I was always interested in how competitive an individual was, how well that person related to a partner or opponent, how accurately he or she called a ball in or out, and whether that player showed leadership potential or blamed conditions and other players after losing a match. It's easy to judge leadership potential in all sports: leaders are people others want to follow and emulate.

Over the years, one of my special delights was to watch new scientific leaders emerge at the Seaview meetings. Leaders in science are easy to identify: they're risk takers who are the most productive scientists and who come up with more new ideas, new experiments to test hypotheses, and new and exciting results in their projects. They attract new recruits because their projects generate scientific excitement. Risk taking is an important aspect of scientific progress. The best scientists are willing, on the basis of a unique understanding of available data, to move their research into exciting new areas in which there are few precedents and therefore a higher probability of failure. Despite the risk, industry depends on these special people for breakthrough products, and I knew they were the key to the future of MRL and Merck.

***

Despite the abundance of productive activity in my early months at MRL, I was in no danger of suffering from hubris. On the contrary, I was acutely aware of the mistakes I was making as I tried to transform this large, proud organization. Determined to produce the research turnaround that had convinced me to leave Washington University, I pushed too hard on the recruitment process early on. When I encountered resistance from outstanding candidates suspicious of "applied research," I gave away too much. I began to promise some of them that they could continue with their own projects, just moving them from the university to MRL. Certain that they would shortly get caught up in the excitement of drug discovery, I thought we could gradually refocus their research if it turned out not to have any practical implications.

I was wrong. They happily toiled away at their own basic research, paying no attention to what was happening around them. So much for infectious excitement. When I tried to get them to take part in any of our leading projects, they reminded me of the promise I had made. I keep my promises. So I was left with a small group of extremely talented people doing hot science that was more likely to help their publication records over the next twenty years than it was to help Merck. I stopped making that promise and began to be explicit about what we were doing and what I expected at MRL. We employed many outstanding scientists who regularly published their research results, but we didn't pretend to be a university. Merck Research Laboratory's goal was to be the best laboratory in the world for drug discovery. After recovering from my initial mistakes, I tried to keep that objective fixed clearly in the minds of our new scientific personnel – especially when they were being recruited.

Another situation I was slow to come to grips with was the "backup problem." When I arrived at MRL, I didn't even realize there *was* a problem. My background in university and NIH research hadn't prepared me for this one. But what I began to see as I settled into my new job was that once basic research produced a promising compound, the team stopped working on the entire project while their candidate went through safety assessment and moved into clinical studies. The scientists who had discovered the molecule might be holding their breath, fearful their candidate would fail the tests. After all, many have worked in pharmaceutical research their entire career and never developed a successful drug. Failures are far more numerous than successes. But I wasn't worried about their state of mind. I wanted them to be preparing MRL for two possibilities. If the first compound was toxic or otherwise unsuccessful, they should already have in the wings a second, related backup candidate different enough in structure that it might lack the toxicity problem. If the first compound succeeded, they should be working on the improved follow-up drug – one with fewer side effects or that could be given fewer times a day.

We established a new rule. We never stopped work on a discovery project until the candidate cleared the final clinical tests. This kept the people in basic and clinical research talking to one another. It also provided us with some outstanding follow-up drugs in the cardiovascular field. The rule worked, but I should have moved in that direction faster and more forcefully. I was learning, but Merck was providing me an expensive, on-the-job education.

Most disconcerting to me was the mistake that resulted from my unwillingness to push harder at West Point. I had made some inroads there, but resistance to my proposed research strategy was deep and strong. The leaders there, distinguished scientists who were experts in their disciplines, were not accepting the molecular targeting approach. They were convinced the traditional methodology of screening random chemicals would be most likely to yield product candidates. They were entirely convinced of their future success, and I let them continue their way for many months. Looking back, I can see in very precise dollar terms what that cost our company.

At that time, the West Point researchers were working on a potential treatment for peptic ulcers, a compound able to suppress the secretion of acid in the stomach of animals. When I talked to them about their "lead," I quickly realized that they didn't know *how* it worked. I tried to coax them into figuring out just what their compound did. Their response was always, "Our product is going to be great. Look what it does to the acid secretion." When problems developed in the safety tests, they tried to solve them by tinkering with the molecule. Each time they told me, "Now we've got it," always convinced that the next variation on the molecule would do the trick. But meanwhile, Merck was losing ground in the race to develop new therapies. The field of ulcer treatments saw decisive breakthroughs in the 1970s. At a SmithKline laboratory in England, James Black developed a histamine$_2$-receptor antagonist. Histamine is the chemical that sits on a specific receptor and signals the stomach to start producing acid. Black discovered a molecule that resembled the structure of histamine and thus could substitute for it on the receptor. By blocking the action of histamine, Black's molecule suppressed the secretion of acid. Since peptic ulcers had been treated with acid neutralizers (antacids) for many years, stopping the secretion of acid in the stomach made enormous sense. This was just the kind of molecular targeting I wanted MRL to conduct. In Black's case, the result was *Tagamet*, a breakthrough treatment for peptic ulcers.

On one of my trips to West Point, I discussed what Black was doing. "This is a rational approach," I said. "SmithKline has a specific receptor antagonist, a molecule that resembles histamine. That's the approach we ought to take." I'd already made this speech several times, but this time I was certain the new evidence about Black's accomplishments would enable us to turn the corner – at last. But it didn't. "We have a superior compound," they said. I leaned harder: "They've shown that their approach will work in humans. I don't know that the compound they have will be optimal. So why don't we use that approach to find a better one?" No luck this time either.

The Merck researchers circled the wagons around their project. They believed they were on the verge of identifying a potent, safe compound that reduced acid secretion in dog stomachs (the animal model). They felt they had a winner even though they didn't understand how it worked. They studied only the end result – acid secretion. I had little confidence in this approach because it was not based on a scientific understanding of the molecules involved.

I wasn't one to bludgeon people, but I didn't give up. I talked to them every time I visited, which was once or twice a week. Each time I was there, they showed me new data, new curves on the graph demonstrating improvements to their compound, making it longer acting. I was growing increasingly nervous as the months dragged past and SmithKline was getting closer to market.

At last my colleagues decided they had optimized their compound, and they then sent it into safety assessment in animals. It turned out to be grossly toxic and was finally dropped. I wasn't surprised because they didn't know the compound's mechanism of action. I knew it could be reacting with several molecules other than those targeted by Jim Black, and I was surprised that some of the senior scientists involved didn't seem to learn much from the experience.

Because I wasn't persuasive enough, or wasn't tough enough, or perhaps because I was uncertain of myself in this new setting, Merck lost several years of lead time in peptic ulcers. Did that matter? It certainly did. We finally ignored the advice of our own research team and licensed from Yamanouchi a compound (famotidine) that was given the trade name *Pepcid*. In its prescription and over-the-counter formulations, *Pepcid* became a billion-dollar-a-year product.

I took some consolation from the fact that *Pepcid* was the first product Merck had ever licensed from an outside source. For years the laboratory had resisted licensing, largely because of an NIH (Not Invented Here) mentality. Only MRL discoveries, the scientists maintained, were good enough for Merck. *Pepcid* blasted that myth, setting the stage for later transactions that were critical to the company's future.

But consolation prizes seldom console, and this one didn't leave me happy with my own performance. Had we shifted our approach earlier, we might have discovered our own compound and avoided paying royalties for a licensed product. Add that to the roughly three years of revenue we lost, and it should be clear why I put this experience on the liability side of my personal ledger.

One reason I was hesitant to knock heads over research strategies was the stunning success achieved with ivermectin. This amazing antiparasitic drug was discovered shortly after I arrived in Rahway, and it was discovered in the old style. A product of random screenings of natural products (microbial broths), it became the leading animal health product of the 1980s and 1990s. Ivermectin kills parasitic worms in the gastrointestinal tracts of horses, cattle, sheep, and pigs. It also kills biting flies. The worms cause the animals to produce less meat, milk, and wool and to derive less energy from their feed, thus requiring more feed to support their growth. Farmers earn higher profits from herds that are free of such worms, and around the world, wherever animals accumulate parasites, one of the several formulations of ivermectin has long been the overwhelming drug of choice. In countries like Australia and New Zealand, which have more livestock than people, raising and exporting sheep and cattle products are a major revenue source, and the impact of ivermectin on productivity is extremely significant to their economies.

Reflecting on ivermectin, I reached two conclusions. First, I saw that the traditional techniques could still produce important products. Although molecular targeting would be our future, in the transition we could continue where we might have an advantage through uniqueness. I thus favored scientists who developed animal model screens unique to MRL and that used unique sources of new compounds. That was the case with Bill Campbell, who had devised a special rodent model of parasitic worm disease. Second, this encouraged me to be tolerant of scientists who thought they were on the edge of discovery. Perhaps a few more months would actually make a big difference.

I could see that resistance to my strategy came largely from those who thought their scientific position was strong. Those with no leads were eager to climb onto my bandwagon. The provenance of ivermectin also made me understand how important it was to my leadership role to demonstrate as soon as possible that a more rational, targeted approach could actually produce successful new therapies. Especially drugs that were a big hit in the marketplace.

***

So the real test of my leadership in research was the program in cardiovascular disease, where Al Alberts and his group played a

central role. This was my own particular area of expertise, where I
had made important contributions to the basic science. Here I had to
show that MRL could convert knowledge about biosynthesis in microbes into new drugs for people suffering from the effects of high
cholesterol.

When Al and I reviewed the literature coming out of the laboratories
at Munich (Lynen), Purdue University (Rodwell), and Dallas (Brown
and Goldstein), we had quickly agreed to target the rate-limiting enzyme HMG-CoA reductase. It was less clear how to proceed from that
point. There was a fork in the road with chemical synthesis down one
side and screening for natural substances down the other. Within MRL,
leads were sought from two sources. One was the library of compounds
that our chemists had developed over many years. The other source
was nature. Art Patchett, along with our microbiologists, had devised
a technology based on soil microorganisms from various parts of the
world – a technique that in the past had mainly yielded antibiotics. The
microorganisms were isolated and grown in small cultures in the laboratory and then in larger fermentation broths. The resulting microbial
broth was extracted to separate any interesting microbial products for
testing in our various screens. These cultures were a potential source
of interesting new molecules.

Merck Research Laboratories had strengths in both processes, but
the chemists were on the more traveled route in Rahway. They had
long been the kings of research at MRL and when we first launched
the cholesterol program, they put significant resources into the search
for a compound to inhibit our vital enzyme. On the basis of my advice
during one of my consulting visits, Mike Greenspan and Lew Mandell
had for some time been screening chemicals for inhibitors of HMG-
CoA reductase in cell cultures. But without success.

The fermentation path was the territory of Merck's microbiologists,
who had logged some significant successes in past years. During the
Second World War, Merck had made important contributions to the
process of mass-producing penicillin, and, after the war, the company's
microbiologists had played a leading role in the discovery and development of streptomycin. But after those front-page successes had come
a long dry spell. Still, I was an advocate of fermentation broths so
long as we targeted a specific molecule – especially an enzyme. My
science mentor, Earl Stadtman, had been trained originally in soil microbiology, and I inherited his respect for nature's ability to develop
ingenious new substances of potential interest to man. Also, Merck

screens could be designed to search for a very specific kind of chemical activity – in our case, an inhibitor of the rate-limiting enzyme in cholesterol synthesis.

So the chemists set off down one path and the microbiologists down another with Al Alberts leading the combined charge and the millions of people with elevated levels of cholesterol standing to benefit so long as one of the teams was successful. Both Al and I had a hunch that microbiology might cross the finish line first. We knew that Akira Endo, a scientist who had earlier worked with Konrad Bloch and was then at the Japanese pharmaceutical firm Sankyo, had reported on a compound called "compactin" that inhibited HMG-CoA reductase. According to the reports, Sankyo's product was a potent natural substance that could be taken orally. We were encouraged by this news but nervous, of course, because Merck was in a competitive race.

Fortunately, Al was still working long hours and unable to stay away from his laboratory when awaiting results from an experiment. He had the support of Art Patchett, who had introduced the practice at MRL of screening microbial extracts for active substances other than antibiotics. Art provided the extracts produced by his team. But what we needed now was a new screen to target the molecule we were after. That's what Al and Julie S. Chen devised in 1977: a rapid, high-throughput enzyme assay that allowed tests to be carried out in large numbers. At that point, things began to move much faster.

Suddenly, in 1978, Al and his team found what they wanted. After developing a screen capable of testing thousands of extracts of soil microorganisms, they got results on number eighteen. It was unbelievable. But the assays clearly indicated that *Aspergillus terreus*, a common soil microorganism found around the world, was producing something that was active against our target enzyme. This particular sample, along with many others, came to Art Patchett's group from a screening operation in Spain.[†] Art's group made the extracts and forwarded them to Al and Julie, who suddenly and surprisingly got positive results.

[†] C.I.B.E, a small Spanish laboratory, had a contract with MRL to select soil microorganisms and send fermentation extracts that might produce an inhibitor to another enzyme, dihydrofolate reductase. At MRL, however, Al Alberts discovered that, although the extract did not inhibit dihydrofolate reductase, it did inhibit HMG-CoA reductase. The inhibitory substance was lovastatin. The Spanish laboratory received a royalty on the sale of lovastatin until Merck acquired C.I.B.E. several years later.

Not until the chemists isolated the active substance from the broth and Georg Albers-Schonberg determined its structure, however, were we certain we hadn't just rediscovered Sankyo's compactin. We hadn't. Although related structurally to compactin, *Mevacor* (the trade name for lovastatin) was a unique new compound. It was the first statin in the world to become a drug.

At this point, we put MRL on red alert and concentrated all the resources Al could effectively use on this single promising compound. In a research organization the size of MRL that's a large number of people with many different talents. In addition to the chemists and microbiologists, the growing team now included chemical engineers, spectroscopists, pharmacologists, and toxicologists. The microbiologists determined the optimal conditions for growing the microorganism. The chemical engineers isolated the lovastatin in large quantities. Spectroscopists determined its chemical structure. Pharmacologists studied its effects in live animals, and the toxicologists studied lovastatin to demonstrate any possible harmful effects by feeding it to mice, rats, and rabbits. We also started to assemble a clinical research team and alerted marketing.

Although the tempo in basic research increased rapidly, the initial reactions from both clinical research and marketing were tepid at best. Both had been burned by their experience with halofenate. To them, the "cholesterol hypothesis" was still just a hypothesis. They were willing to get started, but they wanted to see more evidence that lowering blood cholesterol was good for you before getting as excited as we were. In addition, they had no reason to believe that lovastatin would be any safer or more effective than halofenate and other older drugs – none of which was very effective. Al and I, on the other hand, believed in lovastatin because it was targeted on a specific enzyme in the cholesterol pathway and thus likely to be safer and more effective than any drug previously available.

Although the emotions rippling through basic research were not infectious, they were intense. We were like a small army focusing all its forces on a breakthrough in the enemy's lines. Al Alberts – the scientist without a Ph.D. – was the general in charge, and I was the chief of staff, making certain he had access to every researcher and piece of equipment he needed. As the pace picked up, the excitement steadily mounted. The competition with Sankyo heightened the thrill of discovery.

There was plenty for all of us to do. During 1978 and 1979, MRL carried out hundreds of experiments to improve our understanding of what exactly *Mevacor* did to the enzyme. When we studied the effects it had in animals, the tests indicated that inhibition of HMG-CoA reductase causes a dramatic reduction in blood cholesterol. Although many of the earliest experiments were done in rats and mice, we soon found that dogs responded more readily to *Mevacor* with greater cholesterol reduction at lower doses. Meanwhile, we were preparing large amounts of the drug in the pilot plant (an intermediate-size facility) so that the toxicology experiments could be completed, opening the way for initial studies in humans. All of this was moving at a whirlwind pace.

I must admit I had an emotional commitment to *Mevacor* that went beyond science and drug discovery. For Al Alberts and me, the trail to *Mevacor* had started in the 1950s when we began to work together on lipid biosynthesis at NIH. Now, almost a quarter of a century later, we were still together and on the verge of turning microbial biochemistry and enzyme targeting into a major factor in drug discovery and the treatment of human disease. I believed *Mevacor*'s success would complete the conversion to targeted research at MRL. That outcome was all the more likely because, during these same months, Art Patchett and his colleagues were in fast forward with a new enzyme inhibitor that reduced high blood pressure. There were still doubting Thomases in the laboratories, but I was certain that even the hard-shell traditionalists would now concede that molecular targeting was a good long-term strategy for MRL.

The first results from clinical tests in patients with high blood cholesterol showed that *Mevacor* dramatically reduced blood cholesterol – especially LDL. To a degree, in fact, never before achieved with a drug. Now even the marketing group began to express some excitement, and in the laboratories we were ecstatic.

* * *

By the time the Vagelos clan left for our annual vacation at Martha's Vineyard in the summer of 1980, I had every reason to relish some days at the beach. The turnaround at MRL seemed to be entering its final phase. By 1980 the laboratories at Rahway and West Point were working together rather smoothly, and our accomplishments with research targeted against enzymes seemed to be convincing even the diehards that we had found a better path to drug discovery. *Mevacor* had sailed through the initial, short-term safety studies with excellent marks, and Merck had received a patent in the United States and several countries abroad. Sankyo, which was dogging our steps, had independently discovered an identical compound in Japan (along with compactin) and acquired patent rights in that country and a number of other markets.

But the outlook for *Mevacor* was marvelous. In small numbers of patients, every additional test indicated that it safely lowered blood cholesterol levels. Clinical research was beginning to gather the information required before wide-scale studies could begin in humans. This research was ongoing when we left for the beach, and the preliminary results looked wonderful to all of us – especially to Al Alberts and me.

On Martha's Vineyard, we collected as many family members as possible at Matakesett, a tennis enclave in the southeast corner of the island, on the outskirts of Edgartown. My dad had died of a heart attack in 1978, and so we were down to two grandmothers, both of whom enjoyed cooking and playing cards while chattering in Greek. We rented one house, and my sister Helen and her husband and children rented another. Diana's sister, Thetis Reavis, and her daughter shared a third house with Iris Andris, a cousin who brought her three children from Bethesda, Maryland. Another cousin, Andrea Lambrinides, her husband, and three children rented the fourth house in our little colony. We were twenty-four in all.

On sunny days, the adults played tennis and the children swarmed to the beach. Our daughter Cynthia, finishing at Brown University, was overseer for the younger children when she wasn't on the tennis court. Randy had graduated from Harvard and was able to get away from the College of Physicians & Surgeons of Columbia University long enough to raise the level of our tennis – briefly. Ellen, at twelve, had a bosom friend in my sister Helen's daughter Jonie, and they were inseparable through the entire two weeks. Andrew was my surf-fishing partner, and we had a good omen that summer. When the Vineyard Sound warms up, the fish move out into deeper water, but that summer Andrew and I caught six bluefish on the surf off Wasque Point, which is a family record that still holds. Occasionally, all twenty-four of us ate dinner at our house, and that evening, Andrew and I were able to provide a main course. Hamburgers, hot dogs, and "s'mores" made with marshmallows were more interesting to our small herd of children, but the adults enjoyed the fresh fish and the family stories we all exchanged as the evening set in.

At these family gatherings, we often discussed the day's activities but also careers that the children might consider. Within the family group we had people in law, business, finance, real estate, and, of course, medicine and science. Like our parents, we wanted to be sure the children had educations that would enable them to enter any career they found interesting. These summer gatherings fostered a close relationship within the family – one that we hoped would extend beyond our generation.

Just about every day, the crowd would disperse just before dinner, and Diana and I were able to take a long swim. We talked about our family, the grandmothers, and our warm, intricate memories of Washington University and St. Louis. Merck kept creeping into the conversation, however, and every few days I called the laboratory to find out how things were going. I was obsessed with MRL, and *Mevacor* was right in the middle of that obsession. Reassured by Al Alberts and others that everything was in great shape, I returned to our idyllic vacation. It seemed almost too good to be true.

6 | *Crisis*

One of the executive perks at Merck Research Laboratories was a limo for company business. On a beautiful September day in 1980, in my fifth year as head of the laboratories, the limo picked me up at home after lunch. We drove down through the Pine Barrens to the Seaview Resort at Absecon, New Jersey, where all of Merck's senior scientists were gathering for their four-day annual meeting to survey their accomplishments and plan our program for the next year. I left early because I'd arranged a singles match with my colleague Stan Fidelman. There'd be neither time nor space on the tennis courts for singles once the entire group arrived, so a few of us always tried to get together early for some intense competition before the work began. It was also a good occasion to have some private time with Stan, who was a close friend and a very special person in our organization.

As the car headed into southern New Jersey, my mind drifted a bit as I admired the beauty of the landscape and thought about the history of that area. I'd recently read John McPhee's book on the Pine Barrens, which rekindled my interest in seeing them again. But I quickly stopped musing, dug into my pile of reports, one from each of our laboratories, and became completely engrossed in the strategic reviews. Which programs were making substantial progress? Which had the greatest potential to make an impact on human or animal diseases? Which had the greatest financial potential? How was the effort distributed across the laboratories? Did we have adequate numbers of people? Did they have enough space, equipment, funds? I'd been working on our strategic plan as it was being compiled, but now that I could compare these final reports I was able to refine our priorities. Setting priorities is the key to planning. There are never enough people or funds to do everything, and thus the goal of the meeting at Absecon was to develop a firm set of priorities.

Since I enjoyed that intellectual challenge, the annual meetings were exciting for me. Our scientists always had late-breaking experimental results that they held back and released at Seaview, hoping to make their project the central attraction of the session. There were always surprises – some compelling, some exciting, some just titillating. These late results always stimulated questions and suggestions from an audience that included the senior members of Merck's laboratories from all over the world.

Two hours later, as we approached the resort, I had pretty much finished my review and started to think about my impending tennis match. I felt good about the reports I had just read. In fact, I may have been a little puffed up about myself that fall because we seemed to be on the verge of achieving my major goals at MRL. The improvements in personnel and procedures were making themselves felt throughout the organization. Targeted research was winning converts at both Rahway and West Point. My prize project, Al Alberts's *Mevacor* research, was on the brink of what we hoped would be a colossal breakthrough in cardiovascular therapy. Things were going so well I should have been suspicious. But I wasn't. I was just enjoying the good times and good work as I glided into the resort.

For some scientists headed toward southern New Jersey that fall, the trip had to have been tense and unpleasant. If you were involved in a marginal project that might face the budget axe as a result of the reports we were about to hear, you probably were not thinking about the quiet Jersey countryside. If we were forced to make cuts, we would try to put a positive spin on the change, providing those affected with an "opportunity" to join forces with a more promising project. They might, for instance, become part of the growing team concentrating on *Mevacor*. But no matter how much the change was candy-coated, the losers became dejected. Most of our scientists had healthy egos that were heavily invested in their projects, some of which had been their sole obsession for several years. It was not easy to drop the axe on people we knew very well and respected. That's one of the reasons they were given an opportunity during "show-and-tell" to present those last-minute results that always suggested their project had suddenly become "promising."

These intense four-day sessions were one of the many forms of communication that helped keep an organization as big as Merck effective over the long haul. A great deal of my time at MRL was spent trying to improve communications, formal and informal, inside the division as well as across divisional lines. It might seem easy, but it's not. Most of us tend to fall into a familiar groove, whether at work, at lunch, or at home. Some of the most intense people, those most dedicated to their work, are the least likely to get out of their grooves and meet someone who works on a different project in another building. At Seaview we had scientists from laboratories in Rahway, West Point, and Canada, many of whom met only at these gatherings. So the meetings were important because they encouraged these intense professionals to get acquainted with colleagues they didn't normally meet day to day. Some of those talks took place in the formal meetings, some in the hallways, some on the tennis court, and some over drinks in the evenings.

Keeping communications open was an ongoing effort. I tried to make sure anyone who wanted to talk to me felt comfortable doing so, and I also liked the idea of being available to all Merck personnel. With that in mind, I usually tried to eat lunch in the cafeteria at Rahway or West Point rather than in a private dining room. I used the latter when I had a special business lunch where I needed quiet and confidentiality; otherwise, I wanted to be in a place where I could meet and see other Merck people (and they could see me). This helped keep me in touch with people and ideas at all levels of the organization. Not all of these conversations were about Merck's business. Everyone from the custodial staff to the executive vice presidents would ask me for medical advice for themselves and their families. I always did my best to help, making phone calls to put them in touch with the top authorities in the appropriate field, whether it was a cardiovascular problem, an unusual cancer, or their son's asthma. The talks at Absecon also blended personal and professional concerns, although for researchers whose projects were achieving marginal results, science was the heart of the matter.

* * *

Late Monday afternoon, after the first full day of reports and discussions at Seaview, ten of us, all senior research executives, were having drinks, relaxing in the comfortable living room of the presidential suite. We were all in harmony, feeling confident about our program and Merck's future. A pharmaceutical company's prospects depend significantly on what's in the research pipeline. All of us understood that our major responsibility was to keep our pipeline full, and we also knew that this was especially important at Merck. For years the company's strategy had been to move out of products that were off patent and becoming low-margin commodities. In the 1930s and 1940s, MRL had isolated and synthesized several vitamins. In the 1950s, 1960s, and 1970s, the firm had gradually moved out of that market, leaving the vitamin business pretty much to the Swiss company Hoffmann-La Roche, which had scaled up to satisfy global demand and the narrow margins of a commodity business. In effect, Merck's strategy bet the company's future on the ability of MRL to keep filling the pipeline with important new drugs.

Not just any drug. Merck periodically needed a blockbuster product in order to grow in a way that would keep the company's top executives and investors happy. That's why they'd recruited me from Washington University. During my first four years in Rahway, we rolled out a number of new products, some of which had substantial sales. In 1978 alone, Merck had introduced three important new drugs in the United States: *Clinoril* for arthritis, *Mefoxin* for bacterial infections, and *Timoptic* for glaucoma. These excellent products pushed our sales growth to 15 percent, 20 percent, and 15 percent in 1978, 1979, and 1980, respectively.

But successful as they were, these drugs were not the kind of blockbusters that can change the sales and profit curves of a large corporation for a full decade. The bulge in 1979 sales was already gone by 1980. Despite the growth in sales, the increases in net income in those same three years (12 percent, 20 percent, and 8 percent) were disappointing. We were also concerned because two of the company's major products (*Indocin* and *Aldomet*) would be going off patent in the United States in the next year.

There was good cause to be nervous about the immediate future even though Merck was obviously in better financial condition than most of the nation's businesses. They were being hurt by high interest rates and inflation. Many U.S. corporations were finding it impossible to match the efficiency of firms from Germany and Japan. The oil crises of 1973 and 1979 hurt many firms that were energy-intensive, and the downturn had reached major proportions by 1980, which was one of the reasons the Republicans won the election that year. Although many American companies were going under, Merck was doing very well in both the domestic market and overseas. In 1980, when sales increased 15 percent, the company's net (after taxes) income was over $415 million.

Still, we needed at least one blockbuster product soon, which is why we were all watching *Mevacor* so closely and why we were all upbeat about our research program. We thought *Mevacor* had the potential to become a billion-dollar-a-year product. The results from our initial clinical studies in humans were outstanding. Al Alberts's new compound reduced blood cholesterol faster and to a lower level than any drug ever tested by any company, making us confident we had a medical breakthrough as well as the blockbuster Merck and the investment community wanted.

* * *

But suddenly one telephone call transformed our late afternoon winddown session into a wake. The bad news came from Boyd Woodruff, one of our top research executives in Japan, where Merck was doing a substantial business. Our Japanese competitor, Sankyo, had run aground in its efforts to develop a cholesterol-lowering agent that was structurally related to *Mevacor*. According to the story Boyd had heard, Sankyo's compound (compactin) caused tumors in the animals used in the safety assessment tests. The company had stopped its clinical studies in humans.

This news was devastating. We knew that the Sankyo drug and *Mevacor* functioned through the same mechanism of action: both blocked the enzyme HMG-CoA reductase. If compactin caused tumors because of its specific structure, then *Mevacor* might not be toxic. But if compactin caused tumors through its activity as an HMG-CoA reductase inhibitor, then all drugs inhibiting that enzyme were likely to be toxic as well. We had no way of knowing whether this was the case. We only knew that Sankyo had stopped a crucial clinical trial. That alone meant compactin – and possibly *Mevacor* by implication – had encountered very serious problems.

As evening fell and the first shock wore off, we launched an intense discussion. How could we verify the rumor? What should we do with the clinical trial of *Mevacor*? Bert Peltier and Marvin Jaffe, who were responsible for Merck's clinical studies, demanded that we try immediately to get additional information from Japan. Charlie Leighton, our regulatory expert, was initially too stunned to say anything. When he recovered, he agreed that we needed to run the rumor to ground. As the discussion continued, the noise level shot up and people began to interrupt one another.

By that point, I thought we had already reached three conclusions. First, we should immediately stop all the clinical studies. Second, we should notify the FDA. Finally, I should try to get more information directly from Sankyo. We kept returning to the point that we had seen no evidence, absolutely no indication in our own thorough safety and clinical tests, that *Mevacor* produced these kinds of effects. Our studies were of relatively short duration, but they raised doubts about the rumor. Nevertheless, we knew we had to move forcefully. The news that Sankyo had actually terminated its clinical trials simply overwhelmed us.

I tried to pump some optimism back into the group. "I'm certain," I said, "that any cancer caused by Sankyo's drug isn't due to a mechanism shared with *Mevacor*." But the ensuing silence told me I was the only one at the table capable of believing that. My colleagues knew, as I did, that my optimistic hypothesis was one of two possibilities, and none of us had the evidence that evening to decide which one was correct.

Only one thing seemed certain at that moment: Merck had to stop its clinical trials immediately, and that's what I did. Marv Jaffe immediately left to phone the physicians in charge of the trials to tell them to stop their programs at once. Charlie Leighton went to phone the FDA. If I hadn't been trained as a physician, I might have been tempted to waffle a bit on this decision. If I'd been the nervous president of a small start-up company with only one drug candidate in development, I'm certain the decision would have been more difficult to make. Then I might have tried to reassure myself, mulling over the fact that *Mevacor* had easily cleared all of the hurdles in Merck's early safety assessment tests.

I knew how our professionals in safety assessment approached their job, going after each compound with the goal of doing everything possible to make certain that it failed. The worst thing they could do would be to allow a compound to move forward into human clinical trials and then discover it was toxic. *Mevacor* had sailed through short-term safety assessment with no indication whatsoever that it might produce tumors. We knew, however, that Merck had not completed all of the long-term toxicology studies, and that left a dark cloud of doubt in our minds.

Although our group of senior executives had talked through all the nuances, my personal decision about the trials had been instantaneous. I didn't need any advice to make this call. We couldn't allow anyone to use our compound if there was the slightest possibility it might be carcinogenic. Even an unsubstantiated rumor was a sufficient basis for making that decision. After Marv Jaffe went off to call the clinical investigators, I left to call John Horan, Merck's chairman and CEO. I explained the rumor, its implications for *Mevacor*, and my decision. Horan, who immediately understood the gravity of this situation, agreed that we had no choice but to stop the trials. He asked to be kept informed.

Later, having moved into the bar, our little group was still absolutely stunned, unable to say anything new or encouraging. "I'll contact Sankyo directly," I repeated, "and find out whether the rumor's true. At this point, all we've got is a third-hand report." This promise didn't pump them up anymore than my previous try had.

Before I could call Sankyo, however, I had to make a more difficult phone call. I had to tell Al Alberts what had happened. When two people have worked together as long and as closely as Al and I had, communication becomes almost effortless – like a wife or husband who can almost always finish the sentences the other starts. This time, our conversation was painful. "Al," I said, "I've just heard from Boyd Woodruff that Sankyo's stopped clinical trials on its cholesterol compound. Apparently it caused tumors in the safety tests." When I told Al I had already stopped our clinical trials, there was a long silence on the other end of the line. Both of us knew that the *Mevacor* project was a once-in-a-lifetime opportunity for him. Very few pharmaceutical researchers ever get as close as he was to discovering a major drug. Hardly any has that experience more than once in a career. So Al, normally a quiet, unassuming scientist, didn't just roll over when I told him the bad news. After a moment to collect his thoughts, he tried to find a compromise position, hoping his project wouldn't go dead in the water.

I told him, "We can do more work in safety assessment to determine what, if any, problem exists. But," I added, "we have to assume that *Mevacor* is dead and find a new product candidate." I was trying to project enthusiasm, playing my role to the hilt, trying to get Al excited again. "Let's find another molecule," I said, "one with a structure different enough from compactin that they cannot possibly have similar toxicities." But all the while, we both knew that wouldn't enable Al's project to keep its momentum. When we stopped the clinical studies, our head of clinical research told the physicians who had been conducting the studies that our compound was "presumed" to cause cancer – at least in the animals used in safety assessment. Until we learned otherwise, we had to assume that the report from Japan was true. The physicians had given our compound to only a small number of patients for short intervals, and although I didn't believe those patients were at risk, we asked their doctors to check them carefully for any signs of cancer. None was ever found. But we didn't know that in the fall of 1980, when it looked as if *Mevacor* was heading down the drain.

* * *

As leader of the laboratories, I knew that my role was to help everyone absorb the pain of this reversal and then start to move ahead again, following the research strategy that had led to *Mevacor*. After all, *Mevacor* had been discovered in the eighteenth culture tested at a time when we were planning to test thousands. But MRL had now suffered a devastating setback, and it wasn't easy to jack up morale. We'd been following the research approach I'd advocated, concentrating a high percentage of our scientific resources on our most promising compounds. Now we had to accept the fact that we'd probably lost our most outstanding example of drug discovery based on molecular targeting. Was the strategy wrong?

That dreary winter in Rahway, the strategy question kept humming through our minds as the months dragged by. We went through the motions of doing research, but we were unable to recover the pace we'd lost with the phone call from Japan. We accelerated the search for an alternative to *Mevacor*. Our chemists had high hopes that this time *they'd* be able to develop an effective cholesterol-lowering compound, but their initial explorations were not encouraging. Meanwhile, we pressed ahead with toxicology studies, none of which corroborated the story from Japan. In toxicology, however, results come only after the long-term tests are finished, and they were still in the works.

Although our progress seemed incredibly slow, I always got a mental lift by walking through the laboratories and talking with our biologists and chemists. They were fighting this battle down in the trenches, and they continued to express optimism. When we discussed their work, I came away confirmed in my gut that this group could win any battle. In the case of *Mevacor*, the battle metaphor seemed especially appropriate because we were fighting on two fronts: we were still trying to save Al's compound, but at the same time we were focusing most of our resources on the search for a substitute that would beat the competition.

When an organization goes flat, its worst aspects begin to look more and more prominent. At MRL we had made considerable progress in improving communications, but after we put the "hold" order on *Mevacor*, we could see only what we hadn't achieved in this regard. We still hadn't, for instance, been able to bridge the fault line between basic research and clinical operations. The clinical staff still tended to take hold of a compound and cut off discussions with the scientists who had developed it. The attitude on the clinical side was "Now it's our baby, and as soon as we've finished our work, we'll talk to you about our results." I kept urging them to communicate regularly, to share ideas, but deeply rooted practices are hard to change. This is especially true when they're reinforced by a sense of competition, a touch of jealousy about who gets credit for the discovery, and a powerful desire to protect your professional turf. This was not a make-or-break problem, but it made us less effective than we could have been. In the backwash of the *Mevacor* crisis, I didn't think we could afford anything that was a drag on our performance.

In an effort to break down barriers and improve communications, I usually turned for help to Stan Fidelman, my sometimes tennis opponent and frequent confidant. Stan was a graduate of City College, an engineer by training, and a great communicator long before the newspapers gave that title to Ronald Reagan. Stan had worked for Merck since leaving college, and he seemed to know everyone by their first name. His official title was Head of Project Coordination. He knew everything that was going on at Merck, and everyone, literally everyone, liked him. When I had two groups disagreeing about something, I'd send Stan to find out what the issues *really* were and how to restore peace. He was a knowledgeable, nonthreatening mediator. Because they trusted him, people told him things they wouldn't tell anyone else (including me). I, too, trusted Stan completely. He was incredibly loyal to Merck in an age when many young people were becoming skeptical of any kind of organizational loyalty. Stan, however, never swerved an inch and remained deeply dedicated to making the organization work as effectively as possible. Every corporate officer needs a person like Stan who can keep reopening those communications channels that seem to close every time you stop paying attention to them.

We were struggling to solve these internal problems and get our momentum back, and I was not at all satisfied with our progress or with my own efforts as president of MRL. All I had to do was read the company's *Annual Report* that year to be deeply concerned. These documents are almost always upbeat. There are seldom any internal problems, only "challenges," which of course the organization's leaders will soon have under control. External issues, especially those created by governments, can be identified as problems, and in 1980 one of these was inflation. "We are unable in many instances," our report said, "to raise the prices of our products at a rate sufficient to keep pace with the rate of inflation." Productivity increases were helping. But with an eye cocked on the Republican administration that had just taken office, the report called for new government policies capable of bringing inflation under control.

That was what the report said, but for those who could read between the lines, it said much more. We had new products coming out. In particular, ivermectin, the exciting antiparasitic drug for livestock. In the United States, we also were rolling out *Dolobid*, an analgesic and anti-inflammatory drug. But the report gave too much attention to improvements in sales of older products, including some that were obviously mature and experiencing "moderate growth." Instead of highlighting a new blockbuster, we were touting "continued solid acceptance of our established products. . . ."

From my perspective, the report simply came out too early to capture a true sense of the revolution we had begun at MRL in 1975. Barely mentioned were two early projects based on enzyme inhibition: one was developing a new therapy to control high blood pressure; the other involved a new, broad-spectrum antibiotic. Of course *Mevacor* wasn't mentioned at all because Al Alberts's project was barely breathing in the laboratory. When I looked at the report, I wanted to tell everyone, "WE JUST NEED MORE TIME!" But obviously I couldn't do that, and in the meantime, the report in effect told our employees, the public, and investors that Merck either hadn't broken out of a flat period or was encountering a major internal problem, or both.

When I reported to Merck's Scientific Advisory Board in 1981, I explained that our researchers had pulled out all the stops but still hadn't found a replacement for *Mevacor*. Most pharmaceutical and biotech companies have these external advisory boards, consisting of distinguished scientists from outside the companies who review major research projects and provide their perspective on how the companies are doing. From time to time, the meetings generate valuable ideas, but that wasn't the case in 1981. All of us recognized the problems, but none of us could propose a quick solution.

At another company, I might have seen my research leadership as well as *Mevacor* and Merck's promising new approach to drug discovery all go in the tank together. Fortunately, Merck had been doing first-class research and development since the 1930s. By the 1980s, there was a good understanding throughout the company of the problematic nature of innovation in pharmaceuticals. Company culture sometimes works against you, but in this case it worked in our favor. CEO John Horan was obviously disappointed when I told him about the problems with *Mevacor*, but he never questioned our decision to stop the project, nor did he ever try to alter our strategic objectives in research. He and the company's Board of Directors continued to provide solid support for MRL, and that year, despite the *Mevacor* crisis, they gave me additional responsibilities. I became a corporate senior vice president for strategic planning in addition to being head of the labs. The opportunity to oversee planning for the entire corporation tossed me into a new arena. As I began to dig into that job, I realized for the first time just how complex Merck was and how many needs in addition to new products the company had to satisfy. I was pleased to be promoted, but nothing of that sort could make up for our problems with *Mevacor*. I had twenty-five years of intense research riding on that project, and I was still determined to do everything I could to pull it out of trouble.

* * *

I looked to Japan, repeatedly trying to get more information about what had happened. I wrote to the Japanese company and asked them to share the results of their safety assessment tests. When that inquiry didn't work, I followed up with a phone call: "We have a similar HMG-CoA reductase inhibitor," I said. "I'd like to know the results of your toxicology studies. Please tell me what you found with your drug so we can look for it with ours." I mentioned that patients in the United States had been exposed to our compound and that we wanted to protect them. We could do that better if we understood what complications they'd encountered with compactin. I framed my questions about safety assessment in professional, scientific terms. I thought it was an ethical issue. Scientists routinely exchange vital information, especially when it has medical implications. That, I thought, was obviously the case with this devastating rumor. I hoped, of course, that the story we had heard thirdhand wasn't true. But even if it was, I wanted – as any scientist would – to examine the evidence.

I thought this sort of direct inquiry might be successful because Merck & Co., Inc., had strong ties to the Japanese pharmaceutical industry. Immediately following World War II, Merck had helped the Japanese industry obtain streptomycin, the first effective therapy for tuberculosis, a disease widespread in Japan. Building on that foundation, Merck had begun to work closely with one of that country's medium-sized pharmaceutical companies, Banyu. Merck patiently cultivated this relationship, adopting the kind of long-term strategy that was one of the hallmarks of Japanese business in the postwar era. As a result, we weren't in the position of the U.S. steel and automobile firms that were blindsided by Japanese competition in the 1970s. Merck's products and its reputation for innovative research were solidly established in Japan.

My repeated efforts to learn anything from the Japanese failed, however. We tried to have our pathologists talk to their pathologists. That didn't work either, but the Merck pathologists did talk to personnel at another American pharmaceutical company that was working with Sankyo on a different product. The Americans told them the rumor was true. At that point, I flew to Japan accompanied by Barry Cohen, who was in charge of all of Merck's international businesses. Barry had very close ties to Japan, where he had attended high school. With his help, I once again tried to pursue the question directly. This time I offered Sankyo a business deal: "If you help us solve this problem," I said, "we'll share *Mevacor* with you in Japan and you can share your second-generation product with us when you're ready." The head of the company smiled. He said they wanted to cooperate but others objected to any exchange of data. So I was never able to have a scientific discussion of what they had discovered. Their executives approached it as a problem in corporate competition rather than a medical problem in drug discovery.

I was angry, but I couldn't do anything to change our tense situation. On the one hand, our studies had yielded absolutely no evidence of any problem with *Mevacor*. On the other hand, we couldn't just ignore the rumors from Japan. We were left suspended, unable to move *Mevacor* forward. This made my competitive juices run faster. I pushed even harder at MRL, pressing our biologists to look for another fermentation product and our chemists to try to beat the biologists across the finish line with a compound that would be an effective inhibitor. I didn't care who won this intramural competition, but I did want a winner very badly. As the months rolled past, we struggled on, trying not to be beaten in this important field. But it was a gloomy time for the entire research organization at Merck.

7 | *Blockbusters*

"Look," Dr. Illingworth said, "high cholesterol is killing people." Roger Illingworth of Portland, Oregon, was a prominent heart specialist. He and two fellow cardiologists from Dallas were visiting Merck in 1982 as consultants to give us an outside perspective on our programs at the laboratories. In their clinical practices all three were treating patients with serious artery diseases, their coronary arteries narrowed by plaques of cholesterol and fat. Not coincidentally, these patients also had elevated cholesterol levels that hadn't responded to any of the available treatments. The three clinicians were in complete agreement: "*Mevacor* was doing a helluva job in the clinic," Scott Grundy said. "Why don't you let us try it in some high-risk patients?" Illingworth, Grundy, and his colleague David Bilheimer were eager to restart limited clinical trials because the outlook for their patients was dire.

Having spent several years caring for such patients on the wards of the National Heart Institute, I knew they were right. As the head of Merck's research labs, I was tempted but hesitant. The evidence these and other medical researchers had uncovered pointed to elevated cholesterol levels (hypercholesterolemia) as a major cause of heart disease, and I knew that the high-risk patients Grundy, Bilheimer, and Illingworth were treating had been unable to bring their cholesterol levels down to a safe range either through diets or drugs. In many such cases, badly clogged arteries left the patients facing almost certain encounters with life-threatening heart attacks.

Still, I was hesitant to move back into clinical trials, and this request led to an extended bout of soul searching. I'd been unable to confirm the reports from Japan, but I couldn't just ignore them. That was why we'd launched extensive toxicology tests in animals, looking for any evidence that *Mevacor* might have similar effects. All of these studies had produced favorable results. One of them, a two-year analysis, wasn't completed, but we already had in hand a substantial body of evidence indicating that *Mevacor* was safe. What our three consultants forced us to do was balance the hoped-for benefits of lower cholesterol against the possibility that their patients would suffer adverse side effects from the drug.

The tests we had conducted before stopping the trials indicated that *Mevacor* had a dramatic impact on cholesterol levels and very few side effects. In November 1983, we discussed these results, as well as the information we had from Japan on compactin, with two experts in the field of cholesterol regulation: Dr. Daniel Steinberg of the University of California, San Diego, and Dr. Jean Wilson of the University of Texas at Dallas. Steinberg and Wilson were the type of authorities in their field whom the FDA would consult. They agreed about *Mevacor*: "You should return to your clinical studies," they said.

Convinced now that we should move ahead, we assembled all of the information we'd collected and presented it to the FDA. The agency agreed with our evaluation and authorized trials in high-risk patients. Dr. Jonathan Tobert, who led the Merck clinical team, was ecstatic that the development group was beginning to move – no matter how tentatively. Al Alberts, who had never lost confidence in *Mevacor*, his first major "hit," was even more excited than Tobert when I told him we were restarting clinical tests. As the good news raced through MRL, it boosted the morale of the entire organization. Al told me, deadpan, that he knew all along we wouldn't find anything wrong with his favorite molecule. Beneath the kidding and excitement, everyone at Merck understood all too clearly that we were actually holding our breath as *Mevacor* began its second trip into clinical research.

All the time that *Mevacor* had been on the sidelines, I had been pushing Al and his team of biologists and chemists to come up with another molecule that wouldn't be plagued by toxicity. Although this seemed straightforward at the start, the search had turned out to be difficult and frustrating. Still, we kept the pressure on even when *Mevacor* went back to the clinic. Finally, Bob Smith and his chemists came up with a second HMG-CoA reductase inhibitor, a compound (simvastatin) that would become *Zocor*. We brought this new drug along as quickly as possible so it could serve either as a back-up candidate if *Mevacor* ran into problems or as a second Merck entry into a huge potential market.

Just as the new *Mevacor* clinical studies were getting under way, the National Heart, Lung, and Blood Institute published a landmark study on the relationship between cholesterol levels and coronary artery disease.* The Institute's findings confirmed what we'd long suspected on the basis of the earlier epidemiological data. For every percentage point the level of elevated blood cholesterol is reduced, the chance of heart attack is cut by about two percentage points!

By this time, however, we weren't thinking about one or two percentage points. Our clinical tests were showing reductions of 18 to 34 percent in total cholesterol, with higher figures for the most dangerous (low-density lipoprotein, LDL) form of blood cholesterol. *Mevacor* was also pushing up the levels of high-density lipoprotein (HDL), which helps protect arteries against elevated levels of LDL. The combined effect was a sharply improved ratio of LDL to HDL. Our new drug was also reducing blood triglycerides, the fat found in adipose tissues. This was good news, even though triglycerides weren't considered to be in the same league as LDL as a risk factor for coronary artery disease.

We knew *Mevacor* wasn't a "perfect drug." Despite what you read from time to time in newspapers and magazines, there are no perfect drugs. All drugs have side effects, some of which are dangerous. Even aspirin has side effects. Some drugs have to be taken so frequently or in such large amounts that patients find it hard to stay on the regimen. Some drugs can be administered only in a hospital or doctor's office. *Mevacor* was different. Taking one pill once a day, many patients were able to bring their cholesterol under control with minimal side effects. As our trials demonstrated, most of the side effects were mild. Most passed quickly, and fewer than one percent of the patients had to drop out of the trials. Some (2%) experienced an increase in liver enzymes, but most of these were patients taking higher doses, and we recommended that physicians monitor them. But by the time all of our clinical results were in, I was as pleased as could be with the findings. *Mevacor* was well tolerated, safe, and extremely effective in reducing a major risk factor in cardiovascular disease.

Despite these outstanding findings, *Mevacor* wasn't an easy sell at the FDA. Cholesterol reduction wasn't yet a top priority at the agency. We were ahead of the field, and there was no external pressure to get a new therapy approved. Nevertheless, the Merck team now had good leadership and more than a hundred volumes of meticulously prepared material supporting our case. When the FDA reviewers came

---

* In the years since I'd left NIH, the National Heart Institute had added "Lung and Blood" to its name and mission.

down in our favor, we knew we had it in the bag. I called Al Alberts to congratulate him on his long-awaited victory and learned that he was taking his son Eli on a tour of colleges. We finally located him in Colorado Springs. Al was happy – "It's like a dream," he said – but neither of us bounded about in ecstasy. Having known for some months what the clinical results were, we both had a sense of anticlimax. After congratulating him, I actually asked what was happening with his new experiments on *Zocor*. We were both already looking to the future.

When the FDA officially approved *Mevacor* (1987), Merck held the customary press conference. But this time we had two Nobel Prize winners on our panel. Drs. Michael Brown and Joseph Goldstein, who had done pioneering research on cholesterol metabolism, joined the Merck representatives in a public celebration of this medical breakthrough. For Al Alberts and me, however, the real celebration had taken place many months before, when we studied the initial findings of the clinical tests and reflected on the decades we'd spent together working our way along the path that led to this new therapy. With FDA approval, Merck could at last start marketing *Mevacor*, and, as we knew, about half of America's middle-aged adults had cholesterol levels that increased their risk of heart disease. In this country alone, there were about a million and a half heart attacks every year. We thought we could now make a telling dent in those figures, enabling millions of people to live longer, better lives. That was a rich moment for both of us.

* * *

Before all of those good results could flow out of this discovery, however, Merck's marketing division (MSD) had to get to work and promote the drug. That, as it turned out, was not a simple matter. There were still many skeptics in the medical profession and the university medical departments. "Yes," they said, "you can lower blood cholesterol. But what does that do for the patient? What's the evidence," they asked, "that you're going to stop coronary heart disease?" All we had was epidemiological evidence from earlier population studies indicating that a high incidence of death from heart attacks was correlated with high blood cholesterol.

We were in the same position as those early researchers who thought they could demonstrate that smoking tobacco caused cancer. They could show a statistical relationship and actually tell you your odds of dying from cancer if you continued smoking. They'd shown that cigarette smokers who quit were less likely to develop lung cancer than those who kept smoking. But they still couldn't demonstrate at the molecular level how, exactly, tobacco smoke caused normal lung cells to be transformed into cancerous cells whose growth was uncontrolled. If you looked at populations with high blood cholesterol – Americans, for example – it was apparent that the probability of their dying from heart attack was far higher than populations that had low cholesterol levels. That was good enough evidence for me, the National Institutes of Health, and the American Heart Association. It was also convincing evidence for those physicians in the United States and other countries who quickly began to prescribe *Mevacor*.

But the naysayers persisted (as they did for many years in the smoking controversy) and rallied around an article published in the *Atlantic Monthly* in September 1989. "The Cholesterol Myth" cited what's called a "meta-analysis," conducted by epidemiologists who attempted to patch together statistics from all the various clinical studies focused on lowering blood cholesterol. Some of these studies were for a six-month period, and some lasted two years. Some of them used one kind of older drug and some another, but none reduced blood cholesterol very much. I was suspicious of this technique, which I thought was not rigorous and was likely to skew the results of the clinical tests. At any rate, the epidemiologists pooled all of this information and came to a startling conclusion of the sort that appeals to the media: total mortality was not reduced when cholesterol levels were lowered! In fact, mortality increased! Why? Because people who tried to lower their cholesterol tended to be involved in more accidental deaths. There were more deaths by suicide. There was also a higher incidence of cancer among patients who had taken cholesterol-lowering drugs. Having spent much of my life working in a scientific environment in which evidence was analyzed meticulously, I thought this "meta-analysis" and the article led to bizarre conclusions. They certainly were not as trustworthy as the double-blind, placebo-controlled clinical trials that establish the efficacy of a drug. Our marketing people tried to brush off the article, saying, "Don't worry, we can handle it." But they were wrong, and I actually had plenty to worry about. *Mevacor* sales, which had been growing briskly in the United States, began to plateau within three months. They stayed on that plateau for a year and a half, I'm convinced, because of all the negative misinformation that flowed from the publication of that one popular article.

As it turned out, the meta-analysis was wrong. This began to be obvious when results from state-of-the-art clinical studies that went beyond studying blood cholesterol levels started to surface. These trials used a technique known as computerized angiography, which involved images of injected radio-opaque dye flowing through coronary arteries. Now we could determine whether the narrowing of the arteries caused by coronary artery disease continued, as it normally does with hypercholesterolemia, or whether it was being slowed by *Mevacor*. As we predicted, the process of narrowing was slowed down among the patients taking the drug, and there was even some evidence that the vessels were opening. That new information started to push us off the sales plateau.

A few years later, we released the results of a five-year study of over 4,400 patients (using *Zocor*, our second HMG-CoA reductase inhibitor). All of these people already had coronary heart disease, having experienced a heart attack or suffered the intensely painful choking sensation, "angina pectoris," that results from narrowed coronary arteries. They all had hypercholesterolemia as well. The findings this time astonished even those of us who had anticipated favorable results for patients taking Merck's therapy. The drug cut overall mortality by an incredible 30 percent! Deaths by coronary occlusion were reduced by 42 percent, and the need for coronary surgery was decreased by 37 percent. In addition, the drug's use led to lower overall health care costs. These kinds of statistics excited me and even attracted the attention of some health economists.

We'd now established decisively that lower levels of cholesterol meant there would be less narrowing of coronary arteries and shown that overall mortality was reduced. These findings and the direct experiences of physicians prescribing our drug produced a snowball effect. Soon *Mevacor* and *Zocor* combined had over half of the market in the United States for cholesterol-lowering agents and were being used in more than thirty other countries.

In time we had competition. Once a molecular target such as HMG-CoA reductase is identified and its importance to pharmaceuticals established, it's only a matter of time before other companies target the same enzyme and invent their own inhibitors. The resulting struggles for market share can be fierce. Competition normally has positive results in this and other industries, but sometimes our competitors launched negative "rumor campaigns," claiming for instance that

Merck's products caused sleeplessness. We saw no evidence of this in our clinical studies or in the market, but we were concerned because sleeplessness was mentioned in the *Atlantic Monthly* article along with every other potential side effect. So we did a short-term clinical trial of potential sleep effects with half the patients on *Mevacor* and the other half taking a placebo. There was no difference in sleep patterns between the two groups. But just to be absolutely certain, we did another study in a sleep laboratory, comparing *Mevacor* and *Zocor* with the competitor's product and a placebo. This time we demonstrated that there was no difference between the three drugs and a placebo. We thought that would wipe out the rumors. But no, they continued to circulate. I hear about this kind of misinformation, as well as real news about cardiovascular products, firsthand from our older son, Dr. Randall Vagelos, now a Stanford University cardiologist.

We did one other clinical test that seemed to interest only one physician in the entire United States. I insisted on a trial comparing the impact on cholesterol levels of *Mevacor* as opposed to diet alone or diet plus *Mevacor*. The clinical researchers were opposed to this because they knew doctors wouldn't like the results, preferring to tell their patients to improve their diets, live a healthy life, and reduce their cholesterol levels as much as possible without medication. That made good sense. If cholesterol levels were not reduced to a safe range, then *Mevacor* could be added to the dietary regimen. But all patients were urged to remain on a low-cholesterol, low-fat diet. Our clinical experts thought some of these doctors didn't want to know that the average reductions in "bad" cholesterol (LDL), as well as total cholesterol, were actually rather small when patients were using diet alone. Especially when we told them about the very large reductions that could be achieved using our new drug.

But I persisted because I wanted to know what the results would be. I wasn't surprised to learn that *Mevacor* plus diet was the most effective treatment. Nor was I surprised to see that *Mevacor* alone was just slightly less effective and that diet alone didn't help these patients very much. With my hunches confirmed, I could continue with assurance to tell my friends who had high blood cholesterol that they should take *Mevacor* or *Zocor* and could occasionally eat a juicy steak fixed on the grill. But the rest of the medical profession continued to follow the party line, and we took the advice of Merck's clinical experts and didn't make much use of our evidence. Some walls are just too thick to batter down.

Besides, by that time we had a billion-dollar-a-year therapy in hand. Sales of *Mevacor* and *Zocor* soared around the world. To put this in context, bear in mind that Merck's annual sales for all its products – including specialty chemicals – had not broken $1 billion until 1973, just two years before I'd joined the Merck Research Laboratories. So *Mevacor* was big news in the firm, the industry, and the investment community as well as in medical circles in the United States and abroad. Personally, it confirmed the decision Diana and I had made to leave a comfortable position at Washington University for a challenging encounter with new drug discovery and development.

* * *

Mevacor was all the more exciting because it was part of a great wave of new products that came through the Merck pipeline in the 1980s. It was this wave and the way that Merck was able to extend and take advantage of it that moved the company to the top of the global pharmaceutical industry. First place in total sales shifted from firm to firm as the consolidation movement of the 1980s and 1990s swept through the industry. But once Merck's wave of new drugs began to break in the 1980s, the company became the leading innovator in global pharmaceuticals. Of course that's merely one person's opinion – and an interested party at that – so here's some evidence to support my case.

In the cardiovascular field, *Mevacor* actually went to market after the new high-blood-pressure drug that Art Patchett was championing. Scientists at Squibb had broken open this area of research by synthesizing a chemical that inhibits a specific enzyme (the angiotensin-converting enzyme, hence ACE) that was part of the body's regulatory system for controlling blood pressure. Squibb's prototype inhibitor had been isolated from the venom of a Brazilian snake. But that particular compound could only be administered intravenously, and so they continued their research and invented captopril, which they sold as *Capoten*, a drug that could be taken orally.

This line of research was exciting to me and many of my colleagues at MRL. It was especially exciting to Art Patchett, who now had a project with enormous potential, giving him an opportunity to return to his work on the high-blood-pressure problem. As with *Mevacor*, the target was a critical enzyme involved in a complex biosynthetic sequence that scientists had been studying for many years. So in both instances, we were looking for a molecule that would, with minimal side effects, inhibit and thus control a vital biochemical process, some elements of which had been discovered as recently as 1975. As our understanding of the sequence improved, so did our odds of finding effective therapies.

At MRL we decided to try to improve on the Squibb product. Since the pharmaceutical industry is often criticized for producing "me-too" drugs, the story that unfolded after this decision seems especially important. Near the end of one of our meetings, we diagrammed the captopril molecule, and several of us recognized that one part of it (the sulfhydryl group) was likely to be a significant source of side effects. Merck Research Laboratories was working on another experimental drug (D-penicillamine, a possible treatment for rheumatoid arthritis), which caused a trio of unfortunate side effects: bone marrow suppression (resulting in a decrease in circulating white blood cells), skin rash, and a loss of taste. That particular drug also had a sulfhydryl group that we thought was responsible for its side effects. In my own biochemical research I'd become very familiar with this class of compounds, and I knew they were toxic. In those days, we were rather cavalier about radioactive isotopes and other potentially dangerous substances, but we'd always been exceedingly careful when we handled sulfhydryl compounds.

After pondering this situation a bit, I decided to talk to Art about it. "Art, that compound is going to have serious side effects in the clinic," I said. "If you could make an inhibitor that lacked this sulfhydryl group, you'd have a winner because you already know captopril works in humans." With considerable enthusiasm I told him, "I'm *certain* you'll make a better drug!" Art and our other chemists were so talented at modifying molecules that I was indeed certain they could do this. I soon learned otherwise.

Art gave me another lesson in chemistry: the part we were trying to get rid of played a vital role by combining with an essential metal in the active site of the enzyme we were trying to inhibit. "It's going to be extremely difficult to do," Art said. "Difficult if not impossible." "Gee," I said, "with all of our computer modeling capability, you'll certainly be able to solve that problem." Art, who knew I was teasing him, just gave me a knowing look. In pharmaceutical laboratories at this time there was a great deal of excitement about developing three-dimensional computer representations of molecules. By helping us visualize the physical structure of a molecule – in this instance an enzyme – we could, we hoped, more efficiently design an appropriate inhibitor for a crucial active site. But it didn't always turn out to be easy or even possible, and Art knew that better than anyone. So he laughed at my suggestion, shook his head, and quietly retired to his laboratory to ponder what seemed to him to be an almost hopeless problem.

While Art was plugging away, Squibb researchers reported that captopril was very effective in lowering blood pressure. But they also reported on the drug's side effects: reduced white blood cell count, loss of taste, and skin rash. So the pressure to invent an ACE inhibitor without the offending sulfhydryl group became even more intense. If Art could solve this problem, we were as certain as scientists are allowed to be that we'd have a much better drug for treating high blood pressure.

As the months passed, Art proved correct about the difficulty. Merck Research had tremendous resources, and we gave Art and his group all of the help they could use. They even made good use of computer modeling. But still it took them about a year to work out the solution. What they finally invented was the compound enalapril, which became *Vasotec*, a safe, effective means of reducing high blood pressure.

It would be nice to end the story on that dramatic note, but this narrative of science-based competition continued to unfold. In the next decisive episode, Squibb had the leading role. The FDA approved *Capoten* for treatment of high blood pressure in the United States, but the side effects initially limited its use. When the company conducted clinical research in Japan at lower doses, however, it discovered that the side effects were largely avoided. Blood pressure could be controlled with doses below those that had caused the previous problems.

The use of a low dose of *Capoten* had undercut our primary advantage before we'd even been able to bring *Vasotec* to market. For a time, in fact, it looked like we might never get our product out. Late on a Friday afternoon, I was finishing my shower after playing tennis, my regular doubles match, when one of our clinical pharmacologists gave me some bad news. "Roy," he said, "one of the patients in our Phase I clinical trial for *Vasotec* had an abrupt decrease in circulating white blood cells." I was stunned. We were using a very low dose in this trial, but it appeared that our product was causing one of the very side effects it was designed to avoid. Months later, we finally determined that the decrease was unrelated to *Vasotec* and was probably a result of an unrelated viral infection. Relieved, the clinical researchers built up momentum again and brought the studies to a successful conclusion. Some of our tests involved as many as 10,000 patients. Others were conducted "under duress," using high doses in people with kidney disease. We demonstrated, conclusively, that the new compound lacked the three critical side effects of high-dose *Capoten*.

But while Art's drug design strategy had clearly succeeded, didn't we just have a "me-too" drug? No. *Vasotec* had a big, unexpected advantage. We hadn't tried for a once-a-day drug, but we got one. *Vasotec* is long-acting, and physicians recognize that compliance with long-term therapy is much more effective when their patients take their drug only once a day. As a result, *Vasotec* quickly took a huge share of the market, beating out *Capoten* in the United States and abroad (as *Renitec*). In 1988 it became the first billion-dollar drug in Merck's history.

Even then, the saga continued. In part, the sales of *Vasotec* were due to its effects in people suffering from heart failure. These patients – whose symptoms included shortness of breath, fatigue, and swollen ankles – had damaged hearts that were unable to pump blood efficiently through their arteries. As Squibb demonstrated, their ACE inhibitor improved the symptoms of heart failure by reducing the resistance to blood flow in the arteries. Then the heart could pump more efficiently, reducing fatigue and shortness of breath. Merck followed with studies of *Vasotec* and dramatically extended the research by examining the drug's effect on mortality. Feeling better is good, but staying alive and out of a hospital is even better.

One of the several clinical tests we conducted had a dramatic conclusion. The patients involved were all about seventy years old, and all were suffering serious heart failure. They were short of breath even when they were lying down resting. Naturally, they found any kind of physical activity difficult, and, sadly, about 60 percent of them were expected to die within a year. Among patients this seriously ill, the mortality rate was higher than it was for those suffering from cancer. By treating these patients with *Vasotec*, however, their physicians were able to reduce the death rate by 31 percent. The results were so outstanding that our Ethical Review Committee stopped the trial so that all of the participants could immediately be switched to the new therapy. None of these findings – which gave added impetus to the rapidly rising sales of *Vasotec* – could have been predicted when Squibb and Merck began their research. The favorable outcomes for patients with heart failure were products of a complex, ongoing competitive process involving heavy investments, substantial risk, and a long-term strategic perspective. Allowing that process to continue has helped make the American pharmaceutical industry the world's leader in new drug development.

With two blockbuster cardiovascular products at the same time, Merck's prospects looked great, but in fact the laboratories had even more good news. We had another ACE inhibitor ready to follow *Vasotec* into the market, and our new antiulcer drug (*Pepcid*) was doing well enough to make me almost forget the time we'd lost while struggling to overcome the Not-Invented-Here syndrome. We were also becoming a major world player in animal health as various formulations of ivermectin (the antiparasitic) began to sweep the field. According to our projections, ivermectin was soon going to be the largest selling animal health product in history for any company.

* * *

We'd also made progress in antibiotics, an area of drug discovery that is an accountant's nightmare because it is so unpredictable and involves such long-term expenditures. Most of the world's antibiotics – including ours – have been discovered by testing soil samples for microorganisms that make substances that stop the growth of bacteria. For the most part, these substances work by inhibiting enzymes essential to making the outer cell walls of the bacteria. Unable to grow without expansion of their cell wall, the bacteria die or at least stop growing. Once the scientists discover such a substance, they isolate the active molecule and attempt to improve it by, for instance, eliminating undesirable side effects. This sounds easy, but there is of course a catch: The discovery process is inherently random, and it may take you five or ten years to find the right soil sample and the right active substance. It may in fact take even longer.

To be successful in antibiotics, a firm has to have the kind of long-term commitment to the field that Pfizer and Merck and a few other leading firms have had. At Merck the laboratories had made a major contribution to the development of an improved manufacturing process for penicillin during World War II and had later played a central role in the discovery of streptomycin by Dr. Selman Waksman and Albert Schatz, one of his colleagues at Rutgers University. Streptomycin was the first antibiotic that could control tuberculosis. As a result of these two initiatives, Merck acquired significant capabilities in fermentation research and in the development and production of antibiotics.

Penicillin, streptomycin, and the various tetracyclines were greeted with great fanfare in the late 1940s and 1950s, and, unfortunately, physicians overprescribed these "wonder drugs." By using these drugs to treat the common cold or other viral infections that don't respond to antibiotics, the medical community fostered resistance. All too soon, we began to encounter mutant forms of bacteria that were drug-resistant. When I was an aspiring young doctor, hospitals were already filling up with resistant organisms, one of the by-products of long periods of exposure to the low dosages used for disease prevention. In retrospect it seems inevitable that the search for new antibiotics would be never-ending – in part because it proved very difficult to persuade physicians to change their behavior. Fearful of failing to provide patients with appropriate medication, doctors have continued to over-prescribe the standard antibiotics right up to the present day.

The development of resistance made it all the more important that Merck and other companies keep sifting thousands of soil samples in their "discovery screens" to find nature's antimicrobial substances. In Merck's case, it took ten years of research to develop a single new antibiotic, *Mefoxin*. The company's microbiologists, headed by Jerry Birnbaum, who worked closely with Fred Kahan, had devised a unique technology for screening antibiotics active against resistant bacteria. When I arrived in Rahway in 1975, they'd already discovered *Mefoxin*, which had special properties that would make it the number one hospital antibiotic for years. But before that could happen, Merck had to figure out how to market it. It had been more than twenty years since the company had found a new antibiotic, and thus no one in our marketing and sales division had any experience with this type of product. After the FDA approved *Mefoxin* in 1978, Merck hired new personnel and built up a hospital sales force to get our antibiotic off to a running start.

By the time we next hit pay dirt in antibiotics some years later, I was surprised to find that our new expertise in enzymology was an asset in this field too. None of us anticipated it. This time the active substance Merck discovered (thienamycin) was so unstable it was hard even to purify it. Once we'd purified it and determined its structure, our chemists eventually developed a stable derivative (imipenem), but the new compound couldn't be produced in amounts that would make it commercially viable. So we launched another round of research, and Burt Christensen and his fellow chemists finally solved the production problem by coming up with the first totally synthetic process for making an antibiotic in Merck's history. It was probably the most complex synthesis in the history of the industry, and it made possible large-scale production of a compound that was actually a better antibiotic than the original natural substance we'd discovered. For the moment, we were ahead of nature.

It was better, that is, if you could keep the drug in its active form in the patient's system long enough to do some good. That's where enzymology entered the picture. We learned that the antibiotic was being degraded and inactivated as it passed through the kidneys. That sent us searching for the critical enzyme that was causing the degradation reaction. Our scientists found it in the nephron, which is part of the kidney, and designed a molecule to inhibit the enzyme. We combined the inhibitor with our antibiotic, and the result was *Primaxin*, which was effective against more disease-causing bacteria than any other drug on the market at that time (1985). *Primaxin*, which enabled physicians to save the lives of patients dying from resistant organisms, soon earned a nickname: "gorillamycin." It was so effective, in fact, that many hospitals held it in reserve as the final line of defense against infections that wouldn't respond to other drugs.

* * *

Of course the best way to deal with infection is to prevent it. To a physician this is so obvious it's astonishing that our society spends so much on cures and so little on prevention. This is true even though immunizing large populations against disease has become extraordinarily efficient and cost-effective. Given our ability to immunize against infection, you would expect the government to be very supportive of the firms that discover and manufacture most of our vaccines. Not so.

During the 1970s, the federal government, which purchases vaccines for clinics and for large-scale campaigns such as the one against polio, barely seemed to notice when several major U.S. vaccine manufacturers left the business. Part of the problem was liability. Vaccines are administered to healthy people, but there's always a small, relatively predictable number of side effects for each shot. These side effects are especially devastating when they involve children. Executives at several companies decided they were unwilling to deal with those problems since the profit margins on large government purchases were very tight. It was simply more profitable to invest in new drugs than in new vaccines.

Merck, which had an outstanding program, also reconsidered its investment in vaccines. The Merck operation was spearheaded by Dr. Maurice Hilleman, a terrific virologist who had developed every vaccine Merck was producing, including a measles-mumps-rubella combination used throughout the United States and many other countries. Anyone vaccinated for these three diseases any time after the 1960s is very likely to have received Hilleman's (and Merck's) vaccine in their arm. Maurice was a gruff, frequently profane scientist who knew how to get results. He ran the entire vaccine program, from laboratory through production line, in a meticulous, dictatorial fashion, along the way cowing some company employees, including a few who were, theoretically, his superiors. For my part, I enjoyed talking science with Maurice. I soon figured out that once you got beyond the expletives you were dealing with a deeply committed family man, a sentimentalist at heart, who was as well a prolific, high-energy scientist.

In the late 1970s, after many years of struggling to develop a vaccine against hepatitis B, Maurice and his troops were at last successful. This is a terrible disease that attacks the liver, causing chronic liver disease and in some cases liver cancer. Merck's breakthrough vaccine was produced from a particle (a surface antigen, a portion of the outer membrane of the virus) that could be recovered from the plasma of persons infected with hepatitis B. I thought it was phenomenal that we would soon have a vaccine against a disease that was a leading cause of death in many Asian and African countries. In China, where 13 percent of its massive population consisted of infected "carriers," hepatitis B was the nation's number one public health problem.

Knowing this and having closely followed Maurice's progress, I was upset when a Merck planning team produced a report for CEO John Horan that was highly critical of the economics of our vaccine program. I couldn't argue with the figures, which were correct. One curve showed the total revenue from vaccine sales, and another the costs of Hilleman's vigorous research program. The two lines were drawing together ominously for the future of Merck vaccines. It was numbers like these that had persuaded several of our U.S. competitors to leave the business.

When the management committee met to discuss the report, I was nevertheless determined to shoot it down. Merck, I insisted, was different from the companies retreating from the vaccine business. Merck had a well-deserved reputation for social responsibility. It was *the* major American vaccine innovator and producer, and it had a powerful obligation to carry forward in that role and to try to make the business profitable. "Preventive medicine is the best medicine," I said. "That's what Merck should be making."

Was my background in medicine and in scientific research showing through? You bet. I chose not to emphasize the immediate profit potential, which was the primary focus of the report. Instead, I took a long-term perspective shaped in large part by concern for the health-care implications of the decision. A Harvard Business School graduate would probably have reached a different conclusion. But I was absolutely certain my position was best in the long run for Merck as well as for society. Fortunately, CEO John Horan agreed, and Merck decided to stay the course. Some years later, I'd have a chance to return to that decision and reevaluate it with the advantage of hindsight.

In the short-term, however, the numbers on the vaccine business looked bad, and the outlook turned even gloomier in the early 1980s. The economic planners were probably muttering, "I told you so," when, to our surprise, events none of us had anticipated undermined Maurice's latest innovation (trade named *Heptavax-B*). Just as Merck was bringing out America's first hepatitis B vaccine, the AIDS (acquired immunodeficiency syndrome) pandemic hit the United States. For a time, no one understood the new disease, but soon doctors and patients became suspicious of any plasma-based vaccine. In this case the plasma had to be obtained from persons chronically infected with hepatitis B, many of whom were gay or intravenous drug users. These were the two major high-risk groups in the U.S. population identified with the HIV (human immunodeficiency virus) infections that led to AIDS – and at that time almost certain death. Our purification methods ensured that there were no live viruses of any kind in the vaccine. The FDA was certain of that and so was Merck. But no amount of scientific evidence could convince people to take a vaccine that had even the slightest possibility of causing a viral infection for which there was no known cure.

This left us standing at one of those crossroads that every company faces. Since Hilleman was approaching retirement at that time, it would have been relatively easy just to let his hepatitis B vaccine dwindle. And with it, our entire vaccine program. But I was still determined to keep moving ahead in vaccines, and even before the AIDS crisis began I had started pushing Merck down a different scientific path. Up to this time, every viral vaccine was made from either a killed or attenuated virus or a particle from the virus. But I thought we might use a new approach, recombinant DNA (rDNA) technology, to produce a vaccine that was effective and entirely safe. Since my sabbatical year in Paris, I'd been following with great interest the advances in molecular genetics. I'd never worked directly in nucleic acids, the macromolecules that store and transmit all genetic information. But we'd made good use of genetic mutations in our research on biosynthesis, and I'd taught elements of molecular genetics at Washington University. So I knew what was being done with recombinant DNA technology and thought we might be able to insert the hepatitis B viral DNA, which directs the virus to make the surface particle, into a safe, noninfectious organism. That organism, instead of the virus, would make the particle we needed. In effect, the new technology turned cells such as *E. coli* into tiny factories. The process wasn't simple, of course, and so I looked outside MRL for help. I knew Bill Rutter, an outstanding scientist at the University of California in San Francisco and one of the leading authorities on rDNA technology, and I decided to talk to him about Hilleman's vaccine.

When we got together, Rutter immediately made a proposal. "Roy," he said, "why don't I use recombinant technology to make human insulin for Merck?" We weren't in that business, I explained, "but we are making the hepatitis B surface antigen by isolating it from infected plasma. That's potentially a very dangerous thing to do," I said, "because when manufacturing plant workers are isolating the antigen from the plasma, which also contains live virus, they could be infected." Then too, I was concerned because people are afraid of any plasma-based vaccine. "But if that antigen particle could be made in a safe microorganism," I said, "that would be much superior." Rutter agreed to try to get *E. coli* to produce, or "express," the surface antigen we needed. We set up a collaboration, with Merck's Jerry Birnbaum operating as the go-between. After considerable effort, Rutter and the *E. coli* appeared to be successful, but we soon discovered that the bacterium produced a form of the antigen that was slightly different from the natural substance. We had to change course again.

Now we turned to Ben Hall, a leading yeast geneticist at the University of Washington in Seattle. He and Bill Rutter collaborated in a new effort to put the hepatitis B surface antigen gene into baker's yeast cells. Bill and Ben already knew each other, and so it was easy to get them going on a joint project. This time the yeast cells produced an active surface antigen that in turn evoked the kind of immunological response we needed to make a vaccine. That was still a long way from having a successful product, but some years later, after intense process development efforts, Merck was able to bring out the world's first rDNA vaccine for humans, *Recombivax HB*. Leading that effort was another terrific scientist, Ed Scolnick, who came to Merck from NIH in 1982. From that point on, he led the effort that enabled us to save Merck's vaccine against hepatitis B.

Recombivax HB was an immediate shot in the arm, so to speak, for our vaccine program and had some unanticipated long-term effects as well. At first, it was used only with people facing a high risk of contracting hepatitis B, but the group of recipients was gradually increased until eventually it included all children in the United States. Our recombinant vaccine also became important internationally. It laid the foundation for what in the next few years would become an expanded global program of vaccine research, production, and marketing and had a significant impact on Merck's relationships with the People's Republic of China – but that's a story for a later chapter. In the United States, the successful cooperation between Merck, Bill Rutter, and Ben Hall helped launch two biotech start-ups. Rutter and Hall both became wealthy entrepreneurs, and royalties from the sales of *Recombivax HB* were major sources of revenue for their start-up firms, Chiron and Zymogenetics, as well as the University of California, San Francisco, and the University of Washington in Seattle, where the early experiments were carried out. Innovation tends in these ways to spill over and have positive results that never show up in the balance sheet of your firm. They are as important to society as they are to the business system.

* * *

While we were still struggling to develop this important vaccine, I was already beginning to sense that Diana and I were approaching another one of those ten-year turning points. Several projects were coming to fruition. Most of our research and development teams now had strong leadership. I had passed my fifty-third birthday when we began to contemplate the next big career move, and as usual, we discussed it for months and months. We were happy living in New Jersey, still in the house we thought would be "temporary." Since we both love music, dance, and theater, it was a big advantage to be within an hour or so of

Lincoln Center for the Performing Arts and the city's theater district. We enjoyed the New York City Ballet and went to Broadway shows fairly often. But our favorite was the Metropolitan Opera, where we had season tickets. Living in Watchung, Diana was also able to visit her mother, the only one of our parents still living, in Washington Heights at least once a week. We also swam in our pool, and we jogged three or four times a week early in the morning.

Diana was developing her tennis game. Having grown up in Washington Heights, where she played stickball against the steps and sides of buildings, she had a good feel for racket sports. She was now playing both women's and mixed doubles and taking tennis lessons, which included pointers about strategy. So when we played together, she was the tennis strategist and I used my energy to chase down the lobs. Although I was stronger and faster, she often kept us in the match, winning as many points as I did. That was good because I hated to lose even a casual club match. When we did, I'd come off the court muttering to myself. Diana would laugh and hustle us into another activity. Sometimes that meant playing against our kids, all of whom had quickly taken to the sport and could beat us easily. Those were the only matches I didn't mind losing.

By the early 1980s, we were only occasionally able to muster the entire family for any special event. Cynthia graduated from Brown University in 1981, having developed what would be a lifelong interest in protecting the environment. Whether leading student biking tours, mastering photography, or taking part in Outward Bound, she stayed close to nature and gave more and more thought to how America's natural environment might be protected. After a year's experience working in government offices in Washington, DC, she decided to pursue her environmental goals through the legal system. She entered law school at Fordham in New York City.

That gave us another reason to go into the city. Randy, who'd followed a path similar to mine, was then at the College of Physicians and Surgeons of Columbia University. Often we all met at grandmother's house for a traditional Greek meal with Nona and a chance to trade stories. Oddly, Cynthia, the friend of nature, was now loving New York, whereas Randy was always grumbling about his rundown apartment, the weather, and everything except medical school, which was interesting enough to keep him absorbed. At Columbia he developed a passion for cardiology, the specialty that had also attracted me. But then he went his own way. Instead of research, he turned decisively toward clinical practice. After graduating from P&S, he decided he could stand a few more years in New York and became a resident physician at Columbia Presbyterian Hospital. That experience nailed down two decisions: he would become a practicing cardiologist for the rest of his career and would find a home as far as possible from the drug dealers who infested the area around 168th Street and Broadway.

Through Randy, Cynthia, and their friends – girlfriends and boyfriends – we stayed in touch with young people. And we broadened our intellectual lives. Diana frequently arranged family theater parties, and Cynthia's friends gave us a window on life from the vantage point of an aspiring young law student. We realized then that we'd spent so much time with scientists and physicians that we had very little appreciation for the intellectual life of many other professions. Diana's social world had always been broader than mine, but both of us found ourselves learning from Cynthia, Randy, and their friends.

At home in Watchung, Andrew and Ellen were charting two different paths through middle school and high school. Andrew, focused and serious, was, and still is, the family perfectionist. Ellen was the family's free spirit, moving in a cluster of similarly free spirits. Diana was doing the heavy hauling with both of them, concentrating on their needs, whether it was driving Andrew to his soccer matches, helping with a difficult research paper, or just providing a hug at the moment when it was absolutely needed. Whatever she did worked because Andrew was as successful in his course work as he was on the high school soccer team, and Ellen suddenly and inexplicably (to me at least) decided to become as serious about school as she was about field hockey.

Neither of these scholar-athletes knew exactly what they wanted to explore later, but both were well on their separate paths to becoming accomplished young adults by the early 1980s. That gave their parents some additional degrees of freedom about a career move. If Diana and I had decided that our next ten years should be spent someplace other than New Jersey, neither Andrew nor his sister would have been heartbroken.

***

Once again, the desire to move on was rooted in success. We'd been able to leave Washington University because we agreed that we'd accomplished our major goals together. At that time we faced a new situation in corporate research and development – something we'd never done and never even imagined doing. But we were certain it was important, not just to us, but to all those who would benefit from the drugs we might help Merck discover. Once we had *Mevacor* moving toward completion, *Vasotec* ready to go, and other therapies squeezing through the pipeline, it was clear to both of us that we'd pretty much achieved the goal that had brought us to Merck. Merck Research Laboratories was far from being a perfect research organization (is there one any place in the world?), but I thought we were the best in the industry, that is, the global industry. We had overcome the hubris that was the foundation assumption for the Not-Invented-Here prejudice. We weren't the quickest organization because we set very high standards for our products and were convinced that we didn't have to cut corners on any part of the R&D process to be successful. Throughout the laboratories, there was now a powerful sense of accomplishment that reinforced the dedication to our new style of drug discovery. Targeted research had proven itself.

Starting about 1981, after I had been heading MRL for more than six years, I began to look for a successor. Although at that time I wasn't ready to leave my job, I knew that the preparation of a succession plan is an important responsibility of every senior executive. At times, the pressure of daily events keeps you from thinking about replacing yourself, but you need to keep this problem up near the top of your priority list because the process can be lengthy. The first decision was whether my potential successor existed among the senior people in MRL or whether to consider scientists outside the firm. We clearly had great strength in several scientific disciplines. Ralph Hirschmann, who had made important contributions to peptide chemistry, had been promoted to senior vice president and was providing leadership to the basic research group. Marvin Jaffe, who was directing Clinical Research, had his teams working smoothly and was coordinating his work with Charlie Leighton, our accomplished head of Regulatory Affairs. Jim Lago and his process development group were providing Merck with a significant competitive edge in the production of our drugs.

We'd also built up a very strong crew in my fields of biochemistry and enzymology, and it would have been easy to find a leader for the labs in those areas of research. That would have been a way of cloning myself, and I suppose that approach is pleasing to many executives. I think that's how some of America's largest and most successful businesses faltered when they began to feel the pressure of foreign competition. Instead of looking for new leaders who could take their organizations in different directions, the top executives promoted people who'd be certain to stay on the same path that had carried their firms to the top. But of course that trail no longer led to the top.

I decided Merck needed a research leader who could develop MRL's capabilities in some of the most promising newer areas of research: molecular genetics and rDNA technology. He or she should be able to do this while continuing to utilize the laboratories' proven strengths in chemistry, biochemistry, enzymology, and virology. Our strategy was explicit. We wanted to take advantage of molecular genetics to help identify protein molecules that were promising targets for chemical attack, but, with some exceptions such as the hepatitis B vaccine and a few other projects, we still didn't want to use the new technology to make proteins because they all had to be injected. Our goal was to continue to discover enzyme inhibitors or receptor antagonists that would be active and effective when taken orally. Used this way, the new technology and science would complement perfectly what we had built up during the previous seven years. At that time, however, we had no scientist in molecular genetics of the stature and experience called for by this job. So we looked outside of Merck.

We found our scientist in Bethesda, at the National Institutes of Health. Ed Scolnick was an M.D., a physician-scientist who, like me, had been an intern and resident at Mass General and then gone on to the National Institutes of Health. I'd been trying for some years to increase the number of M.D. scientists throughout our laboratories. Merck's central mission was the development of new treatments of disease, and it was easier for scientists who had been through medical school and had some clinical experience to make connections between new developments in science and their potential application to new drug discovery. They also had a better feel for different diseases and the effects they have on people because they recognized firsthand the shortcomings of available therapies.

Although Scolnick and I had these experiences in common, he was no clone. In most other regards, he and I had chosen different paths into medical science. Right from the start, Ed had been intrigued by molecular genetics. He was my junior by about ten or eleven years, and in that decade, gene-based science had become a more exciting biological frontier than biochemistry and enzymology. Both were thriving, but by the early 1980s, molecular genetics was newer and hotter. At the National Cancer Institute of the NIH, cancer research had become Ed's lifetime obsession, the counterpart of my dedication to unraveling the mysteries of lipid biosynthesis.

Scolnick thrived at NIH. His explorations of the genetic basis of certain kinds of cancers were of central importance in the field, and by the early 1980s he had collected a number of major awards for distinguished scientific contributions. He had breadth as well as depth. I knew he'd be the kind of high-energy science leader who would stay personally engaged with the wide variety of projects under way at MRL. I persuaded him to join our laboratory in 1982, starting out as head of research in Virus and Cell Biology under Maurice Hilleman, who was scheduled to retire shortly. Scolnick saw Merck's rDNA vaccine against hepatitis B through to completion, which was a difficult task for a scientist who had no previous experience with the practical aspects of vaccine development.

Ed knew from the beginning that I was grooming him to take on the responsibilities of running our large R&D organization. I was confident that whenever I left and wherever I went, the laboratories would be positioned to take full advantage of their existing strengths while building new capabilities in recombinant technology and in Scolnick's style of molecular genetics. With this blend of new and established talents, I thought we might even be able to conquer the deadly retrovirus that we knew was causing AIDS.

8 | *On-the-Job Training*

By 1984, Diana and I knew exactly what we wanted my next job to be. We just didn't know where it would be. After acquiring some new responsibilities outside the laboratories during the last few years at Merck, I'd become intrigued by what made the company tick. And what might make it tick even better. Those experiences with on-the-job training whetted my appetite for an executive role somewhere. Neither my education nor my experiences before Merck had prepared me to become a "suit," but that's what we decided my next job would be.

Fortunately, Diana and I were practiced at surviving these transitions together. In a sense, we repeatedly relived the NIH years, when I'd started with a textbook and launched my explorations in biochemistry and enzymology. I'd started at square one, with all its attendant doubts and insecurities. About ten years later, we made a less drastic turn into a university career. Add nine more years and we were headed to the Merck Research Laboratories to immerse ourselves in drug discovery in an unfamiliar corporate setting. Each time there'd been a few big problems and thousands of little problems for both of us to solve.

As I survey that trajectory, it seems evident that at each shift in direction we were captivated by the complexity of the problems and spurred by the results we hoped to achieve – results that would make a difference to a large number of people. That was true in hot science and in university administration. Certainly that was the case at MRL, where we advanced the development of new drugs with the potential to help hundreds of thousands, maybe even millions, of people around the world. That was indeed exhilarating.

The competition was also exciting. I found some aspects of the business world distressing, but I loved the competition and still do. It brought out the best in me and, I've observed, in most of us. Competition is what keeps my juices running, and I'm absolutely convinced it's what keeps capitalism productive and efficient. Feeling at home in the business setting, Diana and I decided it was time for a third career, preferably as CEO of a pharmaceutical firm and preferably at Merck, whose corporate culture and operations were compatible with our values. But if not Merck, then another leading firm in the industry.

* * *

When this objective first took shape in our minds, it was obvious that my résumé was missing a few items that any board of directors worth its salt would want to see. For starters, I'd never taken a course in business. Or accounting. Or business law. As late as 1982, my résumé announced that Roy Vagelos, M.D., had never, throughout his entire education and early career displayed the slightest interest in being a business executive.

Before leaving Washington University, I had never read an issue of the *Wall Street Journal*, *Business Week*, or *Fortune*. That's probably why, in 1974, I really didn't know if Merck made plastic combs along with prescription drugs. Even after we'd landed in New Jersey, I paid no attention to the business press unless someone handed me a particular article dealing with Merck or another pharmaceutical company.

Once at Merck, however, I diligently read our competitors' annual reports, a gold mine of information for the careful reader. I used them to figure out what biochemical pathways the other companies were exploring and how successful they seemed to be. I also kept up with the scientific and medical literature. Most of Merck's breakthroughs would come from placing our bets – and they were big bets – on the therapeutic possibilities inherent in the newest scientific understanding. Luckily, I didn't care for television and didn't need a great deal of sleep (I still don't), because the technical journals kept my briefcase and my evenings full.

Busy as my professional life was, we continued our regular family dinners when I wasn't on the road. Andrew and Ellen, both in local public schools, kept us up to date on their activities and interests – at least on as much as they thought their parents should hear. Diana and I would attend the various evening school meetings for parents, and we also provided a family cheering squad at the soccer and field hockey games after school and on weekends. My family and MRL kept me racing. There was just no slack time to devote to corporate affairs.

So if the Board members had interviewed me before 1982, they would have noticed plenty of liabilities. I couldn't read a balance sheet.

During my previous six years at MRL, I'd kept a tight focus on the people and their research programs, not on the corporation as such. My primary concern had been developing new therapies, not making money. I appreciated the significance of a billion dollar drug, and I knew we were in the business of producing pharmaceuticals, not science. But my passion was the solution of significant medical problems. I understood that a reasonable Board member might conclude that this just wasn't the right mind-set for Merck's CEO.

Although I'd been running a research organization with a $300 million annual budget, I still had only the most rudimentary knowledge of accounting procedures. I'd gratefully left the business details to the financial experts, whose efforts let me focus on the work at the labs. One of these experts was my comptroller, Judy Lewent, a talented, hard-working graduate of MIT's Sloan School of Management. Since one of her jobs at Merck was to make a large group of scientists toe their budget lines, she was both tough and clever. She had to be because the researchers considered all accountants "bean counters" who were obviously less creative and less important than any bench scientist. I didn't feel that way, however, in part because Judy was so accomplished and in part because I needed help so badly. It was very apparent to me that her ability had put her in the fast lane to senior management. In the meantime, she helped me keep MRL's expenditures in line with company policy and running close to our budget figures.

* * *

In the early 1980s, John Horan, Merck's Chairman and CEO, began giving me opportunities to fill some of the holes in my résumé. He appreciated the energy, judgment, and people skills I had displayed in running the division of the company he clearly identified as the key to successful growth. Now Horan set out to develop my ability as a line officer – a senior vice president as of 1982 – handling a broader range of responsibilities and people to make me a more attractive candidate for a top position at Merck. Not the top position – at least not yet. Once again, I found myself on the steep part of the learning curve, taking home stacks of reading material in order to pass this new "course." Once again, I had an instructor. Frank Spiegel, Judy Lewent's boss, was my guide to the mysteries of the corporate world. Frank, who was patient, friendly, and above all, knowledgeable, had immigrant roots (German and Irish in his case). In the 1950s he had worked his way through Lehigh University by driving a beer truck for the family's distributing business. He said he always sat at the back of the class because he drove the truck to school and had to keep his eye on it. Besides, the other students didn't appreciate his clothes, which always smelled, sometimes rather strongly, of stale beer. In addition to the odor, truck driving gave Frank the common touch, a respect for hard physical labor, and an intense desire to find a successful niche in corporate America. After graduating, he became an officer in the Marine Corps, which schooled him in leadership, and his expertise in accounting opened doors to the executive level at Merck.

Frank and I were thrown together when we began to share responsibility for strategic planning for the corporation. Today, the planning function exudes a mystique that is propagated by business schools and management consultants who claim to have special visionary gifts and complex analytical tools for peering into the future. But when I first became a strategist, Merck's planning process was no mystery, even for a scientist trying to learn on the job. Once a year, Frank collected strategic plans from each division and staff group. These projections were for the coming year, and the plans generally looked forward to improvements in performance. I knew all about these divisional reports because I'd been doing them since becoming president of MRL in 1976.

In the labs, our annual projections were always conservative. In these matters and, in fact, in anything involving budgets, I've never overcome my upbringing during the Great Depression. Nor have I wanted to lose touch with the values I acquired during those difficult years. As a result, I'm an instinctive fiscal conservative with an intense desire to see each case grounded as solidly as possible in hard data. Having no flair for "boosterism," I submitted brutally honest projections for the laboratories. By the early 1980s, of course, due to our new research strategy, MRL could dramatically understate its future and still look forward to some impressive results. Judy Lewent helped us transform our scientific estimates into dollars. She developed a financial model that combined data from research and marketing and projected the value of R&D's output. Using her model, we could give Merck's corporate executives the kind of estimates they needed to plan capital expenditures. All of these contributions to Merck's annual strategic plan were, like my budgets, conservative. My approach to running the labs was to work very hard at making better use of the resources we had. I didn't want more money; I wanted more output. As I understood my job, it was to make my operations more efficient, not just bigger.

When Frank started walking me through the reports from the other divisions and the staff, however, I learned that not everyone took the projections seriously and not all of them were conservative about the future. Some divisions seemed to approach the process as a bureaucratic game. The international group's motto was "THINK BIG!" They provided outlandish projections, which prompted me to ask the leaders of the division, "Do you believe these numbers?" "Oh no," was the reply, "but it gives the people in our division something to hope for." The domestic pharmaceutical division apparently needed less "hope" because they played the game differently. By turning in very low projections, they tried to ensure that they'd always exceed top management's expectations.

Frank Spiegel was experienced and very clever, and his response was to massage the figures. He knew how the divisional performances had compared with their plans in the past, and so when he received a number like +15 percent from international, he just lopped off almost half of the projection. He added a percentage point or two to domestic pharmaceutical's plan, and so on, to construct an imaginary but impressive corporate strategic plan. After I learned how the yearly plan was created, I asked CEO John Horan about it. "I hope you're not paying a lot of attention to the figures that are submitted," I said. "They're ridiculous." But he assured me they were "very important," and I dropped the matter.

I began to recognize that the basic strategy was predetermined – deeply rooted in Merck's history. Actually, I could now see that CEO Henry Gadsden had explained it to me before I accepted Merck's offer to head the labs. In effect, his successor, Horan, had reaffirmed it every year when he looked at my budget for MRL. The CEO always approved my budget requests without asking difficult questions. Why? So far as I could tell, it was in part because our requests were conservative and in part because MRL was the centerpiece of Merck's strategic plan. Since the 1930s, Merck had been investing heavily in research. The founder's son, George W. Merck, had launched this policy innovation, and all of the subsequent CEOs had followed the same basic strategy, looking to the labs to provide the new patented products that would enable the company to keep growing. From time to time the CEOs added something special to the strategic plan: John Connor

(1955–65) emphasized expansion overseas – first in Latin America and then in Europe. After Henry Gadsden (1965–76) became convinced the federal government would impose price controls on pharmaceuticals, he started a modest diversification plan to hedge against controls and also to reduce profit margins. John Horan (1976–85) built up Merck's operations in the Far East, especially Japan. But all of these strategic additions were secondary to research, which was always Merck's first priority.

When the company added something to its strategy, it was usually a target of opportunity, not a product of formal long-range planning. That was how Merck's new policy of making strategic alliances with other firms developed. The Swedish pharmaceutical firm AB Astra approached Merck with a list of twelve product candidates it had in its pipeline. The company didn't have the resources or organization needed to move the drugs through the U.S. regulatory system and into the large American market. AB Astra was too small for that, but not too small to develop very promising compounds. When I saw its list, I said, "Wow! If these product candidates are real, this is terrific! One of the compounds alone, a new type of antidepressant, could be worth all of the money we're going to invest in the project."

So I took part in the negotiations that followed, but as head of research, not as a strategic planner. As a scientist, I recognized that the Swedish firm had first-rate laboratories and innovative products that Merck could develop effectively and profitably. I was wrong about the potential of the new antidepressant but right about the general quality of the compounds and the benefits of an alliance with an organization with its scientific capabilities. In 1982 the two companies signed an agreement permitting Merck to develop and sell the Swedish firm's new drugs and committing us to establish a new joint enterprise, Astra/Merck, if our sales of AB Astra products reached a certain level within ten years. This was an important shift in strategy for Merck, which had to that point given almost exclusive emphasis to products developed internally, and the origins of this corporate innovation were entirely ad hoc.

In the early 1980s Merck's corporate strategy continued to evolve in this incremental, ad hoc fashion, and I didn't try to change that pattern of development or the role of the divisional projections in the process. I didn't think I could. I nudged the CEO once or twice, but for the most part, Frank Spiegel and I just massaged the numbers and kept cranking out the kind of reports Merck had been producing for some years. I could see that there were reasons to introduce a different approach to planning. We could, for instance, have taken the process out of the hands of the departments and divisions and introduced elements they were overlooking such as changes in the regulatory environment. But I didn't think I could muster the support needed to change that aspect of the company's operations. So I spent my time learning as much about the business side of pharmaceuticals as I could from Frank Spiegel and from visits to the marketing, sales, and manufacturing divisions. There I learned that the divisions were actually pursuing their own long-term strategies, which they weren't sharing with the corporate planners, who were considered extraneous.

* * *

Marketing interested me because soon after joining MRL, one of the top marketing executives had said, "Roy, you have to understand that this company is used to breakthroughs." New to the industry, I asked what he meant. "Well," he said, "you've got drugs coming out of the pipeline that we simply can't sell." Now I got the point: "You mean the incremental improvements are going to be difficult for you to handle?" "Yes," he replied, "that's it. We need breakthroughs. That's what we're used to selling."

I mulled over that distressing conversation for a long time. I had thought every physician wanted to give patients the best drugs, even if they were only modest improvements over current therapies. Surely that's what all patients wanted too. I thought our marketing organization should be strong enough to promote a drug that might be the third in its class to reach the market but represented important improvements, or even a modest improvement, over the competition. I began to tuck these ideas away for future use along with the other things I learned about marketing.

At Rahway, where I spent most of my time, the MRL scientists looked down on marketing as an inferior, low-status activity. Marketing was at best a necessary evil in a company whose glorious accomplishments all came out of the laboratories. Or so they believed – with some justification. At Merck, the scientists were industrial royalty and the marketing folks were commoners. These ideas and the related status hierarchy were so deeply ingrained that marketing personnel were never allowed to take part in MRL meetings.

I quickly decided that was a mistake and asked Stan Fidelman, my peacemaker and confidant, to help me bring the two groups closer together. I wanted to eradicate Merck's corporate class system. I wanted research and marketing to work together, to communicate with less effort, to work toward our common goal, which was to get the best medicines into the hands of people who needed them.

We achieved this incrementally, with Stan negotiating each step in the process. We started by inviting marketing representatives to attend the meetings but to sit away from the table around the borders of the room. They could listen but were not allowed to talk! After the researchers and marketers became accustomed to being in the same room, marketing was at last given a voice. They could comment and actually make suggestions, some of which proved to be extremely important. They told us, for example, what kind of clinical information would help promote particular products. But we never allowed marketing people to participate in meetings in which we determined which basic research projects MRL should bet on. Those were scientific, medical decisions, and I adamantly refused to have anyone make them except scientific, medical people.

On other matters, however, marketing and research began to communicate more frequently, and the tension between the two groups gradually began to subside. More and more scientists – including me – came to appreciate one of the great strengths of Merck's style of marketing. "Fair balance," invented by John Horan, was the key concept. Merck's marketing and sales persons were taught to explain the weaknesses as well as the strengths of our products. By the time I joined the company, the marketing and sales crews were devoted to achieving "fair balance" in everything they did, and I thought they were the best in the industry at making an evenhanded, informative sales pitch.

Horan's idea was simple. After leaving medical school most physicians have little time to read, and thus drug company marketing personnel become their major source of information about new therapies. Otherwise, they'd just go on prescribing the compounds they'd learned to use in med school – ten, twenty, thirty years ago. What doctors hear from sales reps does indeed affect their decisions about prescription medicines. A pharmaceutical company's marketing and sales force is therefore constantly tempted to exaggerate either the high quality of its own products or the low quality of competing drugs. That's what induced Merck's competitor, trying to get an edge, to put out false information about *Mevacor*.

In most industries, exaggerating the benefits of your own product and demeaning a competitor's isn't particularly harmful. If a salesman tells you Coke is better than Pepsi for quenching your thirst, he may or may not be right, but the choice won't seriously affect your health. The pharmaceutical industry is entirely different. Whether the drug works or has side effects can have a decisive impact on people's lives, and your busy physician is likely to choose between two or three possible treatments on the basis of a five-minute conversation with a pharmaceutical representative who leaves him or her a handful of free samples and some literature that may or may not get read.

Merck used those five minutes to present accurate, balanced information about its products. Every piece of paper leaving the company was subjected to a Medical-Legal Review. Every pharmaceutical rep was drilled in the proper procedures. "Fair balance" was deeply ingrained in the company culture. The reward system didn't look just at sales figures but assessed the ability of sales and marketing people to present balanced information. If anything, Merck was overly stringent in what it allowed its people to say, but the great advantage was that, if you worked for Merck, you knew your firm wasn't disseminating dangerous misinformation. You could sleep well.

I appreciated "fair balance," but I could still see there were opportunities to strengthen the company's marketing. We had to be more innovative and also to adjust more quickly to changes in the marketplace. We certainly had to be able to market products offering modest advantages, even when they weren't "breakthroughs."

* * *

By 1984 I had tucked into my mind quite a few ideas about the pharmaceutical business. I was increasingly interested in tackling a senior executive position that would enable me to introduce some of the changes I had in mind. CEO John Horan, who was by that time facing his own succession issue, already seemed to have me in mind as a potential replacement. At least that was the way I interpreted my promotion that year to executive vice president (EVP).

My family and friends weren't too impressed by my new status. Neither, for that matter, was I. For Diana and me, the critical circumstance was to find a new position that would challenge me in the next decade of my career. That was far more important than my title. Most of our close friends were scientists who had no idea what the title meant anyway.

I had to interpret the significance of the promotion myself because no one told me what, exactly, was going on. The CEO and I were friends but not confidants. All John Horan said when I was promoted was "Roy, I'd like to have your input to these manufacturing and marketing groups. I'd like them to report to you." I said, "Fine. I'd like to learn that part of the business." I didn't ask any questions. He must have assumed that, if I was smart enough to be a candidate for the top position, I should be smart enough to understand that he was grooming me by giving me some experience as an operating officer. As EVP I was directly responsible for Merck's pharmaceutical, animal health, and specialty chemical divisions, as well as research.

This appointment jumped me over the other candidates for the top job. There are almost always at least three or four possible successors, and that was the case at Merck in the mid-1980s. Merck and most large corporations are organized into divisions and functional departments, and the CEO normally looks to the several senior executives heading those operations when he or she starts to think about retirement. Customarily, the CEO chooses and the Board of Directors approves. The process resembles the role the U.S. Senate plays in setting foreign policy. The Board, like the Senate, gives its advice and consent, but the real power usually rests with the CEO, who should by that time have carefully weeded out the nonstarters and carefully groomed the leading candidate.

If the CEO is considering an executive in a staff position, the grooming usually involves a stint in operations. That, I assumed, was why Horan had promoted me to EVP and given me responsibilities in marketing, sales, and manufacturing. As president of MRL, I was immune to the familiar caveat "He never met a payroll," but being in charge of a production line was definitely an item missing on my résumé.

As EVP, I also became one of the three company representatives on the Board along with CEO John Horan and President John Huck. I already knew that we had an excellent Board composed of accomplished people with knowledge and experience in corporate enterprise. They had good judgment and did their homework and were thus able to contribute to the firm's success. Some knew the pharmaceutical business; some were more familiar with other industries. They were willing to speak their minds and could not be cowed by management to approve policies they opposed. For instance, they flatly turned down management's proposal to diversify further by acquiring a medical equipment firm. Merck's Board included people like Dr. Richard S. Ross, for many years the respected Dean of the Medical Faculty at Johns Hopkins. Ross thoroughly understood the medical side of our business, and like many of his colleagues on the Board, knew how to ask tough questions. Another long-term member was Dr. Jacques Genest from the Clinical Research Institute of Montreal, who had a good grasp of what we were trying to achieve at MRL. From business, we had Frank T. Cary of IBM, Dr. Ruben F. Mettler of TRW, and John K. McKinley of Texaco, among others. Al Merck represented the family on the Board, and former Merck CEO John T. Connor also participated.

* * *

In my new position as an executive vice president, I was more concerned about marketing than production, but two manufacturing issues in particular concerned me. One of them was generics. About every two years, our management council would discuss the issue of generic versions of Merck products that went off patent protection. There was always a report that was usually presented by someone who looked like a smart high school student. I suspect the project was assigned to a very junior marketing person because the discussion was always short and always reached the same conclusion.

Once generic versions of a drug came on the market, the competition drove down prices. The generic producers had no significant R&D costs, they spent very little for the studies required for regulatory approval, and they did little promotion since they emphasized only the price of their drugs. Merck's strategy had long been to avoid narrow-margin, commodity competition in which products are distinguished solely by price rather than quality. Like "fair balance," this idea was deeply planted in the firm's sales and marketing mentality.

It wasn't planted in my mind, however, and so I asked them to explain why we couldn't manufacture generic versions of our own drugs. This irritated several of my marketing colleagues, but I persisted. "We've already got manufacturing plants producing the compounds. We must have already paid back the entire fixed cost of those plants. If we're at all efficient, we should be able to produce at a lower cost than any of our generic competitors."

"No, no!" came the replies. "You don't understand how this market operates." The marketers explained that they didn't want to undercut the prices of our own branded products by offering generic versions of the same medicines. Many physicians, having little incentive to change to generics, continued to prescribe Merck-branded drugs long after they had lost patent protection. "If we put out generic products under the Merck name," they said, "we'll shoot our own marketing organization in the foot." They argued fiercely to stay on the traditional course, cash in as long as possible on Merck products, and then leave the market to the generic producers as we moved on to sell the new drugs coming out of our laboratories. Control of prescription drug costs was not yet prominent in anyone's mind.

It was hard to argue with success. Merck had followed this strategy since the 1950s, and the labs had always pumped new products into the pipeline to replace those going off patent. Merck Research Laboratories hadn't always kept the pipeline full, but each flat period had been followed by a burst of success with the labs producing the kind of breakthroughs that pushed Merck to a new level of revenue and profitability.

I wasn't convinced, however. I didn't think Merck should produce generic versions of other companies' products, but if our manufacturing operations were truly efficient, we should be able to maintain a strong position in the market for any generic drugs that we'd originally discovered and had been distributing for years. Since I could make no headway against the traditionalists, however, I had to tuck that idea away for future use.

My only victory was to fight off any attempt to claim that generics were inferior to Merck products. "Forget it!" I would say. "The FDA has said they're equivalent. If a patient gets the same blood level of an active ingredient in a brand name and a generic, as far as I'm concerned, they're doing the same thing for the patient." Because of their narrow profit margins, generic manufacturers probably had more difficulties with quality control than companies like Merck, but that was a problem for the government to cope with, and I didn't think Merck should touch that issue.

* * *

The other manufacturing issue that interested me was labor costs, and I had to deal with that problem in 1984 in tumultuous circumstances. Top management and the Board were taking a tough position. Merck's contract with the Oil, Chemical, and Atomic Workers Union had already expired, and, in early May, Merck instructed its union employees not to report to work. The result was a bitter, prolonged struggle that continued into early September 1984.

I agreed completely with the company's position. Over the years, management had avoided work stoppages by making concessions to the unions, gradually allowing its wages and fringe benefits to get far out of line with those of its competitors in pharmaceuticals and with other businesses around Merck plants. Many American corporations had done the same thing and been crippled by competition from more efficient, lower-cost foreign producers. That hadn't happened to Merck – at least not yet – but it didn't take a crystal ball to see that industry conditions were changing dramatically and the future would bring downward pressure on prices and costs.

I'd already learned enough about the business side of pharmaceuticals to know that Merck would need to operate its plants more efficiently in the next ten years than it had in the past. Managed care and the rise of large buying organizations were already supplanting the kinds of individual physician services long familiar to Americans. These new organizations put downward pressure on prices, and that pressure was certain to increase. If Merck didn't respond effectively to these changes, even the best performance by the labs wouldn't protect the company or the workers' jobs.

I also sympathized with the employees and their families. Given my background and my experiences in Estelle's Luncheonette, I understood their feelings about a large corporation that seemed extremely wealthy. But I knew that, over the long term, the workers as well as the company would benefit if Merck was prepared for the intense competition emerging in our field. We didn't want to end up like the American steel or automobile industries.

Something had to give, but since neither side could work out an acceptable compromise, the result was a lockout followed by a painful strike. Although feelings ran high on both sides and there was at least one case of violence against an employee going to work, I never became angry during the struggle. When the union invited me to one of their parties, I went, even though this had never been done before. Some executives in Human Resources worried that doing this might derail the negotiation process, and the head of HR decided to chaperone my attendance to observe our interaction firsthand.

I was happy to meet with any Merck people who would talk to me. When I arrived at the party in the nearby union hall, I spent time greeting people throughout the crowd. They were friendly to me personally, but they knew I represented management, their opponents in the strike. After a while, I addressed the group informally. "Merck," I said, "has to prepare for a very competitive environment. In order to have competitive prices for our drugs, we've got to have competitive costs. I hope you'll consider wages that will *in time* be closer to those of the industry around us. I hope you'll be willing to accept more flexibility in work assignments." There were questions of course. They wanted, quite reasonably, to know what I thought about the long-term future of manufacturing at Merck. "That's in your hands," I said. "Outsourcing is becoming popular in some industries, but I personally don't favor it for Merck." The discussion closed on a friendly note, but I left knowing I hadn't changed anyone's ideas.

Merck management had, I knew, a tremendous advantage over the workers. It did not result from the conservative political environment fostered by the Reagan administration, nor was it a product of the company's resources. Rather, it was a consequence of changes made at Rahway and elsewhere in the 1970s, when Merck had introduced automation and computer controls in all of its chemical and pharmaceutical plants. The same thing was happening throughout the nation's chemical businesses and oil refineries, most of which could now be operated by a few individuals standing in front of a control board. Managers could run the plants, and so eventually the unions would be forced to give way.

That was what happened at Merck in 1984. All of us in management went on extended duty, and we were able to keep supplying pharmaceuticals to our customers from May through September without our unionized labor force. Since I didn't know how to run a control board, I put on an apron and took charge of the sandwich line in the cafeteria. I knew everything there was to know about making a sandwich. I could make them faster than employees who had been doing the job routinely for years. "You're really good at this," my fellow executives and scientists proclaimed. "You're better at this than at your prestrike jobs." I just smiled and kept pushing out sandwiches.

As the strike ground to an end, Merck had to choose between becoming a nonunion operation or simply negotiating an agreement that would enable us to compete effectively. I followed the late-breaking

Roy making sandwiches at Merck during the labor problems in 1984.

developments from Martha's Vineyard, where our family spent its customary two-week vacation. I kept calling the head of Human Resources, afraid that the workers would stretch out the strike and never recoup the wages they'd lost. I didn't want Merck to break the union, and so I was pleased when the company signed a conciliatory contract, opening the way to bring labor costs back into line with those of its competitors and regaining some of the flexibility in work rules that we'd lost over the years.

* * *

With the settlement completed, I quickly slid into a normal EVP schedule, which involved a great deal of travel. Diana made a couple of trips with me, but most of the time she was busy in Watchung with her own schedule and the complex affairs of Andrew and Ellen. Both were doing well in school, and so we stayed in our quirky house with its leaky roof and compromised siding. We talked about moving every time something else needed major repairs. But there was always so much to do at Merck and so much going on with our family that we postponed a move over and over again.

Meanwhile, I was becoming familiar with the lounge at Newark Airport. Merck had plants in twenty-six countries, and I was determined to visit as many as possible. There's no substitute for face-to-face meetings. Absentee landlords don't do well in this business and perhaps not in any business. For one thing, the people running a plant in Ireland or Spain want to know that executives from headquarters are interested in what they've achieved. If they're having problems, they'd like headquarters to share them and make suggestions. That's almost always more important to them than their fear that you'll criticize what they're doing.

I prepped very carefully for all these visits. Frank Spiegel had done a good job teaching me what all the numbers meant, and now I honed those new skills, digging in and figuring out what kind of performance I was evaluating. Then, when I visited, I used every minute to get a better grasp of what the plants were accomplishing and what might be improved. Elaborate social events didn't interest me, although I had to take in the usual round of luncheons and dinners. I was more interested in one-on-one discussions, and I usually started my questions on the way in from the airport: "What do you see as your biggest problem in running the plant? Who are your best people? Are you getting support from Rahway?"

The visits were a bonanza because it was so easy to improve things. With my technical background, I could always see where something could be done better – and almost immediately. One time I walked into a plant in France that was making vials of freeze-dried *Primaxin*, our new antibiotic. There were two different sources of antibiotic for the vials. "Why," I asked, "are you taking antibiotic from different sources? Isn't the *Primaxin* the same?" They said, "No, that one is for everywhere in the world except Japan. This one is just for Japan." "What's the difference?" They explained, "Japanese physicians are finicky, and so you can't have any particles in the solution or they won't accept it. They'll ship it back." My blood pressure started shooting up. "The antibiotic is the same in either case, isn't it?" They said, "Yes, but when you shake up the vials and hold them up to the light, the liquid for Japan can't have any particles floating around." The batches with a few tiny particles, they said, were okay under Merck's specifications – the ones developed in conjunction with the U.S. FDA.

After I exploded, I made an on-the-spot executive decision. "Look, guys," I said, "if we're able to make a batch that's clear of particles, and that's our standard for Japan, we're going to use that as Merck's world standard!" They were stunned. Why take on extra refinements when they weren't required? I understood their reasoning, but I was determined that Merck be a tough worldwide competitor, now and in the future. Japanese firms were beginning to go global; in the long haul they were likely to have a competitive advantage if their formulations were clearer than ours. Distributing an inferior formulation to the rest of the world made no sense at all.

That may seem trivial, but I wanted everyone at Merck always to be concerned about our competitive position in matters large and small. I wanted the plants to improve their quality every year. Instead of hitting the standard and then focusing exclusively on cost cutting, I wanted them to lower costs through process improvements at the same time that they were upgrading quality. Improving simultaneously on both fronts made them sweat a bit, but once they had their organization attuned to this dual approach, they too were pleased with the results. Merck people loved to compete and to win. They just needed leadership from the top, and I loved giving it.

Even more trivial was the matter of the cotton fluff. Walking through one of our plants, I picked up and opened a bottle of capsules, finding the inevitable wad of cotton at the mouth of the bottle. The wad, as you know, has to be fished out with a toothbrush or whatever implement is handy. I asked someone on the line to get me some tweezers, but of course none could be found. Then, a new question occurred to me. "Why do we have cotton in here?" "Some tablets are fragile," they replied, "and the cotton keeps them from breaking during shipment." But, I noted, most Merck tablets are not fragile. "Well, we've always done it that way," they said. Once the question was asked, however, it was apparent that in this case the cotton served no purpose and, indeed, posed an inconvenience unless you always carried tweezers or a toothbrush with you. The plant stopped using cotton, saved three quarters of a million dollars that first year, and listed this innovation among the divisional accomplishments.

I was obviously enjoying myself. Going to the plants was like visiting a class: I always learned something, and I was often able to make useful suggestions. The visits could have been painful for the local managers if they weren't so happy to see an interested executive coming from

Rahway. To them, corporate headquarters often seemed a million miles away populated by "suits" from another planet. As I tried to correct that view, I gathered hundreds of ideas about what I might do if I became John Horan's successor.

* * *

Barry Cohen, head of Merck's international division, accompanied me on many of my trips overseas. He was a perfect guide, a charming, almost enchanting travel companion. He could talk about almost anything and had a marvelous collection of stories about the industry, Merck, and people we both knew. He seemed to have lived in every place we visited and, in fact, every place I had ever been. Articulate, urbane, intelligent, Barry became one of my closest friends at Merck and a friend to the family as well. He was the son of a trader with a British company and had attended a Belgian Jesuit school in India. When his father took a post in Japan after World War II, Barry continued his education at the American school in Tokyo. His first job was for a cigarette company in India, but when his father moved to New York, Barry followed the family and worked in finance. In 1957 he joined Merck's international division – a freewheeling, multilingual organization that suited his style.

Barry quickly shot up the ladder at Merck. After successful stints in the Indian and Pakistani subsidiaries, he became a regional director for South Asia. Moving on to Europe in the 1960s, he played a leading role in ramping up Merck's operations on the Continent. He was so talented it was easy to forget how young he was, but all of us knew that major multinationals seldom promote anyone, as they had Barry, to a divisional presidency at the age of forty-two. Since by this time his international division was providing over 40 percent of Merck's revenue, he too was in the running – near the front of the pack – to become Horan's successor.

Although many of the foreign subsidiaries Barry and I visited were doing very well, I could always see something that could be improved to Merck's long-term advantage. For one, I was distressed to find that the company was using leadership positions overseas to give our executives operating experience, rotating them through these positions regardless of their nationality. I thought the leadership in France should be French and in the United Kingdom, British. A national could do a better job dealing with the government, and in overseas healthcare systems, government decisions are frequently of overwhelming importance. The governments controlled entry to their markets and negotiated the retail prices for drugs. Having a national at the top would also allow potential recruits from that country to see that they too would have a shot at the presidency. The international division saw it otherwise, however, and so yet again I put my idea on file for future reference.

* * *

After reviewing Merck facilities around the United States and the world, I could see that some things we had already established in the labs could be generalized across the entire company. We should, I thought, give more attention and energy to recruitment to get better people in key positions. All too often, we just put an ad in a newspaper and, in effect, took potluck. We weren't making phone calls to get suggestions from leading people in the various fields. We weren't being really tough about schools, recommendations, and records. Too much depended on interviews.

When interviews are paramount, it's the charming people who get the job. One of these was sent around to talk to me after being interviewed on the top floor of Merck headquarters. Afterward I wanted to know: "What do you think of this guy? What do you think of his background?" The answer: "Well, we like the cut of the man. He speaks very well." This rubbed my professional elitism the wrong way. "He has a good vocabulary," I said, "and a nice way of speaking. But I can't find anything else in his record that's distinguished." I thought we could do better and was happy to say so. I wanted to upgrade personnel in every job, from bottom to top. It was just as hard to get managers to accept this as it had been in MRL. It's a lot of hard work. It takes time. But it's absolutely crucial if you want the best organization. Not just a good organization. The best.

* * *

My first year as EVP was my last. On the brink of retirement, John Horan called in each of his four senior executives seriatim and asked each the same question: "Who should lead the company when I retire?" Afterward, I was told that two candidates had named Roy Vagelos, but I didn't believe that for a moment. My competitors all had a great deal of energy, deep experience, considerable talent, and very strong egos. They were not about to recommend Roy Vagelos for the job they all coveted.

In effect, I recommended myself without making a recommendation. "John," I said, "I don't really care who's chosen to lead this company. If I don't get the job, I'll probably become CEO of some other pharmaceutical firm." I knew what was in the Merck pipeline and what I'd done to put it there. So did the analysts who covered our industry. I figured if John Horan and the Board didn't understand what was going on, I wasn't going to argue my case or worry about the decision. The Board of Directors knew me by this time, and so they didn't even bother to interview me. I never found out what they said about the succession and never asked. All I know is that John Horan called me into his office for a chat. "Do you want to be CEO?" he asked. I answered, "Thanks. When do I start?"

9 | *Global Aspirations*

I 'd barely settled into my new office when I made my first mistake, a global whopper. It was just what you might expect from a green CEO who didn't want to acknowledge that his organization wasn't ready to slug it out, toe-to-toe, with a heavyweight international competitor. The details, round by round, blow by blow, are engraved on my memory, but I'll try to gloss over the minutiae.

It was my first deal. ICI, the giant British chemical company, had approached Merck because they needed a modern cardiovascular drug to boost their sagging product line and were focusing on the ACE inhibitors. Merck had an excellent candidate coming along in the clinic, lisinopril, our follow-on therapy to *Vasotec*. Our early clinical results were very positive. Lisinopril reduced blood pressure, was a bit more potent than *Vasotec*, and appeared to have a slightly longer duration of action. On the basis of these results and our experience in the field, we were confident that our new product would be a success. ICI agreed and proposed that we both market the drug worldwide at the same time, competing against each other and using different brand names for the same therapy.

The negotiations, which lasted for weeks, were intense. Corporate Licensing handled Merck's side of the deal while ICI's CEO and I stayed on the sidelines. In exchange for lisinopril, ICI offered one of their compounds, an aldose reductase inhibitor designed to stop the long-term ravages of diabetes. Diabetics suffer from diseases of the nervous system (neuropathy) and kidney (nephropathy), and from damage to the retina (retinopathy) that can result in blindness. A compound that could prevent all three effects would be a major breakthrough. The risk, however, was high. ICI had some interesting results from animal tests but no convincing evidence from human clinical trials. So from our point of view, the offer involved trading a sure thing of modest commercial potential, the third or fourth ACE inhibitor on the market, for a compound with huge potential and high risk.

Merck wasn't working on diabetes, and our laboratories urged me to negotiate for the rights to sell the ICI product. By that time, MRL's scientists had completely overcome the Not-Invented-Here syndrome. "If the drug works in humans," they said, "it'll be used very widely. It'll also give us a foothold in an important new therapeutic area in which Merck Research can probably make some significant contributions." I agreed but wanted to be certain we displayed due diligence before signing an agreement. I said we should first look at what American Home Products was doing with another inhibitor of the same enzyme also directed against the effects of diabetes. After looking at their preclinical data, however, we decided the British firm had the more promising compound.

Then I turned to our marketing group and asked, "Are you going to be able to push lisinopril when you already have *Vasotec*, with similar indications for its use, on market?" It's not always easy to sell a follow-on, especially when the first product is doing very well. "Would you rather we trade away lisinopril?" I asked. The answer was decisive: "No, no, no, don't sell it! We can handle both." Because of their experience with an ACE inhibitor, they said they could go head to head with ICI and beat them in the marketplace.

I welcomed that assurance because ICI was turning up the heat in the negotiations. They were considering, they said, another company's ACE inhibitor. Our negotiating team wanted assurance from ICI that, if their chemical failed to make it, Merck would get access to another ICI product, but the British team rejected that stipulation. As the tension mounted, I became directly involved. With my negotiating team huddled around me, I talked to the ICI representatives by phone. They were unwilling to talk about any other ICI products and wanted an answer from us soon. They were playing hardball, and I flinched. I wanted their potential breakthrough drug and was now convinced we could beat them in marketing our own product.

We agreed on the original proposal, and both firms set out to market lisinopril. Our brand name was *Prinivil*. ICI named the drug *Zestril*, which was a clever choice because most older treatments for hypertension caused a loss of energy – the patients, in effect, complained that the medicine took the zest out of life. Unfortunately, the Merck marketing teams also lacked zest. Our other drugs were booming, and they found it more difficult than anticipated to get enthusiastic about Merck's second ACE inhibitor. ICI's marketing group, in contrast, saw

Zestril as the hot product that could turn around their lethargic drug sales. They cut their price, put their entire operation behind *Zestril*, and took about 55 percent of the lisinopril market. At that time Merck was unwilling to shave even a penny on price. The marketing people told me, "It's a Merck product! We will never give on price!" Each of our marketing and sales groups tried a slightly different approach, but none worked particularly well. In France, for instance, we shifted all our support to *Prinivil*, letting *Vasotec* sales slide dramatically. The increases didn't equal the declines, so there too we found ourselves losing overall ACE inhibitor market share.

ICI looked at the world differently. With its roots in the bulk chemical trade where price competition is a way of life, the British firm knew exactly what to do for lisinopril. We didn't. We were especially vulnerable where the bulk buyers – governments, hospitals, consumer organizations – were large. We couldn't win a bidding war because Merck's *Prinivil* and ICI's *Zestril* were the same drug. Large buyers knew that and were unwilling to pay for the Merck name.

The results were not disastrous, but they were embarrassing for Merck and for me. I was further embarrassed when ICI's breakthrough compound failed in clinical tests. We never learned whether the theory behind the drug was wrong or whether the compound was simply not good enough to block the complications from diabetes. Later, the fair-minded chairman at ICI agreed that the deal was unbalanced and that his company owed Merck a product candidate. But when I retired as CEO, nothing had come of that promise. This outcome in clinical trials for a high-risk, high-potential product was commonplace in pharmaceuticals, but it certainly hurt to have our deal go sour so early in my career as CEO.

* * *

If I'd continued to make deals like that one, my tenure as CEO would have been abbreviated. But I learned two lessons quickly. One was that I had to be able to hit the hardball without flinching. The other was that I had to pay substantial attention to pumping up our marketing and sales forces. Even without any previous experience in this dimension of the business, I knew we had to turn Merck's domestic and international marketing and sales organizations into more nimble innovators and convince them that they could sell a second product in a therapeutic field. Even if it wasn't a blockbuster, even if the differences between our new product and the first entry were only marginal, and even if our new drug was similar to one being sold by the competition, Merck had to be able to market the second product effectively. The trick would be to do this without making any change whatsoever in marketing's great strengths. Once a large group of people is committed to a sound idea like "fair balance," it is wise not to tamper with that aspect of the operation. Marketing was already expanding on the idea of communicating complete information by conducting symposia, empaneling medical researchers to focus the attention of clinicians on therapeutic areas in which Merck was involved and on specific Merck innovations. In addition, marketing was hosting regional or local dinner gatherings where physicians could meet with a research clinician, a decision leader in a particular field. I wanted all these programs to continue.

I started the upgrade with the hardest part: recruiting the best people. I had strong support from the top – in particular from John Lyons, who headed Merck, Sharp & Dohme, our domestic sales and marketing division, and Barry Cohen, who led the international operations. Both had stayed on despite not being named CEO. Both had been in marketing most of their careers and were members of my inner council, an eight-member Operating Review Committee. In effect, we repeated in marketing the process I had already started at the labs, answering the same questions and applying steady pressure in the same way. I insisted that we place more emphasis on a candidate's record than on an interview. I wanted to hire the best, not the most charming.

In the international division, we had a sticky problem with leadership. Many of our top people overseas were not nationals. However talented they were, they simply could not elicit the loyalty of their people or recruit top talent the way a compatriot could. I worried about this and their inability to interact with government bodies as effectively as a local citizen. I insisted on seeking out top national talent, preferably by promotion, to carry the flag for Merck. In time, strong nationals led all our overseas subsidiaries, and our performance in these markets improved.

We also tried new ways to improve our personnel. For example, each year all Merck supervisors evaluated their "direct reports," that is, everyone working directly for them. Since most Merck people did satisfactory work, most of the evaluations clumped around a "satisfactory" level, and many of the numerical "grades" were exactly the same. We announced that supervisors could no longer give the same score to two direct reports. We wanted some differentiation: Who was the best? Groans could be heard throughout the land of Merck, but we stuck with the new approach because we were determined to get the best people in the global pharmaceutical industry working for us in marketing, research, and elsewhere in the corporation. Most important, we wanted to know which of our people were the best – at every level – so that their compensation reflected their quality. Retention of the best was necessary if we were to excel.

We also reorganized the marketing activities, and I became a devotee of restructuring, reorganizing, or reengineering – whatever they were calling it at that time. Every time we reorganized, we had a chance to move the best people to the top and gracefully clean out some of the deadwood. We also tinkered with the company's structure, attempting to make it more efficient by grouping together people who had jobs with similar objectives.

But I continued to be more concerned about people and their day-to-day performance than I was about organizational charts. In marketing we started by creating a headquarters task force to appraise what we were doing worldwide and to propose specific improvements. At the same time, we increased our marketing personnel about 25 percent while steadily upgrading our critically important training programs. These programs focused on the evolving market in each country because they differed enormously. In the United States, regulatory approval from the FDA allowed immediate launch of the product at a price set by the company. In many of our major foreign markets, launch of a new product required not only government regulatory approval but also government pricing approval – a process that sometimes took many additional months of negotiations. The task of educating physicians about our products also required different approaches within our varied national markets.

Overseas, in Barry Cohen's empire, we also made structural and personnel changes. Merck was logging double-digit growth in Europe, but I still felt we could improve those operations with more global centralization. Although centralization cuts costs and lets you develop global performance standards, it can dampen innovation. Further, you can lose the support of local heads who resent the loss of autonomy. To reap the benefits and minimize the downsides, you have to manage the transition carefully and be sure to have effective leadership at the top and throughout middle management. Barry started by restructuring or eliminating some subsidiaries in Latin America, Asia, and Africa that weren't performing up to our standards and kept fine tuning to find the right balance between centralization and decentralization. This process never ends, but by 1994 Merck was certainly a more focused, more centralized multinational better prepared for the intense global competition the industry was likely to face in the next two decades.

***

Managed care was one of the domestic areas in which I thought Merck was responding too slowly. It was obvious by the 1980s that the U.S. healthcare system had to change dramatically and that some form of managed care was the wave of the future. In 1988, about 30 million people were already enrolled in managed care (such as a health maintenance organization, HMO), and our studies indicated that many more Americans would soon join them. Merck had fallen behind in responding to this change in the market. We needed experts in negotiating contracts with large buyers, and so I had John Lyons quickly reorganize, creating a new department fully dedicated to handling HMO accounts. We did the same thing for our hospital business.

After we got this reorganized marketing organization humming, we took the next giant step. In 1991 we created a single worldwide marketing organization, the Merck Human Health Division, under the leadership of Jerry Jackson, who guided the division successfully through the centralization process. Once again, organizational change enabled us to move promising executives like Australian David Anstice, Richard Markham, and Per Wold-Olsen, a Norwegian with extensive experience in European marketing, toward the top. One of the least understood aspects of organizational change is the opportunity it provides to alter the business's leadership cadre. All three of these executives were high-performance leaders with special experiences and skills that we needed near the top of the company. Without reorganization it would have been difficult to promote them this quickly. The presidents of our European subsidiaries opposed this change, but they were on weak ground, defending national autonomy when all of Europe was rapidly consolidating. We, on the other hand, were moving with the flow of history, not against it. Where products had special marketing needs – in animal health and crop protection, specialty chemicals, and vaccines – we kept the operations in separate divisions. But the heart of our business, drug therapies for humans, was now gathered into one marketing organization with unified high standards for manufacturing, marketing, and sales around the globe. This way we could be even more confident of the quality of our products and the quality of the information transmitted to physicians in all of our markets.

We were still vulnerable on one major front. The pharmacy benefit management organizations (PBMs) were revolutionizing the way many Americans purchased our medicines. Labor unions, government organizations (such as the country's largest federal employee benefit program), and many big companies like General Motors provided prescription drug benefits to their employees, including retirees. All these institutions were struggling to hold down their soaring healthcare costs, and they were wisely contracting with the PBMs to provide prescription drugs to their members.

The PBMs controlled costs by high-volume purchasing and by developing more efficient means of delivery – including mail systems – than the corner drugstore. They drove hard bargains with pharmaceutical companies that wanted to place their products on the PBMs' formularies, their lists of acceptable medicines. They also cut the costs of treatment by ensuring that patients received generic drugs wherever possible. Using mechanized delivery systems, the best PBMs developed an enormous database with multiple benefits. They sharply cut the rate of errors in filling prescriptions while vastly improving the speed and efficiency with which orders were filled. They could compare the costs to patients and providers of different therapies that had the same or very similar profiles. They could improve patient care because all prescription information, along with background data concerning the patient's potential adverse reactions, was maintained on the PBMs' computers and made available to a pharmacist whenever a plan member requested a new prescription.

The leading firm in the industry was Medco Containment Services, Inc., which entrepreneur and master salesman Marty Wygod had pushed to the top of the business. Medco was particularly good at selling its services to large organizations, at shifting market share within a class of drugs to their preferred product, and at driving down costs. By 1992 Medco was serving 38 million people – an astonishing number for such a young enterprise.

Since Medco and the other PBMs were now established in a strong position between Merck and its customers, I decided to consider integrating forward into that business. We formed a high-level task force that recommended acquiring the strongest of the PBMs, Medco. We put together a small team headed by Frank Spiegel and launched negotiations with Marty Wygod, who was already talking to Bristol-Myers Squibb and others about a possible acquisition. This sent us into high gear, and I stayed very close to these discussions. Two of our top executives, Judy Lewent (now Executive Vice President and Chief Financial Officer) and Mary McDonald (Senior Vice President and General Counsel), had assured me that Medco was the most desirable acquisition and that the government was likely to approve it. Both were on target, but our first move was to set the right price for Wygod's creation.

Wygod was incredibly smart to have seen what the entire industry missed. He had recognized an unusual business opportunity, built a powerful organization to capitalize on that opening, and created value for his customers and his company. Along the way, he had hired Per Lofberg, a superb strategist, and several other intense, talented executives, who worked together extremely well as a team. Wygod's accomplishment was an outstanding example of what modern American entrepreneurship could accomplish.

Now we had to calculate just how much value Wygod had created, and that was determined in a series of complex, multisided negotiations. From the sidelines I stayed in close touch with my negotiating team, hoping the price would be $5 billion or less. But Wygod's price was $6.6 billion, and that's what we paid to stay ahead of the pack and close to our customers. Four decades after Merck had integrated into pharmaceuticals by acquiring Sharp & Dohme (1953), Merck led the U.S. industry into a new era of improved patient care and cost control. The formation of Merck-Medco was a unique strategic move in response to the needs of Merck's customers – both individual consumers and employers who provided prescription drug benefits. It positioned the firm to communicate directly with millions of patients who could now acquire their drugs more easily, with more accuracy, and at lower cost. Indeed, by 1999, over fifty million persons were covered by Merck-Medco plans. One direct benefit of our acquiring Medco was that Merck drugs attained a higher market share within the Merck-Medco formulary than they had achieved in the broad U.S. market. This gave a strong boost to Merck sales in this country.

All of these experiments in marketing had a latent objective. We were looking for a way to replace the traditional sales reps with a new method of getting information to physicians. I wanted to reduce the sales force, which I considered an expensive, inefficient relic of the past. The experiments failed, probably because they had to be run through a sales force that had every reason to be suspicious of the innovations. Nevertheless, I remain certain to this day that the company that successfully changes the pharmaceutical sales rep paradigm will revolutionize the industry. In this day of high-speed information technology, pressure on physician time, pressure on prices, and intense competition, someone will break this mold. My bet is that it will be broken by a small company with no sales force – a firm that has an important product and a smart, risk-taking CEO. Eventually, the big pharmaceutical companies will follow the leader, but in the meantime they will be stuck with the huge, antiquated sales forces they are all continuing to enlarge.

* * *

In manufacturing as in marketing, Merck had some well-established strengths, including a number of accomplished people with the kind of technical training I considered a big advantage for those who wanted to get to the top in pharmaceuticals. Merck was particularly adept at moving new products from the laboratory into the factory. Some of the credit for that goes to Dr. Max Tishler, one of my predecessors as president of the labs. Max was a first-class organic chemist who delighted in leaving the lab and mingling with the people working at the pilot plant and the factory. He was a high-energy driver who made his business his life and made Merck's research and development organization one of the best in the industry. Probably *the* best. The executives who followed Tishler – Jim Gillen, Jim Lago, and Seemon Pines – were able to build on the organizational tradition Max had established, much to Merck's advantage. By maintaining close, intense coordination between research, development, and manufacturing, they made the process of bringing new drugs to market far more efficient.

I was now satisfied that we were systematically upgrading the quality of our chemical engineering. But once we started to produce a new product like *Mevacor* or *Vasotec*, our manufacturing division seemed content to continue cranking out the drugs without making significant improvements annually in the production process. I thought we were missing opportunities to cut costs and improve quality through process innovations. I insisted on setting higher targets for improvements each year. Instead of raising prices, we should deal with inflation and achieve profit growth by increasing our share of the market. I became a preacher, and my sermons were not always appreciated. One of our experienced production men said I was too demanding. "Right after you win the Olympic high jump record," he said, "you don't want to be asked how high you're going to jump next time!" He was right: I always asked.

To complement the sermons, I looked for opportunities to foster major innovations in manufacturing from the top down. It was apparent to me and others on the Operating Review Committee that Merck's manufacturing operations had grown willy-nilly, driven by political necessity. When the company pushed into Latin America in the 1950s and 1960s, part of the price of entry had been agreements to manufacture as well as distribute pharmaceuticals in the various national markets. The same was true throughout much of Europe when we entered those markets. France was a particularly difficult country in which to grow our business. Negotiations there went through several stages. First you made a deal requiring you to establish a plant and start producing specific products. Then, in a separate deal, you had to negotiate the prices you could charge for your drugs. Finally, you had to sign an agreement saying you had done all this freely of your own will with no pressure from the government, which of course was not true. Finally, in our case, in the last stage of the relationship, the French government cut the prices we had agreed upon in the negotiation that theoretically had never taken place. Even my sabbatical year in Paris had not prepared me for this style of doing business.

Although Diana and I truly love France, I must note that of all my experiences with government manipulation, the worst was with the French. When it was apparent that *Vasotec* would be one of our biggest products, the French asked us to produce all of the active ingredient, enalapril, for all of Europe in a new plant that we would have to build in France. Under our secret agreement, we would in return be allowed a decent price for the finished product. We built the plant, which made Merck one of the largest corporate taxpayers in the country due to our huge quantity of exports within Europe. Soon after we were in full operation, however, the government cut the price. Our executives in

France protested to no avail. The government warned us not to take any precipitous action or we would be punished even further.

We waited, but they didn't reverse the price cut, and my patience finally ran out. We transferred our chemical operations to the United Kingdom and closed the French plant. Then we waited for a political explosion, but nothing happened. Our French subsidiary suffered no negative consequences and to the present day has continued to operate successfully. This experience taught me a bit more about negotiating and probably made me a little tougher when deciding how to reorganize our manufacturing.

When we reviewed the elaborate global production system we had created in this haphazard, ad hoc style for our chemicals and the pharmaceuticals we made from them, it was obvious we were unprepared for the long era of cost containment facing us and the rest of the industry in the 1980s and 1990s. Maybe even longer. We couldn't hold down costs if plants were not running at full capacity. We couldn't cut costs when we were producing the same thing in three, four, or five sites around the world. Globalization was transforming the pharmaceutical business just as it was changing steel production, automobiles, and many other industries. A worldwide merger movement was just beginning to take place in these industries and ours, and one result of that transition would be, we thought, a long period of intense price competition. We had to be more efficient if we were going to be leaders in the global industry.

Recognizing that we needed to become competitive in every aspect of our business, we reorganized manufacturing in two stages. First, in 1989 we combined all of the company's pharmaceutical operations in fourteen different countries under one division. The heads of the foreign subsidiaries screamed just as they had when we centralized marketing. They asked, "How can we deal effectively with our governments, the governments that in most cases set prices on all of our products, if we don't control pharmaceutical production?" They had a point, of course. But it was now more important to unify our operations and lower costs than it was to deal effectively with any single government. We were paying a short-term price to achieve a long-term gain in efficiency. Logic aside, our foreign heads were also angry over losing turf, and they made this transition painful. Gradually, however, they came to appreciate that the new division lowered costs and accelerated the development of international standards in everything from environmental protection to production and marketing issues. Then, in 1991, we pushed the centralization one step further, pulling the bulk chemical production and the pharmaceutical manufacturing into one global organization that included thirty-one different plants.

Once more, restructuring enabled us to float another cadre of executives to the top. These were leaders with the combination of technical training and managerial ability that I favored, people like John Zabriskie, who had a Ph.D. in chemistry and extensive experience in marketing as well as manufacturing. As head of our new manufacturing division, John and his next-in-command, Dave Conklin, were able to close redundant plants, reduce our work force, cut our costs, and still improve output and quality. As a result, our productivity increases began to exceed the rate of inflation and provide a solid basis for growth in earnings.

These changes hurt some people, but many more would have been hurt much worse if we hadn't responded successfully to the new environment for healthcare in the United States and abroad. We tried to ease our employees through the transition with training programs and effective leadership, but we couldn't be in the business of subsidizing inefficient operations – a practice that can't be sustained over the long haul in a competitive setting.

***

With centralization well under way, I was able at last to persuade my colleagues to try an experiment with generic drugs. In the generic market we'd be competing with our trademarked products because they typically continued to sell long after the patents had expired. Some doctors preferred the trademarked versions and continued to prescribe them even though they carried a higher price. In generics, we'd be competing solely on the basis of price, which was not the traditional Merck way to do things. But if our customers wanted generics, I thought we should be providing them, and in the early 1990s, we launched a generic drug business limited to Merck products no longer covered by a patent.

This new policy put additional pressure on manufacturing to keep cutting costs, but that wasn't my major objective. My primary goal was to stay in touch with our customers and give them what they wanted and needed. That's why I persisted, listened to a great deal of grumbling, and finally shoved Merck into this low-margin business. I say "shoved" because my Merck colleagues were for the most part dead set against this strategy. Although generic drug manufacturing of Merck products was a minuscule operation at the start, the plan anticipated the expiration of patents on some of our most important products, including *Vasotec*, *Prinivil*, *Zocor*, and *Pepcid*, to mention only a few. Merck wasn't the first pharmaceutical company to sell its products in both a branded and generic formulation, but change at Merck came with particular difficulty because of the firm's long success with innovative, branded products.

* * *

We were already satisfying a growing number of patients with new drugs like *Mevacor*, but it was evident to me and the Management Council that we could further broaden our drug development front. We steadily increased the annual budgets for the labs until, in 1994, we spent over $1.3 billion on research and development. Ed Scolnick built up our resources in molecular genetics and recombinant DNA technology, starting with specific projects like the one that produced the vaccine *Recombivax HB*. Soon Merck had a generalized capability in the new science and technology that we (and others) thought was the equal of any biotech company in the world.

Nevertheless, the breakthroughs were coming so fast and across such a broad front that we still found it useful to partner with small biotech companies having special skills. The combined opportunities for new drug development through molecular genetics, rDNA technology, biochemistry and enzymology, crystallography,* and medicinal chemistry were awesome. It was evident that even a billion-dollar R&D program couldn't cope with all the changes taking place in the biomedical sciences in the United States and abroad. In my inner circle of advisers, we began intense discussions of what we could do to keep Merck at the front of the pack.

One possibility was to increase the research budget by creating a much larger business through merger or acquisition. Since each of

---

* Crystallography employs X-ray studies of crystals of a molecule such as an enzyme. These studies reveal the three-dimensional structure of the enzyme in enough detail that the active site, where the substrate binds to the enzyme, can be discerned. This information was invaluable in designing inhibitors that bound to the active site and blocked the function of the enzyme.

the world's major pharmaceutical firms tended to emphasize particular therapeutic categories, such as cardiovascular treatments or therapies for nervous disorders, a merger could have a quick impact on the new product pipeline if two firms with products in complementary therapeutic areas merged. Financial analysts watched these pipelines like birds of prey circling a potential meal. Most of our successful competitors in the 1980s and 1990s pulled off at least one significant merger or acquisition. Some completed several deals and quickly built up their total sales. Bristol-Myers and Squibb merged, as did Hoechst and Marion Merrell Dow. American Home Products acquired American Cyanamid Company. After Glaxo acquired Burroughs-Welcome, the combined enterprises moved for a time into first place in total global revenue. Hoffmann-La Roche pushed decisively into biotechnology by acquiring Genentech. Despite this wave of combinations, the worldwide market for pharmaceuticals was still not highly concentrated – a situation that seemed to me and my colleagues basically unstable. Further consolidation was, I thought, inevitable.

The momentum was substantial, but we decided to chart a different course. We saw no advantage to acquiring a firm that was significantly less successful at new drug discovery and development than Merck. We had carefully observed what happened with Smith Kline, which had become a very successful company after Jim Black discovered *Tagamet*. This was an absolute breakthrough treatment for peptic ulcers, and it quickly became the largest selling drug in the world. For a time, the leaders of Smith Kline were kings of the hill: they lectured the rest of the industry on every aspect of the business from research to marketing to manufacturing. Intoxicated by success, they ignored the fact that their prominence was based on a discovery by one talented scientist working in a small British outpost of Smith Kline research. Jim Black soon left the company, just as he had earlier left ICI after inventing beta-blockers, a new treatment for hypertension.

Without Black, the Smith Kline research laboratories were unproductive, as they had been for years, and the money from *Tagamet* sales didn't change that situation. When *Tagamet* lost patent protection, Smith Kline was battered by generic competition and within a few years was a limping giant looking to be acquired. Beecham took up that challenge, restructured, and merged the operations to form SmithKline Beecham, but the long-term future of the combination still largely depended on the productivity of a research organization in need of change. It was not long before another merger followed: Glaxo Wellcome acquired the combine and formed Glaxo SmithKline.

These mergers, as my chief financial adviser Frank Spiegel pointed out, were expensive. This was especially true given the high prices of pharmaceutical stocks during these years. It was also much more difficult to capitalize on a merger than most financial observers realized. The lengthy process of consolidating Merck with Sharp & Dohme offered useful lessons, some of which I had been forced to learn when heading our laboratories. It had taken decades and a great deal of managerial effort to iron out the seams between these two organizations. When that task was successfully completed, however, the combined enterprise was able to move to the forefront of the global industry – and that fact was always in my mind.

Late in my tenure as CEO, I seriously contemplated a merger. We discussed several possible partners – including Glaxo – but I thought only one competing firm in the entire industry really worth all the trouble and expense a merger would entail. That firm was Pfizer. Our product lines largely complemented each other, and I yearned to graft the research potential of Merck to their marketing power. But Merck was so successful on its own that I couldn't persuade my colleagues to pursue this combination, which I thought would have created the strongest pharmaceutical research organization in the world. Nor could I generate the necessary enthusiasm in Bill Steere, the recently promoted CEO of Pfizer. I backed off. It wasn't wise to push hard for this merger when, owing to my impending retirement, I wouldn't be able to help the combination succeed.

Instead of mergers, Merck negotiated strategic alliances along the lines of the arrangement with AB Astra. Fortunately, the Reagan administration had decided to encourage experimentation with mergers and acquisitions by relaxing the structural side of the antitrust policy. Without that change, we couldn't have woven the network of agreements that let us combine some of our selected capabilities with those of other leading firms. This was "win-win" if I ever saw it.

Take, for example, our joint venture with Johnson & Johnson, a company with a leading position in the over-the-counter (OTC) business. We had products with great potential for over-the-counter sales; J&J had marketing capabilities that would have cost us many millions of dollars and several years to develop. Even then, we might not have been successful in what for Merck was a new undertaking. By handling the OTC business through a joint venture (Johnson & Johnson • Merck Consumer Pharmaceuticals Co.) both firms could maximize their existing strengths. We were winners, but so were the consumers and a national economy that needed powerhouse multinational competitors willing to explore new avenues to innovation.

That venture began when Jim Burke, CEO of J&J, and I met in Washington, DC, waiting to board a plane and return to New Jersey. This, I thought, is another advantage of not having a corporate jet. I had repeatedly turned down suggestions from my executive group that Merck acquire a corporate jet. Although private planes obviously would have been a convenience for me and others who had access to them, I disliked the idea of a large Merck group taking a business trip with only part of the contingent in private jets. The planes were not only expensive, but they undermined the unity of management.

Jim Burke and I took advantage of our meeting to talk about the OTC potential of *Pepcid*, our prescription treatment for peptic ulcers. This product had been on the market several years, and we had a high degree of confidence in its safety. *Pepcid* had been, however, the third entry in the field of peptic ulcer medicines behind SmithKline Beecham's *Tagamet* and Glaxo's *Zantac*. Now our question was, Could a Merck–J&J venture get to the OTC market first and achieve an advantage over these two strong competitors? On the spot, we decided we could and agreed to organize a team to bring our companies together. The race was on.

Our collaboration went smoothly. Merck research quickly developed the new OTC formulation and received the FDA's approval. The J&J forces guided the new brand, *Pepcid AC*, onto the market ahead of our two competitors and promoted it with vigor and skill. We developed brand loyalty, which is as important to OTC products as patents are to prescription drugs, and *Pepcid AC* never lost its lead. Together, J&J and Merck increased the value of *Pepcid* enormously by taking it OTC, and in fact the prescription version, owing to these marketing efforts, gained market share at the same time.

Our collaboration with DuPont was a venture with a different twist. When I took over as CEO, some Merck executives were afraid DuPont, huge in comparison to Merck, might mount a hostile takeover of our company. Corporate raiders, white knights, golden parachutes, and leveraged buyouts were big news in the 1980s. I wasn't concerned. I thought I could run Merck perfectly well as part of a larger company with the kind of track record DuPont had compiled over the past century. DuPont, a world leader in research and development in the industrial chemicals business, had especially strong capabilities in chemical engineering. As it turned out, however, our respective market capitalizations shifted. Merck's stock was rising, and DuPont's was falling as a result of intense competition among the producers of several of its important products. This made it difficult to purchase Merck with DuPont stock. So instead of trying to buy us, DuPont decided to move into pharmaceuticals in a way that eased us toward a joint undertaking. DuPont had invented a new type of receptor blocker (an angiotensin II receptor antagonist) for treating high blood pressure but didn't have the experienced development, regulatory affairs, or marketing and sales force that we had in the cardiovascular field. We agreed to license their new drug.

As our two groups worked together, it became apparent that Merck and DuPont people were very compatible. Frank Spiegel and I then suggested to Ed Woolard, CEO and Chairman of DuPont, a new 50–50 joint venture – a proposal DuPont accepted. This cooperative arrangement strengthened both firms. Before 1981, however, the chances that the federal government's antitrust division would have approved such a contract between two very large firms were slim to none. The results in this case were impressive. The product DuPont had invented became *Cozaar*, which later established itself as the most important of the new-generation drugs for treatment of high blood pressure.

I saw the joint venture arrangements with DuPont and with Astra earlier as essential long-term strategic moves for the company. In the Astra deal, the joint venture firm in the United States, Astra Merck, would have access to most of the major products flowing from Astra research in perpetuity. The Swedish company had proven its capability by inventing *Prilosec*, which replaced *Zantac* as the largest-selling prescription drug in the world. The exciting antidepressant candidate, *Zimeldine*, worked through a novel mechanism of action: it blocked the removal (by reuptake) of the neurotransmitter serotonin in the brain and was thus different in action from any known antidepressant at that time. More important, it lacked the common side effects of other antidepressants. AB Astra subsequently launched *Zimeldine* in the European market before we had time to begin our development program in the United States. Sales rose rapidly. But as the number of consumers climbed, reports began to circulate of a rare but serious side effect, Guillain–Barré syndrome. AB Astra pulled *Zimel-dine* off the market, and suddenly the most important product candidate that made our deal attractive was dead. Years later, Eli Lilly developed another serotonin reuptake inhibitor, *Prozac*, that lacked this side effect and became the company's most important new product in over a decade.

Unfortunately, AB Astra research hadn't followed our strategy of pursuing a backup for every product candidate. As a result, what initially looked like a good deal for both firms began to look decidedly unbalanced. Our independent auditors suggested taking a charge against earnings, which would mean giving up on the alliance contract. We resisted because another AB Astra drug, *Tonocard* (to control abnormal heart rhythm), was able to generate modest U.S. sales and also because we heard rumblings from the laboratory that another very important candidate at the bottom of the AB Astra list was beginning to look interesting. But until that drug materialized, our position in favor of a strategic alliance between Merck and AB Astra remained tenuous.

Once *Prilosec* came through the pipeline, however, the alliance strategy clearly was working very well indeed. Similarly, the DuPont–Merck joint venture was able to build on the research output of a pharmaceutical organization that had produced *Cozaar*. Merck owned only 50 percent of the joint ventures, but our access to the research of both DuPont and Astra was crucial in the alignment of experienced manpower and proven scientific talent for the R&D war that I foresaw in pharmaceuticals.

We didn't stop there with our new strategy. We started a joint research venture in therapies for viral diseases, working with Sigma Tau, a leading Italian company that already shared important commercial links with us. We knew that combination vaccines were the wave of the future, and we were determined to strengthen our position in global vaccine markets. *M-M-R II*, which immunized against measles, mumps, and rubella with one shot, was our model. As everyone in the industry knew, the central problem with immunization programs in developed countries was persuading the adult recipients or parents bringing their children to show up for their shots. In the developing world, that problem was exacerbated by rudimentary and underfunded public health organizations and frequently inadequate transportation and communication systems. Combination vaccines were an ideal way to solve the delivery problems in both cases, as *M-M-R II* had demonstrated.

But our efforts to develop new pediatric combinations were blocked because other companies were already producing some of the vaccines we needed. The solution once again was a strategic alliance – this time with a leading French firm, Pasteur Mérieux Sérums & Vaccins. Mérieux and Merck were competitors, but we could now cooperate in a way that clearly enhanced public health as well as the ability of Merck's vaccine division to promote new products and increase global sales.

Our strategic alliances and the improvements in manufacturing, marketing, and sales enabled us to take full advantage of the wave of new products emerging from the Merck Research Laboratories. We could, of course, simply have ridden that wave, enjoyed life, and looked forward to retirement with a nice package of Merck stock and a clear conscience. But that would have left the firm poorly positioned for the coming era of intense global competition and downward pressure on prices. I wouldn't even contemplate a passive strategy. I wanted Merck to be able to exploit every opportunity opening up in the biomedical sciences, and I wanted everyone in the company to help achieve that goal. Literally, everyone.

* * *

To maximize our opportunities – or even come close – we had to tighten our focus. Merck had dabbled with diversification, acquiring a specialty chemicals operation that made everything from granulated carbon to thickeners for salad dressing. We didn't make combs, but our Calgon Corporation provided water management services to a broad range of industrial and residential customers. In the years that followed our diversification, each of these enterprises acquired a momentum of its own. They kept growing, innovating, and making profits (though never at prescription drug margins), and so there was no good reason to disturb them.

When I became CEO, I was advised to consider further diversification. But I didn't think Merck needed to camouflage its profitability, and I didn't want management to spend time thinking about water coolers, activated carbon, or salad dressing. Merck leadership had little expertise in these businesses, none of which had a high-tech component, and as a result they had been left to make their own way. I was uncomfortable with this arrangement. I was convinced that we could be the best in pharmaceuticals, and if we couldn't, salad dressing wouldn't be our salvation even though it was a large, profitable business. I began looking for ways to spin off our diversified operations at decent prices.

One of our first spin-offs made some former Merck executives instant millionaires. The group running Calgon Carbon Corporation brought off a managerial, leveraged buyout, and shortly after the deal with us was done, their new company's major competitor failed. They were left sitting on a gold mine. Personally, I was as happy for them as I was for Merck, which had narrowed its focus and deepened its commitment to its core business.

We continued to divest noncore businesses. We started withdrawing from specialty chemicals by selling Calgon Water Management in 1993. I thought we shouldn't have entered this business in the first place, and I was certain we could use the capital and personnel to better effect in pharmaceuticals. Last to go were Kelco and a smaller operation, Calgon Vestal Laboratories. Kelco had become a world leader in manufacturing alginates and biogums, some of which were produced from seaweed harvested in California waters. In addition to thickening salad dressing, Kelco's products were used in everything from oil exploration to skin care. Although Kelco and the Calgon Vestal Laboratories (which specialized in wound dressings) were both successful niche players, they too were peripheral to our central strategic goal. Both were sold because they couldn't help us be the most innovative and successful firm in the global pharmaceutical industry. To achieve that goal, we made plans to exit all of Merck's remaining nonpharmaceutical businesses. This job was not completed when I retired, but by that time we had already significantly restructured the business and established the strategy for the future.

* * *

The more we concentrated on pharmaceuticals, the more pressure we put on the Merck Research Laboratories, where Ed Scolnick was running the show. As CEO, I made certain that Ed and MRL had all the resources they could use successfully. We increased the research budget by 13 percent during my first year, added 18 percent two years in a row, and provided an additional 12 percent in 1989. At that point, we were spending over $750 million a year on research and development, which enabled us to open the Neuroscience Research Centre in England (which later developed *Maxalt*, Merck's new migraine drug), to double our R&D program in Canada (which later discovered *Singulair*, a break through treatment for asthma, and *Vioxx*, the company's important new osteoarthritis and analgesic product), and to complete a new $80 million John J. Horan Research Building at Rahway.

When I was head of MRL, the company had concentrated substantial resources on rolling out big winners, including *Vasotec* (for hypertension), *Primaxin* (an antibiotic), *Mevacor* (to reduce cholesterol), *Recombivax HB* (hepatitis B vaccine), and *Pepcid* (for ulcers), but the labs were also working furiously to have backup and second-generation drugs ready. This kind of work doesn't make banner headlines or win prizes, but it was crucial to Merck and any other firm in the industry with global aspirations. Drug development is so slow and expensive that this follow-up work must be under way long before the blockbuster drug hits the market. One thing any investor should look for in a company report is information about plans to develop second-generation drugs and to extend the application of an existing therapy by conducting additional (Phase IV and V) clinical trials. If the business doesn't seem to be pursuing this route, it's reasonable to conclude that it will soon lose its market share on some major products. Or worse.

Merck Research Laboratories was doing a superb job looking for improvements on each of our drugs and learning through clinical trials exactly what each could do for patients. This may seem elementary, but I'd seen many pharmaceutical companies fail to do this systematically, and it was one of the things I'd worked hard to change when I was heading Merck's research. Now, Merck was harvesting the fruits of that transition. Under Scolnick's direction, MRL established through extensive clinical trials that *Vasotec* was an appropriate therapy for patients suffering from congestive heart failure as well as hypertension. By combining *Vasotec* with *Hydro Diuril*, an older medication now off patent, MRL produced *Vaseretic*, which enabled physicians to give patients a diuretic, an antihypertensive, and a treatment for congestive heart failure in one dose – a convenience for many people. Merck Research Laboratories won no headlines for meticulous attention to this aspect of drug development, but the aggregate impact on the company's bottom line was significant. By 1990 Merck had eighteen drugs with annual sales reaching or exceeding $100 million, and the list included *Vaseretic* as well as *Zocor*, our follow-up to *Mevacor*.

In the late 1980s and early 1990s, MRL also began to add significantly to our core group of blockbuster products. The stars included four cardiovasculars, one antiulcer drug, and *Primaxin*, our leading anti-infective. In 1988, we started our rollout of *Prinivil*, the new ACE inhibitor we had developed as a backup to *Vasotec* and then used in the unfortunate deal with ICI. The following year we brought out the major innovative therapy acquired from AB Astra, an acid pump inhibitor, *Prilosec*, which strengthened our position in the market for ulcer treatments. Virus and cell biology contributed to the new wave of products with a pediatric vaccine against Hib (*Haemophilus influenzae* type b), a major source of meningitis in children.

* * *

Our research pipeline was full, and two of MRL's newest products moved us forcefully into the rapidly growing field of therapies for older people. One came directly out of our labs, and we licensed one from Italy. *Fosamax*, the Italian discovery, prevented loss of bone mass due to osteoporosis, a disease affecting about one-third of all women over fifty. For men in the same age group, MRL developed *Proscar*, a treatment for prostate enlargement (symptomatic benign prostate enlargement), a problem confronted by more than half of males over fifty.

The *Proscar* story was a long, convoluted research tale with some Gothic touches. It began in the 1960s when Art Patchett and other Merck scientists began studying male sex hormones, seeking an effective treatment for acne. They focused on a particular enzyme that helps convert testosterone into an even more potent hormone (dihydrotestosterone or DHT). Alas, this was one of those projects that couldn't seem to work up a full head of steam. The prospect of giving adolescent children steroids was unappealing, and at last the laboratory's Research Coordinating Committee decided to terminate the project in the 1970s.

Then, miraculously, a pseudohermaphrodite from a backwoods area of the Dominican Republic saved the entire project. Brought into a hospital for abdominal surgery, this young girl turned out to be a boy! Other young males from the same area were found to have developed in the same way. Through their preteens, their genitalia appeared to be female (hence the "pseudo") because they had undescended gonads. But the Cornell University and Southwestern Medical Center scientists who studied them discovered three interesting facts: first, the youths were males who later in their lives had obvious male genitalia; second, they had relatively tiny, underdeveloped prostates; and third, they never developed male pattern baldness. Our attention focused on the

Roy (center) touring the Italian manufacturing plant in 1990.

underdeveloped prostates. As the scientists reported, all of these Dominicans were genetically deficient in an enzyme that converted testosterone into DHT.

Dr. Glen Arth, head of the acne project, and I read the same journal article at the same time. We burst out of our offices, meeting in the hall with our index fingers in the air, saying "Ah hah!" Both of us had seen that the goal of our research should be the prostate gland, not acne. By blocking this crucial enzyme, we might prevent prostate enlargement. Sixteen years after starting the project, Dr. Gary Rasmussen and his associates gave Merck a new product, *Proscar*, the first oral therapy for this disease. *Proscar* actually did more than we anticipated. It not only stopped excessive growth of the prostate but also caused a 20 to

25 percent reduction in the size of the gland. Further clinical studies demonstrated a marked reduction in the need for surgery – just what we had hoped for.

Although Merck research and marketing people were excited about *Proscar*, urologists were not eager to prescribe a therapy that might make their surgical procedures unnecessary. Surgery was quick; *Proscar* required prolonged treatment. This presented Merck with a serious marketing problem. The pharmaceutical industry is often criticized for spending too much on marketing, but *Proscar* illustrates why it is essential to market drugs just as effectively as you discover and manufacture them. With *Proscar*, we decided to go directly to the ultimate customers, the patients who stood to benefit by an alternative to surgery. So we mounted our first large-scale advertising campaign aimed at patients – a campaign that led Merck and other companies to experiment extensively with this style of marketing. As a result, *Proscar* made steady progress, although it did not become a blockbuster.

By vigorously pressing follow-up research, however, MRL generated at least one additional chapter to a story spanning four decades. Knowing that the young Dominicans didn't develop male-pattern baldness, once *Proscar* was on the market we began to research whether a different formulation might not help the millions of men concerned about their receding hairlines. Add a few additional years of intense study and several million dollars more and you have *Propecia* (launched after I retired), a follow-on drug that might be just as successful as the initial breakthrough product. Especially if the marketing is carried on vigorously, as it certainly has been in the last few years.

There is also the possibility that *Proscar* may some day play a role in prostate cancer prevention. Prostate cancer had never been identified in these particular Dominicans, who lack the enzyme blocked by *Proscar*, which is an observation that prompted Merck and the National Cancer Institute to conduct a large, long-term clinical study of the new drug with results still pending. But if the findings show that *Proscar* reduces the incidence of prostate cancer, the results will appear in major headlines because this cancer is common among elderly men.

***

If we summarize Merck's strategic plan and present it in the bullet form characteristic of business and business school presentations, this is what we get for the years 1985 through 1994:

- We were steadily improving our personnel throughout the organization.
- We were pumping more resources into research and development while adding substantial new capabilities in molecular biology and genetics.
- We were systematically following up on the development of each of our new products, whether they came out of MRL or were licensed from another firm.
- We were upgrading our marketing operations.
- We were cutting costs and improving quality in manufacturing.
- We were tightening our concentration on the core business: developing and selling pharmaceuticals.
- We were increasing our capacity for breakthrough research and innovative marketing through strategic alliances.

This kind of strategy made sense to me. It was entirely different from compiling projections from the different divisions and departments, which was the kind of plan Frank Spiegel and I had worked on when I was "learning by doing." The new Merck plan challenged every division and demanded innovation from every individual.

The industry was shifting with hurricane force in the 1980s and 1990s, but by successfully implementing our strategy, we were able to keep Merck growing vigorously and producing the kind of profits that attracted the attention of Wall Street and Main Street. Between 1985 and 1993, we increased the company's total sales from $3.5 billion to $10.5 billion. Our growth in Europe, where we were the leading U.S.-based competitor, was in double digits. Net income almost quadrupled, from $540 million to a little under $2.2 billion. When you add stock price appreciation to dividends to get the cumulative total stockholder return, we had created a compound annual growth rate of 24 percent during the ten-year period ending in December 1993. These figures would have been even more impressive if the Clinton administration hadn't blindsided our entire industry, but more on that will follow in a later chapter. Despite political problems, neither our stockholders nor our employees could complain about Merck's performance. We had fulfilled most of our aspirations by that time. We were the largest pharmaceutical company in the world and, in my opinion, the most successful innovator in an industry with a great track record for entrepreneurship.

In addition to attracting attention and investors, Merck was winning some impressive awards. For seven years in a row, the senior executives, directors, and financial analysts who vote in *Fortune* magazine's annual poll chose Merck as their "Most Admired Corporation." Since 1985, we had also won several other honors for our management, our technological breakthroughs, and the quality of our manufacturing. But the two awards I was proudest of involved our employees and their working conditions. For six straight years, *Working Mother* magazine rated Merck among the top ten places in the United States for mothers to be employed. Another magazine, *Black Enterprise*, gave us a similar rating for the opportunities we were providing African American professionals. We had superb affirmative action programs in place, were dedicated to flextime, and had shattered the glass ceiling that kept women and minorities out of top executive positions.

It was a pleasure for all of us to contemplate these accomplishments when Merck & Co., Inc., celebrated its centennial in 1991. When we looked back over that century in business, it was apparent that some aspects of the firm had remained relatively stable for many years. The emphasis on high-quality products could, for instance, be traced back to 1891 and even further if you crossed the Atlantic and looked at E. Merck, the German fine-chemical producer that had been our parent organization. But from my perspective, the variables far outweighed the constants in the Merck formula. Just in the time that I had been with Merck we had completed two major transitions in research and development, two significant reorganizations in manufacturing and marketing, and several substantial changes in staff operations and basic corporate strategy. Given our dedication to change and recognizing that everyone in the company, from bottom to top, had contributed to our success, we granted stock options (100 shares) to all 34,500 of our employees throughout the world. For some years I had been looking for a way to make everyone an owner as well as a worker. The centennial gave me the opening I needed to give everyone at Merck a chance to acquire an owner's stake in our future.

* * *

The centennial was heartwarming. It was nice to win awards, several of which had come my way. In 1990, *Manage* magazine named me

"American Manager of the Year." The following year, *Industry Week* decided I was one of the best CEOs in the country, and in 1992, *Chief Executive* proclaimed that Roy Vagelos, M.D., was "Chief Executive of the Year."

This type of acclaim, however, didn't stop me from obsessing on what we hadn't yet accomplished as well as the obstacles ahead for Merck and the society in which we lived. In the early 1990s, millions of people all over the world were still not receiving the treatment they needed for their cardiovascular problems. In New York City, next door to Merck, the entire hospital system seemed on the verge of collapse. Hundreds of millions in developing countries had inadequate medical infrastructures and budgets that wouldn't support even the most rudimentary treatment programs. These were some of the social problems I was contemplating.

Looming before the entire world was the unfolding HIV/AIDS pandemic, a public health crisis with no known solution. In the age of modern scientific medicine, this new plague seemed to have returned us to the epoch before sulfa drugs, penicillin, and the new viral vaccines had transformed medical practice. Once again, physicians were helpless to prevent a disease that in its final stages killed virtually every person who was infected.

In 1986 Merck had embarked on a major HIV research effort. This was risky because the virus had been identified only in 1983. Randy Shilts's book *And the Band Played On*, and the movie version, recounts how mysterious and controversial the origins and epidemiology of this disease were at that time. Much basic research remained to be done. In the normal course of medical innovation, that research – on the virus itself and the nature of the illness it caused – would be carried on primarily in government institutions like NIH or in nonprofit organizations like Washington University. Then pharmaceutical firms would use the accumulated knowledge of the disease and virus to find a vaccine or a specific therapy. That's the way the cardiovascular research that produced *Mevacor* developed. Our applied research in the 1970s and 1980s built on a basic research foundation established in the 1950s and 1960s. But the AIDS pandemic was too threatening to wait for basic science to make its discoveries. We moved ahead knowing that Ed Scolnick's teams at MRL needed to do significant basic research as well as the normal applied research if they were going to be successful soon enough to stop the spread of the disease and save millions of lives. We were looking for either a vaccine to prevent infection or an antiviral drug that would effectively treat the infection, and we moved down both paths at once.

I was convinced that our researchers would succeed. I may even have been a bit cocky. We had, after all, just produced the world's first recombinant DNA vaccine for humans, *Recombivax HB*, which prevents hepatitis B, and our success persuaded me that we could follow the same road against HIV. We would find a surface particle from the virus to serve as an antigen, triggering the immune system to action without causing the disease. Then, when the virus attacked a vaccine recipient, cell memory would kick in and the immune system would fight off the infection just as it did in those vaccinated with *Recombivax HB*.

Merck Research Laboratories started searching for an appropriate surface antigen, but just to be safe, we also began researching two other lines of attack. As we soon discovered, HIV is more evasive and dangerous than the hepatitis B virus, attacking the very cells in the immune system, the CD4 cells, that we wanted to stir into action to combat the infection. The virus actually uses these cells to manufacture new viruses. Even more baffling was the way in which the infection seemed to have a long quiescent period following the initial infection. Then, years later, this retrovirus would suddenly defeat the immune system. Patients in the AIDS stage of the infection then died from one of a variety of opportunistic bacterial or fungal infections.

HIV taught us a series of lessons in humility. Our initial vaccine research failed because we couldn't elicit the immune response we needed. Monoclonal antibodies, one of the new products of immunology, were also unsuccessful. We didn't give up. Indeed, Scolnick and his colleagues took each defeat in stride and came roaring back to try a different approach. The hours that Merck employees put in on their various projects and the level of emotional commitment were always outstanding, but there was a special attitude toward this project throughout the organization. The level of dedication to HIV research, from the top of MRL to the bottom, was unbelievable. So was the level of investment Merck was making in what threatened repeatedly to be a total failure. By the end of 1994, we had already spent over $400 million on HIV/AIDS research. That figure would go much higher in the next few years.

Having failed with a vaccine, we now concentrated on inhibiting the enzymes crucial to viral replication. (By now enzyme inhibition was the dominant strategy for drug discovery at Merck.) One of these enzymes was reverse transcriptase, which was the target of azidothymidine (AZT), the major drug used against HIV. Another was a protease critical in the development of the virus. An individual virion (a single virus) lives only about twenty minutes, but it replicates at an astonishing rate. If we could find a chemical that blocked replication better than AZT, we would perhaps enable the patient's immune system to conquer the infection. Scolnick targeted both critical enzymes and sent MRL's medicinal chemists in search of an inhibitor. But each time they came up with a likely candidate something went wrong. One was too toxic; others failed because the virus created mutations that enabled it to resist our drugs. This was the problem with AZT, which nevertheless remained the most common treatment for HIV infection worldwide.

In the course of this research, MRL did some brilliant basic research that improved everyone's knowledge of HIV and of the disease. Our scientists published their findings, in some cases giving away an advantage that Merck might have exploited for its financial gain. But this was not business as usual. Too many people were dying. The infection was spreading and its epidemiology shifting. At first it appeared that the disease would primarily affect gay men and intravenous drug users who shared needles. But then evidence of heterosexual transmission mounted, as did indications that infected mothers were giving the disease to their newborns. We were so determined to develop a new therapy that Scolnick and I promoted a cooperative venture with our erstwhile competitors in pharmaceuticals. In 1993, this proposal led to the organization of the Inter-Company Collaboration for AIDS Drugs Development, which enabled several leading firms to share knowledge, develop standard assays, and obtain drugs for clinical trials with combination therapies.

As my 1994 retirement date approached, however, we still hadn't solved the HIV puzzle. We had a promising lead candidate, a protease inhibitor that passed safety assessment and Phase I clinical trials for tolerability, bioavailability, and antiviral activity. But these trials involved small numbers of patients. And there was always the threat, the very real threat, that HIV would develop resistance during the second phase of the trials.

I wasn't happy about leaving these large-scale research programs in such an unfinished state, nor was I pleased with my efforts to anoint a successor as CEO. I had been grooming candidates for several years,

doing what John Horan had done for me when he and the Board appointed me a senior vice president and then executive vice president.
Each time a promising executive emerged, I would provide a new range
of experiences and watch carefully as he or she grappled with those extended responsibilities. One candidate stood out, demonstrating many
of the attributes that I sought, but he left Merck abruptly for personal
reasons. Still, I ground away at this problem when I wasn't worrying
about our AIDS research or the Clinton Administration's heavy-handed
efforts to reform the U.S. healthcare system, including the pharmaceutical industry. All of these unsolved problems left little time to enjoy
being head of America's Most Admired Corporation. There was too
much to accomplish to spend time reflecting on our past achievements
or present honors – either corporate or personal.

10 | *The Moral Corporation*

The 1980s provided every reason to think all business was corrupt. The newspapers were full of insider trading and Wall Street scandals. The most upsetting news was about the gross profits made by people widely described as financial parasites, who sucked off billions of dollars through complex schemes that most people had difficulty understanding. There were junk bond crazes and hostile takeovers by financiers who broke up organizations instead of building them. Much the same picture appeared on television, in local movie theaters, and in popular magazines. Fiction, nonfiction, it was all the same: People in business are not like you. They are fundamentally immoral, and the richest are making no positive contributions to our society.

Recently we have had another burst of business scandals. In the last few years some of the country's largest firms have collapsed as a result of corruption, leaving their shareholders, former employees, and entire communities in deep distress. This time some of the leading firms in the accounting profession have been caught up in the scandal for abandoning their watchdog role and approving the illegal practices of their corporate clients. Once again, men in powerful positions lined their own pockets while presiding over a devastating slide into bankruptcy.

During the nation's previous bout with business scandal in the 1980s, it was especially easy to believe that business was corrupt because millions of lives were changing in dramatic, often devastating ways as a result of changes in corporate America. As global competition hit companies and industries that were unprepared for the onslaught, layoffs and downsizing (later renamed "right-sizing") occurred all over the country. White-collar as well as blue-collar workers were hurt when U.S. companies tried to cut costs to meet those of more efficient foreign competitors. Frequently, the layoffs followed hostile takeovers, and the relationship between what was happening on Wall Street and what was happening on Main Street was all too obvious.

My own experiences in the 1980s and early 1990s took place in an entirely different business world – one populated by people who were actually like most other Americans. And for that matter, like most people I've met around the world. I could see no difference in moral terms between my colleagues and competitors in business and the colleagues and competitors I'd known as a university administrator, scientist, and physician. In the university and in business, a few people were reasonable candidates for sainthood, and some were fundamentally immoral. But most were someplace in between, trying hard to do the right thing, to lead productive lives, and to make positive contributions to society. We weren't always succeeding – and yes, I place myself in that large middle group – but we kept trying. Here are some of the things we tried to do at Merck during those years.

* * *

One of the most difficult issues I struggled with for years involved the prices of our products. It's not surprising to see this issue popping up in the news again recently. It will always be a thorny issue because drugs and vaccines are literally matters of life or death for many people. When a physician prescribes a particular medication, the patient seldom has a choice about which one to buy. The physician has already made that choice. Health insurance, a health maintenance organization, or Medicare is likely to pay the physician's bill but is unlikely to pay for prescriptions, which as a rule are expensive. If patients are not covered by a plan that provides low-cost prescription drugs, the pain of payment is immediate and memorable.

As a physician who grew up during the Great Depression, I understood that distress, and as CEO at Merck I became very concerned about our pricing policy. At first, I didn't really understand the nitty-gritty of what was going on in the marketplace. When things are going well, the CEO doesn't press the managers very much. He wants to give them freedom to do what they do. But I was fretting about prices, and so, rather early in my years as CEO, I started a dialogue within the firm about this issue. In general, Merck priced according to the value that its products contributed. If our new drugs made a substantial difference in treatment of a disease compared with earlier products, our price was going to be higher. We knew that many of our medicines, even when they were expensive, reduced overall healthcare costs and kept people on the job. They also improved the quality of life. We tried to set the price so that a majority of the potential users would be able to afford the drugs, but we also never lost sight of the fact that our research and development costs were steadily increasing and that sustained innovation by the laboratories was the key to Merck's success. In effect, we were trying to achieve a successful balance between public good and private gain.

Once we had set what we considered to be a fair price for a product, we had to deal with the issue of annual price increases. Here I had a different view than most of my marketing executives and certainly the rest of the industry. I wanted to keep increases low because I wanted to continue to get medicines into the hands of people who needed them, and clearly they were distressed about prices. When I pressed our marketing people about price increases, they had answers for all but one of my questions. Their story went like this: "We had a long period of severe inflation in the 1970s, when costs went up faster than we could increase prices. Our margins got tighter and we weren't certain we could pay for our expensive R&D if that continued indefinitely." Because I'd headed MRL when that was happening, they thought I would be susceptible to that argument. I was. But not enough to let this matter slide off the table. I continued to worry about whether we still needed to raise prices to make up for an "inflationary gap" that had developed long before I was CEO.

I began to watch the statistics on prices very carefully. I kept pressing – in part because I thought the "gap" had disappeared and in part because it seemed that we were frequently making up for our failure to increase the volume of our sales by increasing our prices. We weren't doing that with vaccines because there volume was increasing and prices were more stable partly as a result of large-volume government purchases. In fact, prices for vaccines were too low and were driving competitors out of the business. At one point, I stunned the management group by suggesting the price for a hepatitis B vaccine could be $100 per person (three shots were required). The marketing group reacted as though I were crazy at the time, but the price they came up with several years later when we had the vaccine was $100 per person. We could stay in the business at that price – especially after the liability problem for childhood vaccines was largely solved by a new law (prompted by Merck and others) that added a tax to each vaccine proportional to the incidence and importance of the side effects. Children who had side effects could receive compensation without resort to courts. This law and our new approach to pricing permitted Merck and a few others to continue to invest long term in this important field.

But we were increasing the prices of prescription drugs faster than I thought we should. It was one thing to charge a relatively high price on a breakthrough drug like *Mevacor*. Patients were paying for value delivered, a new therapy that didn't exist before. And of course a drug like *Mevacor* initially faced very little competition. It was another thing to raise prices with mature products still covered by patents. In fact, however, we could raise prices and increase total revenue even on products facing generic competition because many physicians prescribed our branded drugs long after generics were on the market. Some doctors were just doing what they had done for years without thinking about the economic consequences for their patients. Others were confident about the quality of Merck's products and somewhat suspicious of generics. Whatever the reasoning, many physicians were behaving just as our marketing experts said they would and, without knowing it, sustaining the pricing policies that were causing me concern.

In the late 1980s, my anxiety about pricing intensified. By that time, the "inflationary gap" had been closed by annual price increases. When I talked to people outside of Merck, people in my local community and elsewhere, I heard a great deal about the trouble they were having paying for prescription drugs. I could see a wave of discontent building up in the American public.

I wasn't the only one to react to these tremors of concern. The media hyped the subject, focused and personalized the concerns, and began to offer specific suggestions about how to solve what was now identified as a national problem. That quickly brought the politicians into play, and they too began to develop ideas about measures that would appeal to the public and have some chance of being implemented by Congress. This is the normal stuff of democratic politics. When the process works properly, our national and state governments solve problems on a regular basis. That is, they respond to new situations by changing our laws and regulatory systems. Of course, the solutions always take longer than we want and entail compromises. As Winston Churchill said, "Democracy is the worst form of government, except all those other forms that have been tried from time to time."

But even in a democracy, the best form of government, the political process has many opportunities to go awry. The greatest danger is implementing short-term solutions that have unintended consequences over the long term. That's especially likely to happen when problems are multifaceted or have vague origins. There was nothing vague about people's concerns over the prices of prescription drugs. People without drug benefits from insurance plans had quite specific stories to tell usually involving a $40 or $60 bill that they were likely to have to pay again very shortly to refill a prescription. Often they knew exactly how much each pill cost. But mixed in with that issue was another, related national problem involving the large number of Americans not covered by medical insurance. This was – and still is – a national scandal. Many of these people were forced to go to emergency wards when they were ill, which is an incredibly inefficient way to deliver healthcare in large cities, both for the individuals as well as for the municipalities as a whole. Individuals, who normally have to sit for hours in the emergency ward, do not get the kind of personal attention they would receive from a regular family practitioner. Further, this situation stresses the capabilities of the emergency wards and the resources of the municipalities that support them. Without insurance and without money, people can't go regularly to a doctor, and instead of a $15 co-pay charge for medicine, they are faced with a $60 or even a $90 bill for their prescription drugs.

What would we do, I asked our marketing folks, if this volatile situation resulted in price controls? That was the question for which they had no answer. The price control strategy in Europe had already cut deeply into the ability of European firms to innovate. Two-thirds of the pharmaceutical innovations were coming out of the United States, where markets still had a major influence on prices. Recognizing that these two issues – increased prices and the threat of price controls – were being joined in the public mind and that Merck and the rest of the industry were drifting into a dangerous situation, I finally forced the issue and developed a new approach to pricing. As far as possible, I wanted to encourage all the other pharmaceutical firms to follow our lead without breaking the antitrust laws. I never discussed prices with any Merck competitor. From time to time, other CEOs delicately introduced the subject of prices, but I always quickly changed the subject. Talking prices was a quick way to get into deep trouble, and besides, our strategy was to succeed by continuing to be the industry's premier innovator. Price fixing by business was, to my mind, as undesirable as price controls by the government because both undercut the kind of competition that makes our economy successful.

So in 1990, I proposed that Merck change its entire approach to pricing pharmaceuticals. Since Merck was the market leader in the United States, I thought we had a good opportunity to make our policy the industry standard. From now on, I said to our top executives, we should unilaterally adopt a policy of not raising our prices any faster than the increases in the Consumer Price Index (CPI). That didn't go down well with our marketing experts. "You're leaving money on the table," they cried. They repeated this several times because they were absolutely convinced they were right. Actually, I knew they were right. The marketers were deeply concerned about attaining revenue growth, a measure of their success each year. I was too, but I was also deeply concerned about the health of the research organizations in our firm and the rest of the industry. If we adopted this pricing policy, we would certainly be leaving money in the pockets of the people who bought our products. But if we didn't do this, I maintained, we were headed toward a major political crisis.

After a series of memorably intense discussions, we decided to adopt the new standard and to use an average figure for any increase in our prices. We took into account all of our products and keyed the in-crease to the CPI. Using an average figure was a compromise that gave marketing a little flexibility and served to stop most of the grumbling within the company. But once we announced our new policy, a burst of grumbling arose from outside Merck. Although some of our competi-tors quickly adopted our new standard, others were angry with Merck and with me personally. At least that's what I heard. Since I wasn't go-ing to change my practice of *never* talking to other CEOs about prices, they couldn't get a direct shot at me. But they were obviously upset.

Then, slowly, even the companies that were kicking and screaming followed the leader – probably for fear of being subjected to intense criticism. In time Merck's policy became the entire industry's policy, and we avoided the creation of a new government bureaucracy to con-trol prices. At that point, we had clearly signaled our willingness to cooperate in solving the country's healthcare problems. Alas, some im-portant politicians misread that signal, as I will explain in the next chapter.

* * *

We applied a similar strategy to environmental, safety, and quality is-sues. We wanted to solve the problems before a new government policy had to be imposed. The entire chemical industry – bulk chemicals, specialty chemicals, pharmaceuticals – had a long history of creating environmental problems, often because the hazards were not initially understood by either the firms or the government. For more than a century, society had little good scientific knowledge about how most chemical substances affect humans and other animals. But gradually, researchers accumulated epidemiological evidence pointing to particular substances as causing disease, including various forms of cancer. In the 1950s, when they began to put that information together with animal testing for toxicity and an improved knowledge of biochemistry, the environmental movement for the first time acquired a firm scientific foundation. We were no longer guessing about the need to limit certain chemicals in order to maintain clean air, water, and soil.

The manufacturing wing at Merck, especially the chemical operations, had been working for many years to decrease the gases and chemicals released into the atmosphere or local waterways. Merck had stopped dumping waste into the Atlantic Ocean long before that practice was prohibited. But when I returned to Rahway and the Merck Research Laboratories in the 1970s, I could see and smell that the company still had a good bit to do on the environmental front. Even before seeing the plume coming out of the TBZ (thiabendazole) plant, you could smell the mercaptans and other substances being wafted into the city. You could also detect a change in the weather by noting the intensity of the local smells, but back then, these byproducts seemed acceptable both to our people and to the local community. When I complained about the odors, the managers of the plant and crop protection business said, "You should be happy when you smell that. It means business is good. You should worry when you don't smell it." That was not a good answer for me. I began to think about ways to improve Merck's procedures, but it was several years before I was in a position to take decisive action on that front.

After I became CEO, the government sounded a wake-up call by publishing data on emissions of known or suspect carcinogens. Several chemicals that industrial processes released in huge quantities into the environment were listed in the second category, suspect carcinogens. Merck was heavily involved in the production of organic substances, which were our medicines, and some of the chemicals used in our operations got us placed high on the government's list of polluters. In Georgia, we were at the top of the list! There, a suspect carcinogen was critical in the production of an important antibiotic. When we built the plant, there had been no reason to worry about that chemical because its toxicity was not known. Now it was known, or at least suspected, which was good enough to persuade me to do something about this problem. After talking with Dorothy Bowers, who directed our environmental group, and Dave Conklin from chemical manufacturing, we decided to change our policies in two important regards. First, we voluntarily established a specific target with a time limit for the reduction of toxic emissions from our plants. We announced this policy in 1989 with a target date of 1995. The goal was to cut the environmental releases of the listed substances by 90 percent – a formidable hurdle to clear. Some of the engineers in our manufacturing division thought 40 percent would be more reasonable, and even the Environmental Protection Agency wanted an initial cut of only 50 percent. I doubt that any chemical company in the world had adopted more stringent standards than these, and it wasn't clear at first that we'd be able to achieve our objective.

We had more than forty plants operating around the world. Some of the chemical manufacturing operations, like the TBZ plant, were dedicated to a single product and had been running for years. Now, suddenly, they were going to have to change some important aspects of their operations, sometimes decisively, because the corporate executives, "the suits," had decided to cut emissions without any legal or political pressure to achieve the 90 percent goal. I knew this policy didn't make as much sense in Albany, Georgia, or Kilsheelan, Ireland, as it did in corporate headquarters, where we were also pressuring manufacturing to cut costs while simultaneously improving quality. The environmental initiative would be time-consuming and expensive: we initially estimated it would cost about $75 million.

Strong leadership in manufacturing, combined with good engineering, got us started quickly. I've always felt that one of the hardest things to do in the corporate world is to encourage people to take risks and not stay in their current, comfortable situations. Many of Merck's chemical engineers were very talented – they just needed to be pushed. "How can we change our processes so that we no longer use a chemical like benzene?" we asked. Our engineers found a way to do it. In making our antibiotics, we used a solvent – methylene chloride – that we bought by the ton. When we started using these substances, they weren't known to cause any problems, but now they were on the list.

"Let's get rid of methylene chloride," we said, and the first response was, "You've got to be kidding!" But we kept the pressure on, and our chemical engineers came through even better than we expected. They eliminated the toxic substances *and* enabled us to cut the cost of production at the same time by completely reengineering the processes used to make some of our products. I was amazed. By 1993, we had hit the 65 percent level of reductions, and two years later, Merck crossed the 90 percent line. Rahway (where the company no longer made TBZ) and several other sites around the world smelled better and were safer for both our workers and for the local residents.

Our second innovation was to make the new environmental program uniform for the entire world. Our plants in Ireland or Latin America would now have to meet the same standards as our factories in France, Japan, or the United States. The highest standard for any of the Merck sites became our global standard, regardless of any less stringent local or national regulations. All around the world we pulled up all our underground tanks and stored everything above ground. Then we put double piping in sewers so that we could see when a leak developed. Where we had evidence of past leaks, we cooperated with regulatory groups to ensure that the soil was not contaminated around our factories. This policy, which made environmental sense, also made good business sense because it was consistent with the objectives of a company in the business of curing and preventing diseases. It positioned us at the forefront of the pharmaceutical industry and prepared Merck for the day, soon approaching, when high standards for the protection of the air, soil, and water will prevail all around the world.

We took the same approach to smoking cigarettes or cigars on Merck sites. How could a company dedicated to improved healthcare allow its employees to damage their health and the health of others while on the job? Years before, in my second month at Merck research, I had made my first move against smoking. I had all the ashtrays removed from the backs of the seats in the research auditorium. Some colleagues grumbled, but they realized I was serious about health risks in a health-dedicated company. Now as CEO, I was really able to confront this problem. Our policy was harsh. At Rahway, we didn't allow smoking even outside the buildings. Executives, managers, all employees, from top to bottom, had to leave Merck property to smoke. They did, of course. There they were, huddled outside the gate, smoking in the middle of the winter. At Whitehouse Station, New Jersey, where we had built our new international headquarters, we had to make an exception to this rule. The wooded area around the large central building is so large it wasn't feasible to require smokers to leave the site. Instead, we constructed a shelter in the woods where they could smoke among the deer and geese.

Not surprisingly, these antismoking rules produced a great deal of distress. Our policy was international, and the French were especially vehement in opposition. But I wasn't about to waver on tobacco when our manufacturing organization was spending $75 million to eliminate other carcinogenic emissions.

During these same years, Merck universalized its quality controls and standards. We established a single worldwide standard for quality on every product. As with the environmental programs, we were positioning Merck for global competition over the long term. I thought both policies gave us a strong, forward-looking, competitive position while encouraging countries around the world to adopt the same high standards for all their pharmaceuticals. When they did, Merck would be ahead of the competition, moving at our own pace.

We followed the same logic when it came to safety in our plants – an area with which I had little direct experience. At NIH and Washington University, we had been very lax in handling dangerous substances, including radioactive isotopes. We sometimes went around the labs with glowing isotopes dancing along our arms. In the 1970s and early 1980s, however, stringent regulations were introduced in science laboratories, and at MRL we religiously followed all of the new rules.

The major safety problem wasn't in the labs but rather in manufacturing. There we were running large-scale, complex operations – some involving chemicals so volatile they could ignite merely by touching a warm surface. Dave Conklin, head of chemical manufacturing and thus our chief safety officer, said our record for safety was "good but not great." Using statistical measures like the lost-time index, he evaluated our manufacturing plants around the world and compared our performance with the rest of the industry. According to Dave's numbers, we were still short of matching the performance of DuPont, one of the leaders in industrial safety, but we'd made significant progress since the 1970s and now had safety professionals at every Merck manufacturing plant.

This precaution, however, didn't save us from a crisis in 1986. It came in Barceloneta, Puerto Rico, where we had manufactured chemicals

Paul Newman and Roy Vagelos accepted prizes from Columbia University for their respective companies.

for many years. An explosion in our methyldopa plant killed three people and injured seven others. Our plant was an up-to-date, modular facility where we could quickly switch from one product to another. Most of our pharmaceuticals are very potent and many can be taken only once a day; thus, we don't need as much of the basic chemical as we used to. With that in mind, plants like the one at Barceloneta were designed to be flexible; each module could be changed within a day or so to produce a different drug. The plant was flexible, but the work was stultifying. Once an employee started on a particular process, he or she might stay on that same job for years. Experience was an advantage, but boredom, as we now discovered, could be a serious threat. I flew to Puerto Rico to visit Barceloneta and meet with the victims' families. After digging around a great deal, we discovered that one employee, who had been working on the same process for fifteen years, had apparently fallen asleep on the job. Human error caused the explosion, but proper procedures could very well have prevented it.

Conklin and his co-workers undertook a full study of the implications of this tragic accident for all our manufacturing operations. They instituted several changes to improve our safety organization and

President George Bush presented Roy, on behalf of Merck, with the National
Medal of Technology in 1992 for innovative human and health products.

practices, focusing responsibility in the line officers who ran our factories. Reinspecting our plants, we found opportunities to set higher
standards for our equipment – standards that we implemented worldwide. Before long, we could see a total change in attitudes at all levels
of the company, and Merck began winning awards for its global safety
record. We no longer left anyone on the same operation for fifteen
years. After two years, we retrained and rotated the workers. If they
fell asleep at the switch, it wouldn't be because of boredom.

By 1994 we had developed uniform global policies on all these
fronts – safety, quality, and environmental protection. We anticipated
that, in future years, this explicitly international focus would enable
Merck to avoid some crises and to deal from strength with governments
around the world. In an industry at the forefront of globalization and
with a high public profile everywhere, this would be no small advantage. Although some dividends from these policies might not be realized for many years – even decades – we were confident of a long-term

payoff for Merck. In the meantime, we had helped to create the kind of enterprise with which we wanted to be associated.

* * *

We also made progress in providing new opportunities for women and minorities. Was I influenced by my own origins and experiences in setting these policies? Of course. As the son of Greek immigrants, I was unusually sensitive to anything that smelled of privilege at the expense of performance. In my own family, I had seen what happened when young women, my sister Joan included, were guided toward marriage while young men, myself included, were guided toward the advanced education and professional careers that are the bridge to success in our society. I wanted that bridge to be open to everyone smart enough to cross it and willing to do the hard work that awaited on the other side. So I pressed for equal opportunity at Merck with unusual vigor.

In doing so, I was able to build on a solid foundation laid down long before I became CEO. In the 1970s, when the United States began to change national policies toward minorities and women, Merck had moved quickly to establish a strong position on what came to be labeled affirmative action. John Horan, my predecessor as CEO, had guided the development of Merck's aggressive program, which focused almost exclusively on African Americans and women. Under his leadership, management was so successful that one of the videos the company used to teach employees the standards Merck had adopted was purchased by several other companies and was actually employed by some government agencies trying to achieve the same goals. As CEO in the 1980s and 1990s, my job was to ensure that everyone in the company understood that we were dedicated to further progress on both these fronts.

Active recruiting was critical in increasing the number of excellent African Americans working for Merck, but it took aggressive monitoring to keep them moving ahead at a brisk pace. We lost some superb candidates for top jobs when other firms offered them opportunities we didn't have available. Two who made the most of the opportunities they found at Merck were Brad Sheares and Ken Frazier. Brad, a promising young scientist, had moved from Fisk University, a black college, to Purdue for a Ph.D., then to MIT, and, following the usual postdoctoral fellowship, into the Merck Research Laboratories. He did a first-rate job at MRL, but after about five years of research, he came to see me. "Roy," he said, "I've got to talk to you." "What's the matter?" I asked. "I want to try something else," he said. I was stunned. He had been doing such a good job that we had been giving him more and more support, which in research means more and more people for his team. Off balance, I blurted out, "What are you talking about?" And he told me: "Roy, I know I can do research, but I'd like to try marketing." Further off balance, I said, "God, you must be crazy!" But Brad, who was calmer than I was, explained, "I'd really like to try it. You see, my father was a preacher." That's all he had to say. I could see that he wanted to focus on people rather than research, and I saw him off into the marketing division with my corporate blessing (and only a pinch of regret). By the time I retired as CEO, Brad was shooting up through marketing and sales like a rocket. Just recently, I learned that he is now president of Merck's U.S. Human Health division. He is indeed his father's son.

Ken Frazier also came to Merck through the professions, but in his case the specialty was law. Harvard-trained, Ken was working for a distinguished Philadelphia firm that had long provided counsel to Merck, and we were able to persuade him to jump ship and become general counsel for our joint venture with the Swedish firm AB Astra. His combination of technical and people skills, energy, and self-discipline put him on the corporate fast track. He's completely open and honest, which are qualities extremely important to me. Veering away from law temporarily (under some pressure from his CEO), he became head of Merck's public affairs department. Just recently, I was pleased to see that he's moved back into law as the new head of the company's entire legal department. As a senior vice president and member of the Management Committee, he provides the kind of role model that aspiring young African Americans need at the same time that he's providing Merck's CEO with astute counsel.

The bridge these men took into the corporate world is the same one I crossed – an advanced professional degree. For African Americans, the journey through the educational system to that degree is always tougher. We recognized that at Merck, and we tried to help more African Americans down that road toward the professions most relevant to what we were doing. We began working with historically black colleges much as we had years before at Washington University. But this time we could provide some funding to about ten schools to encourage students who were studying science and mathematics, hoping that in a few years some of these talented young black scholars would come in the door at Merck ready to work with us. I can remember only one who did so, Brad Sheares. But we were satisfied that we had Brad on board and that we had helped enlarge the pool of young African Americans interested in the kind of scientific careers that lead to good jobs in education, government, and high-tech industries like pharmaceuticals. Meanwhile, we had expanded our internship program as another means of recruiting minorities.

Affirmative action is under fire today, but my experiences at Merck convince me that we will need these policies for another generation – perhaps more. Shortly before we lost one of our top candidates for senior management, he asked me to meet with a small group of African Americans to get an update on affirmative action from their perspective. I was surprised and saddened to learn that, in their opinion, an African American had to be 15 percent better than a white colleague to be promoted at Merck. I couldn't see this from my position at the top of the firm, but I believed them because they were intelligent, credible, sincere people. That's why I think our educational and corporate institutions must continue with forceful policies if we are ever going to achieve equality of opportunity for African Americans.

The situation with women was somewhat different. The pool of well-educated female university graduates and professionals was relatively large, and soon we were hiring about as many women as men in most divisions of Merck. Still, we had a twofold challenge. First, we had to make Merck stand out as the best place to work in order to attract the most talented members of this pool. Second, we had to ensure that opportunities for advancement would be available at all levels, including the very top, to keep our most successful recruits. Because women normally experience the tension between the demands of career and those of family and childrearing more acutely than men, it was important that we accommodate that situation. It wasn't enough just to proclaim a level playing field and say that the best person, regardless of gender, would win. We had to provide good facilities for childcare, which we did at all our major locations. When we built our new international headquarters at Whitehouse Station, New Jersey, the architects designed a modern building, separated from the main offices, specifically for the purpose of childcare. We built a similar facility at Rahway and made other equally attractive arrangements at all of Merck's major sites. Flextime also helped both men and women employees juggle family and corporate responsibilities. We ensured that women who took pregnancy leaves would get their regular jobs back when they returned – a practice now required by law but not always honored by employers. When we made all these policies an integral part of our day-to-day operations, we had an organization that won a series of awards as one of the best places in corporate America for women to work.

The toughest barrier was the glass ceiling about which women frequently complain, a barrier evident in every large corporation with which I am familiar. I was determined to crack that ceiling at Merck, and I had been around the company long enough to know that I would have to crack a few hard heads as well. By 1989, more than half our new hires were women and almost 20 percent were minorities, but the Operating Review Committee – my top eight advisers – was still a white male preserve. The Management Council, a group of twenty-one in addition to me, included one woman. I had been working on this problem since taking the helm as CEO, and I had one woman in the second-tier of the top executives to show for my efforts.

Why was progress so slow? Of course it took years for anyone to move through the ranks and become a president or senior vice president, and Merck's decisive new policies on African Americans and women – a decisive break in corporate policies at Merck – had only begun in the 1970s. But that was just one part of the story. Another aspect involved resistance to change on the part of some of our leading executives. The top management in any large institution tends to become a tightly knit community. That happened at Merck even though we had a considerable amount of turnover, which worked against solidarity. Nevertheless, the men running the company got to know each other extremely well, both on and off the job. Some had come up through the ranks together. Many shared an interest in golf, belonged to the same clubs, and dined together regularly. Although I never caught the golf bug, I loved to play tennis and sometimes played doubles with my fellow executives. We shared problems, interests, and the kind of chitchat about our families that fills the empty spaces in every organization's social life.

All these activities had a heavy male orientation that made it difficult for a woman to get accepted. Because most of my top executives had begun their careers before the 1960s, they were being forced to change some deeply grooved attitudes about gender roles in society. Like me, most of them had traditional marriages. A few were simply prejudiced against women, certain they couldn't withstand the pressures of the executive suite. Raised in an environment with two distinct tracks, one for men and one for women, they thought corporate leadership should remain a male preserve because it worked better that way. They weren't outspoken about these ideas, but I knew how they felt. Others – the majority – were simply comfortable with their current golf partners and convinced that all of their decisions about promotion were unbiased even when all the best jobs went to men. They believed in equal opportunity in the abstract but just weren't prepared to do anything about it in real life, that is, in their life.

To change this situation, I found a few unusually strong candidates for promotion to the Operating Review Committee. Mary McDonald had been with Merck's Legal Department since the mid-1970s under the tutelage of Robert Banse, our general counsel. She'd played an important role in handling discrimination and labor relations matters and had gained valuable experience with international operations. When Merck began to develop strategic alliances with other firms, such as Astra, Mary was a key player who helped keep the ball rolling when successful business negotiations had to be translated into sound contracts. With Banse's support, she was promoted to vice president and general counsel, becoming the second woman to join the eight-member Operating Review Committee. When Bob Banse retired, Mary succeeded him as head of the Legal Department, Senior Vice President, and my close adviser on all legal questions. I had complete confidence in her. Nevertheless, I had to field the usual sorts of questions about the appointment.

Although Mary is a strong, intelligent person with a firm grasp of the law, some colleagues suggested she might not be forceful enough for the top position. It was hard to tell exactly what this meant. It could have been a way of saying that women executives are generally not as aggressive as their male counterparts. It could have been suggesting that Mary, in particular, was too soft-spoken, too inclined to yield the floor, for us to make her a member of the club, the clique at the top. I just treated the opposition as if it were completely impartial and pushed the appointment through on the grounds that Mary had passed all of the tests and was the strongest candidate for the position.

When Mary McDonald joined the top group of Merck executives in 1992, the way had been paved by Judy Lewent, who had been elected vice president and chief financial officer (CFO) in 1990. After graduating from Goucher College, Judy received an MBA in finance from the Sloan School at MIT and then worked briefly at Pfizer before moving to Merck. I had first worked with her as president of MRL, where she was controller, and had followed her career through the early 1980s, when her boss, Frank Spiegel, was coaching me on how to be a businessman. Frank and Judy were a great combination: Frank was especially strong on accounting and the policy side of business, and Judy's great strength was the analytical aspects of business finance and strategy. At the labs she developed a computer model that predicted the value of our projects right through product development and a success-ful launch. Her projections were very useful when I was dealing with corporate officers who had a better understanding of finance than they did of science. But Judy Lewent wasn't just some narrow technocrat. Her kind of analysis blended into business strategy and enabled the rest of us to make effective decisions involving long-range planning. It was evident to me and to others that Judy had CEO potential.

When we discussed promotions for Judy, even the most traditional of the Old Boys couldn't say she wasn't tough enough, not aggressive enough to handle one of the top rungs in the firm. Frank Spiegel, a Marine veteran, paid Judy the ultimate compliment he could offer. He said, "She'd make an excellent Marine officer!" I agreed. This made it easy for Frank and me, approaching retirement together, to ease Judy in as a senior vice president and heir apparent as CFO of a Fortune 50 U.S. corporation. The only obstacles to the top job at Merck or another large corporation were her age and lack of operating experience. She had spent her entire career in a staff position, and to run a company like Merck, you normally need the sort of experience I had gained as executive vice president. In a more perfect world, I would have had more time before retiring to give her that experience, grooming her to vie for the position I was vacating. I am encouraged to see lately that Judy will now be getting the line experience she needs as a president of Merck's Human Health organization in Asia.

Did it make any difference that we added two women to the top rank of executives and that at least two African Americans were on target to join them in the future? I'm convinced that it did matter throughout the ranks at Merck, where women and minorities could see they wouldn't have to bump their heads on a gender or racial ceiling. It mattered to the company because it enlarged our pool of potential leaders and gave us a marginal advantage in recruitment. Every large corporation searches endlessly for managerial talent. Skillful, energetic risk takers who have solid technical backgrounds and can lead are always in short supply. By increasing and diversifying the supply, Merck had established a position that some of our foreign and domestic competitors would find very difficult to match.

That was certainly true in Japan, where we had acquired the Banyu Pharmaceutical Company. When I visited Dr. Koichi Iwadare, head of the firm, he complained of great difficulty recruiting top people as sales representatives because the top male university graduates preferred other industries. "Why don't you have women in the sales force?" I asked. He explained that in Japan sales reps traditionally took physician clients out for drinks and did other favors that wouldn't be appropriate for women. I agreed, "Those activities aren't appropriate for women." But to his surprise, I added, "They aren't appropriate for men either." As a result of that visit, we started a broad program at Banyu to retrain their representatives in the professional techniques used by Merck in every other part of the world. Once the men were working in this new style, we recruited women. By offering good professional jobs, we were able to recruit top Japanese women, who often performed better than the men. Banyu management was impressed by the women's performance, and within a few years women made up about 40 percent of their reps. Soon after, other Japanese pharmaceutical companies followed Banyu's lead.

* * *

We had other opportunities to get ahead by doing right. One of our best business decisions earned us no profits in the twentieth century, but it promised to save more lives than anything else Merck had ever done. It further promised us a unique position at some time in the distant future in the world's largest national market. The decision involved *Recombivax HB*, our genetically engineered vaccine against hepatitis B. The market was the People's Republic of China, where the leading public health problem was hepatitis B.

The Chinese government approached Merck about transferring our technology for the production of *Recombivax HB* to their country. We were eager to do this. Our response was influenced to some extent by our previous success helping an Asian country deal with a major public health problem. Following World War II, the Japanese were starving and a tuberculosis epidemic swept through the population. Merck had helped to develop streptomycin, the first drug that controlled tuberculosis.* Destitute, the Japanese could not afford to buy streptomycin, and several Japanese companies approached George W. Merck, who was president at that time, to request access to the drug. He granted them an unprecedented, royalty-free license to produce the antibiotic. The Japanese observed the Merck manufacturing process and then returned to Japan where they produced enough streptomycin to stem the epidemic. Merck received no remuneration for this assistance, but I'm convinced the company's long and favorable relationships in the Japanese economy grew from this seed of life-saving philanthropy.

In the early 1980s Merck acquired a majority share (later, a 100% share) of Banyu, which was by that time a medium-size pharmaceutical company. Here was another unprecedented move – this time by the Japanese in favor of an American company. The Bank of Japan and the Japanese government agreed to permit this acquisition, which resulted in Merck's having the largest pharmaceutical market share of any non-Japanese company. The Japanese who made this decision of course never mentioned an "obligation" or anything specific about Merck's help in providing streptomycin to postwar Japan.

Hoping for a similar outcome, we launched discussions with the People's Republic on our hepatitis vaccine. Initially we wanted to sell it, but we quickly learned they could not afford it even at a very reduced price. So we then began to negotiate a technology transfer and found ourselves deeply mired in talks that promised to go on to the end of time. At least that's the way it looked to me in my anxiety to make a

---

* Supported by a Merck grant, Selman Waksman and a colleague discovered streptomycin at Rutgers. As a consequence of the grant, Merck held the patent on streptomycin, at that time the only known cure for tuberculosis. After the implications of the discovery became clear to Waksman, he became concerned about the patent. George W. Merck decided to return the patent to a Rutgers University foundation because he thought maintaining good long-term relations with university science was more important than short-term profits from a new drug. After giving up its exclusive rights, Merck licensed the antibiotic (as did other firms), developed it, and sold it in the United States and elsewhere.

deal that would start saving children from a deadly viral infection. The facts seemed clear. Our proposals were dirt cheap, but the discussions meandered as if no one were dying of liver cancer, no newborns were being infected, and no one needed to get around to making *Recombivax HB* in China. It drove me up a wall. I can be patient, although it takes an explicit effort once I think I understand a situation. But I was no match for the Chinese. My concept of long term included the first half of the twenty-first century. Their concept seemed to look beyond that to some epoch I couldn't even imagine.

Months dragged by, and so I finally decided to get something done. I told them we would charge a rock bottom price of $7 million and they could take it or leave it. Since I knew we would spend more than that to train the Chinese engineers and send Merck personnel back and forth to China, I thought this offer would quickly yield a contract. Well, they thought about the offer for another several months before accepting it. Then, at last, the real work of technology transfer could begin. The Chinese sent a team from Beijing to West Point, Pennsylvania, bought all of the necessary equipment in the United States (it wasn't available in China), and assembled the processing equipment here under our supervision. After we helped them run several batches of the vaccine, they took the equipment apart and shipped it back to Beijing along with the crew that would run it. We sent the Merck chemical engineers who had trained them to assist in building the plant, assembling the equipment, and starting up the process. The two sets of engineers worked over a year putting together this splendid new stainless steel plant and getting it into production.

This episode also demonstrated to us how the Chinese Communists tried to create some of the benefits of American capitalist competition. They sent a second team of chemical engineers, from Shenzhen, about six months after the Beijing group arrived. Knowing they were behind in the race, our new guests asked if we could slow down their compatriots. "No, we can't do that," we said, "but we'll try to get you in operation as fast as we can." We then repeated the entire process of helping them buy equipment, set it up, run it, dismantle it, and ship it to Shenzhen. We never learned how the team competition turned out, but we knew that China now had two state-of-the-art recombinant DNA vaccine plants capable of producing 20 million doses of hepatitis B vaccine a year – enough to immunize all their newborns. Eventually, they'll be able to bring the disease under control, and when they do, I hope they, like the Japanese, will remember that Merck helped them save all those millions of lives.

* * *

Sub-Saharan Africa, which also suffers massive public health problems, has even fewer resources than mainland China for treating or preventing disease. Some of these poverty-stricken nations can budget only a few dollars per year per person for public health, making the development of an effective health infrastructure impossible. Deadly infections like HIV/AIDS sweep over helpless populations with a loss of life reminiscent of the Black Death of the fourteenth century and the great influenza pandemic of 1918–19. Other debilitating diseases, including malaria and onchocerciasis, which causes river blindness, are endemic to the region. At Merck, we became involved with onchocerciasis (pronounced onco-sir-KI-isis) as an unanticipated result of one of our most profitable discoveries. The outcome is one of the best arguments I know for having diverse organizations if you want fruitful innovation.

This story began about a year after I took over as head of basic research at MRL. Then (as we saw in an earlier chapter) parasitologist Dr. William C. Campbell and his colleagues had discovered a substance, ivermectin, that was active against worms that plague livestock. They didn't do this by following the Vagelos guidelines for targeted research. Instead, they did it the good old-fashioned way by screening fermentation broths from endless soil samples in live rodents infected with worms. Finally, they found a microorganism that produced a broth capable of killing the worms. Sample OS3153 from the Kitasato Institute of Japan was the only sample of the 40,000 tested that produced a broth that had a powerful impact on parasites. Once the active substance was isolated and identified, chemically altered, and thoroughly tested for efficacy and safety, Merck had a product, ivermectin, that soon become the world's leading veterinary product, the largest selling animal drug in history. Owners of cattle, sheep, swine, horses, and finally dogs all adopted it.

Ivermectin was a spectacular medicine for cattle. Not only did it kill all gastrointestinal worms after a single dose, but it also killed biting insects that cause weeping sores on the hide of a cow. In early experiments designed to demonstrate its effectiveness, cows treated with the drug were compared with animals that received a placebo.

After one week the treated cows could easily be distinguished by their clean hides as compared with the hides with weeping sores on animals in the placebo group. Ivermectin also killed heartworms in dogs. If your dog is taking monthly medication to prevent heartworm disease, it is probably ivermectin.

When Bill Campbell and Mohammed Aziz, an infectious disease specialist in Merck's clinical research group, came to see me however, it was not to talk about Merck's sure profits from ivermectin. Nor was it to slyly twit me about this important drug's having been discovered in a distinctly pre-Vagelos style. What Bill Campbell and Mohammed Aziz wanted was to spend more money to see if ivermectin could be used against the parasite that causes river blindness. Mohammed had seen many victims of this disease when he worked in Africa with the World Health Organization. When the black fly, which breeds in the fast-flowing rivers of Africa and Latin America (hence *river* blindness), bites humans, it deposits parasite microfilariae (*Onchocerca volvulus*) it has picked up from the skin of already infected humans. In the victim's skin, the microfilariae develop into adult worms that live in lumps under the skin for fourteen years and can reach two feet in length. These adult worms produce millions of microfilariae, which crawl through the skin, causing intolerable itching, but worse, when they gather in the eyes, they cause inflammation and then scarring, leaving a hard, blinded eye. Given that ivermectin was effective against a related parasite with a microfilarial stage of development in horses, Bill thought there was a good chance that a new formulation for humans might provide the first effective treatment for this terrible disease.

There was a catch. Eighteen million people were infected in Sub-Saharan Africa alone, and in some West African villages 60 percent of the population over fifty-five years of age was blind. The World Health Organization (WHO) estimated that 90 million people lived in areas threatened by onchocerciasis. The existing therapies were not very useful. If ivermectin worked against the river blindness parasite, there was bound to be vigorous demand for it in Central and South America as well as Africa, but there was no way the impoverished people or their governments could pay for the treatment. That was of no interest to the scientists. Nor, at that time, to me. The important question was whether ivermectin could control river blindness. I moved quickly to learn the answer by dispatching Mohammed and a small group of Merck people to Dakar, Senegal.

Luckily, I hadn't been in business very long and still thought of myself as a physician first, scientist second, and president of an industrial laboratory third. This was, after all, still early in my presidency of Merck Research. Our big innovations were in the pipeline, but until they emerged, Roy Vagelos was unproven as a leader in new drug development. My drumbeat for targeted research had begun to exert some influence throughout the laboratories. But not all of us were marching to that beat, and now I was being asked to spend a great deal of money on a compound in a field none of us knew very well. As a doctor, I decided to crawl out on this limb and see what our medicine could do against a disease that blighted the lives of millions. At this point the risk to the company was small: if it didn't work, we wouldn't pursue it. But the potential payoff to the afflicted African populations was huge. I liked the odds.

I told Campbell and Aziz they needed more information and to "keep pushing." Mohammed was soon discussing ivermectin with WHO parasitologists he knew. By this time, we had all seen the tragic pictures of African children leading blind adults, some of them very young, around their villages. The initial studies were positive. With an acute sense of the need for a breakthrough therapy, in early 1980 we pushed ahead into expensive and complicated clinical trials that would tell us whether ivermectin would be effective against this insidious parasite. We had to conduct the trials in African countries where onchocerciasis was endemic and where, unfortunately, the normal networks of professionals and health organizations that support clinical research didn't exist.

That's where our diversity came into play. Merck had an unusually high number of foreign nationals in very important positions, and we sought out foreign researchers in all of our non-U.S. research facilities. Our clinical research staff for this project was led by Aziz, an experienced traveler on jungle paths and unmarked trails. His own path to Merck had been far from normal. It began in Bangladesh, wound through college in Calcutta, to Dacca for a medical degree, and then to Minnesota, where he received a Ph.D. in clinical pathology. Further training at the Johns Hopkins School of Hygiene and Public Health was followed by study at the London School of Hygiene and Tropical Medicine. He was a coordinator for WHO in Sierra Leone, and then he moved to Merck just a couple of years before Bill Campbell found evidence that ivermectin might be effective against river blindness.

For Aziz – the only Merck researcher who knew anything about the disease – the new therapy, renamed *Mectizan*, became a crusade. Trips to Paris and Dakar, Senegal, yielded support for the first tests in humans. Coordinated through the University of Dakar, these initial studies were relatively simple. Infection was evident because the worms formed lumps in people's skin. Aziz and his crew took tiny skin snips from infected persons, counted the number of microfilariae, and then treated the people with the new drug. Testing the same way some weeks later, they were amazed to find that the microfilariae were all gone. Completely. With a single oral dose. When Aziz had confirmed the safety of the therapy in these patients and determined a proper dosage, Merck prepared to move ahead.

Aziz invited experts from WHO to review the results of the initial clinical study in Rahway. At that time WHO was running a large, expensive, modestly successful program of aerial spraying to suppress the black flies that spread the disease. Our researchers were convinced that *Mectizan* would be far more effective than spraying, but the WHO representatives were unenthusiastic about our experimental results. "Too preliminary to be meaningful," they said. "By testing more people, you'll probably get the usual drug-related side effects." After that discouraging chat, Aziz and I had lunch with the WHO reps. By the end of the meal I was no longer discouraged; I was hot under the collar. But I admit to some prejudice because they all looked like bankers, wearing elegant suits and handcrafted neckties. This, I sensed, was a turf problem. I quizzed them about the expense and success rate of their spraying program, but they insisted their approach was problem free. They left expressing no interest in *Mectizan*.

That was all I needed to turn on a major Merck effort! I told Aziz he had all the resources he needed to find out how good *Mectizan* was and what its side effects would be. Aziz didn't need encouragement to get excited, and now he had the funds to mount a large, multinational clinical trial. After double-blind, placebo-controlled tests in Senegal, Mali, Ghana, and Liberia, followed by Phase III studies, Aziz had solid evidence that oral *Mectizan* was safe, that it was far more effective than the current leading treatment (diethylcarbamazine), and that it needed to be taken only once a year. As Aziz proceeded and the exciting results of his initial tests were discussed by infectious disease scientists, the WHO researchers returned to Merck and asked to participate. We eased their way back by suggesting that WHO should also continue its fly spraying and keep its air force aloft. But tensions continued. When WHO reported on tests of *Mectizan* conducted in its clinics, the organization sometimes failed even to mention Merck's involvement. I protested rather fiercely; they backed down, and we became good partners after that.

I followed the progress of Aziz and the clinical trials with great interest, first as president of the laboratories and then as CEO. I was now worrying because, although a single annual dose worked effectively, an organization had to supply bottles of *Mectizan* for distribution in developing countries, some of which did not have established health-care delivery systems or even roads to the interior. We were already spending millions on this project, supplying both financial aid and the *Mectizan* for the trials. We were rapidly approaching a go-no-go decision about production. Should we build a plant to produce the drug? If so, who would pay for it? We explored U.S. government support, but neither the U.S. Agency for International Development nor the Department of State had room in their budgets for a new program along these lines.

In 1987 we were on our own. I'd had some practice with a similar issue in 1979, when Merck had considered closing its vaccine business. At that time, I'd helped keep us in vaccines, but with *Mectizan* the issue was drawn more sharply. There were only two possibilities. If we decided to sell *Mectizan*, it wouldn't reach those who needed it most regardless of how low we set the price. This was unacceptable for a company dedicated to improving human health. If, on the other hand, we decided to give it away, we would set a dangerous precedent for a pharmaceutical company that needed profits to sustain the sort of research and development that had made *Mectizan* possible. Not only that, other groups suffering from virulent diseases such as malaria or AIDS might expect similar donations of medicines. Giving *Mectizan* away would be expensive for Merck in any case. At that time, 18 million people were infected, and 80 million more were at risk worldwide. I worried that our giving the drug away might discourage some organizations from developing other drugs for impoverished countries. But I also felt we were in a unique situation: we hadn't originally set out looking for a cure for river blindness, but we were now in a position to help millions of people.

These discussions were taking place, as I've already mentioned, under mounting pressure to control the prices of pharmaceuticals and an unstable political setting for healthcare issues. As CEO, I was responsible for protecting the long-term future of the organization. I had to answer to the stockholders and our Board of Directors as well as to the employees and the communities in which they worked and lived. In brief, the decision was not obvious.

Nor did I have much time to ponder the alternatives. The French government suddenly informed Merck that it was about to approve the drug. We had gone to France for approval instead of the FDA because there was no river blindness in the United States. France had expatriates from its former African colonies living in Paris who had the disease and could participate in clinical tests. Our tests there proved successful, and the government was prepared to move ahead at once. As we hastily arranged a press conference in Washington, DC, I met with my staff and decided what Merck's position would be. There was no time to convene and consult with our Board. I reflected on my training as a physician and Merck's mission statement: "to provide society with superior products and services." *Mectizan* was an incredibly effective medicine that could improve the lives of millions of people around the world. It was deliverable – it took one dose a year to do its work, not, say, three doses a day on a strict schedule.

I decided Merck would give the drug free to any person endangered by river blindness anywhere in the world for as long as it was needed, and that was what I announced to the press. We would of course work through organizations capable of distributing the drug to the endangered populations. Shortly after that, the Board convened and was completely supportive. But there was a tense moment or two before I explained why I had been willing on my own authority to commit Merck's resources ad infinitum to the fight against river blindness.

The next step was to create an independent committee of experts to decide which distribution programs qualified for supplies of the drug. This humanitarian initiative attracted an astonishingly high level of volunteer experts. I asked Dr. William H. Foege, who had served as director of the U.S. Centers for Disease Control and was then the executive director of the Carter Center in Atlanta, to chair this group. Other members included Dr. Bruce M. Greene from Case Western Reserve University, Dr. Michel Lariviere from the University of Paris, Dr. Adetokunbo O. Lucas of the Carnegie Corporation, Dr. Eric Albert Ottesen from NIH's National Institute of Allergy and Infectious Diseases, and Dr. Guillermo E. Zea-Flores from Guatemala's Ministry

Roy and Diana Vagelos in Chad in 1994. They accompanied Jimmy and Rosalyn Carter for the second annual distribution of *Mectizan* to prevent river blindness.

of Public Health. Merck shipped *Mectizan* free to any program this committee approved. We also tried as far as possible to make special provisions for populations not served by a large-scale program.

President Jimmy Carter and his wife Rosalyn were very supportive of our efforts and, in 1994, they accompanied Diana and me on a visit to a village in Chad when the second annual dose of our drug was being administered. We arrived on foot because even our Land Rover couldn't make it into this part of central Africa. The trip was moving – unforgettably so. The heat, the flies, and the mud huts without electricity or running water were overwhelming. So was the presence of so many blind people, old and young. We saw a blind seventeen-year-old mother suckling her infant. *Mectizan* couldn't restore her sight, but happily it could protect her baby from river blindness. Equally unforgettable was the people's excitement upon meeting an American president.

When the first dose had been administered, I was told, Chadians had been suspicious of the pill. "Why," they asked, "should we take a medicine that no Americans are taking?" But after a few people took the pills, stopped itching, and passed dead worms in their stools, the doubters were persuaded. The dead worms, unrelated to river blindness, had been living in their intestines as parasites, but they too were killed by *Mectizan*.

When we arrived, the entire village eagerly formed straight lines (like British queues) to take their one dose a year. Over the next ten years, we delivered more than 96 million treatments. Some villagers walked for three days to reach a distribution point. In 1997 alone (the tenth year of the program), between 19 and 20 million people received *Mectizan*, largely through ministries of health and nongovernmental organizations.

River blindness is likely to be eradicated after a decade or so of further treatments – much like smallpox. Only humans are hosts for the parasite *O. volvulus*. Thus, if most people in a large region are treated with *Mectizan*, all the microfilariae will be eliminated, and the black flies (which transmit this infection) will have no source for the parasite. The disease cycle would end. To my knowledge this would be the first example in history of a company contributing a drug to eradicate a disease, and it would please Diana and me enormously. This was the goal that had persuaded us to leave Washington University and take our chances in a world of business entirely new to us.

After my retirement, I was encouraged to see Merck expanding its *Mectizan* donation program to cover elephantiasis (lymphatic filariasis, which also has a microfilarial stage), another parasitic disease affecting millions of people in Africa. The good works flowing from Bill Campbell's discovery, Mohammed Aziz's incredible efforts, and Merck's generosity continue to mount and will do so for many years to come.

* * *

Is Merck's *Mectizan* donation program wise corporate policy? The plan eventually cost Merck over $200 million. The company has made many other donations through The Merck Company Foundation, including a very large grant to build the Children's Inn (for families of children suffering from cancer) at the National Institutes of Health and gifts to universities (including Harvard and the University of Pennsylvania) and hospitals (Massachusetts General Hospital, for instance). Some argue that corporations should not be in the business of making donations, contending that their first obligation is to reward their stockholders with higher dividends and not squander company resources on gifts. I disagree. Our policy on *Mectizan* and other gifts made Merck a place where people were proud and excited to work because they wanted to make lives better around the world. It helped us recruit the best people and build company morale. It was consistent with Merck's fundamental corporate philosophy of doing well by doing good. It served the global society Merck serves. It also served Merck's stockholders because corporate social generosity is often followed by higher profits as the corporation becomes a better, more attractive workplace for the best talent.

My only regret about the *Mectizan* program involves its timing. We couldn't launch the first donations until we solved all the organizational problems in late 1988. By then, Dr. Mohammed Aziz had succumbed to stomach cancer. He was able to attend the Washington press conference in October 1987, when we announced our donation policy, but his cancer had just been diagnosed and he was already in obvious pain. He died just as the first delivery of *Mectizan* was being completed, but he will never be forgotten by those still working to eradicate the scourge of river blindness.

* * *

So where does Merck fit in the moral array of the hundreds of thousands of companies in all lines of business in the United States? Or in a similar, much larger array for the entire world? Of course objective, systematic comparisons of corporate social responsibility are impossible because no one knows very much about most of these organizations. If you can still read small print, scan down your newspaper's list of the firms on the New York Stock Exchange, NASDAQ, and the American Stock Exchange. Every business day, they all get graded by the market, which sets a price for their stocks. But only a few are evaluated for moral behavior, and that's usually done on the front page of your local paper, the *New York Times*, or the *Wall Street Journal*. When they do make the front page, it's usually bad news for the company and its employees.

Merck & Co., Inc., became big news in the 1980s and 1990s for the first time in its long history. The profits from those billion-dollar drugs we were rolling out attracted attention as did our innovations in pricing policy and even some of the unusual things we did like donating *Mectizan*. The firm won several awards for its environmental and employee policies, and as I've noted, the company was elected seven years in a row as *Fortune's* Most Admired Corporation. Judging from that evidence, Merck seems to be far on the right side of our moral bell curve, right at the top of the good guys.

Pleasing as that might be to Merck people, I'm not satisfied with that answer. The policies we followed in the 1980s were, I thought, consistent with Merck's guiding philosophy in the 1970s, when the company was not yet big news. We frequently reminded people inside and outside the firm what George W. Merck, the founder's son and company leader from 1925 until 1957, said about the Merck mission: "We try never to forget that medicine is for the people. It is not for the profits. The profits follow, and if we have remembered that, they have never failed to appear." He and Merck faithfully followed those guidelines. But most of what Merck did for many years wasn't big news and wasn't noticed, even though it was indeed moral behavior.

What we had at Merck in the 1980s and 1990s was a series of special opportunities – some related to medical science, some to economic performance, and some to what we might call social responsibility. We vigorously and effectively took advantage of those opportunities and that attracted the attention of the media. We were quick to respond to the unusual situations developing in the medical sciences, especially in enzymology and then in molecular genetics. We implemented a business strategy appropriate to our changing markets and the national and global economies. We were also vigorous and innovative about our social responsibilities. But remember, we didn't create the medical sciences, nor did we shape the national and international political economy in which Merck thrived. Absent those two settings, few would have noticed that we were, indeed, a moral corporation.

Why am I so certain about that? Because I am now chairman of two small start-up firms. I'm the same person I was before I retired from Merck in 1994. Both companies are focused on producing products needed by patients in the United States and around the world, and both have the same moral standards that George W. Merck expressed so eloquently. Neither company is front page news – yet – nor do many people know anything about them. But both of these companies are, I believe, close to the norm in moral terms for American business and for business around the world. When the current wave of corruption is swept aside, Americans will recognize that, although their business system is far from perfect, it is the most successful in the world. They should perhaps reflect on the fact that even Merck dropped out of the top position on *Fortune*'s most admired list after Bill and Hillary Clinton launched an attack on the pharmaceutical industry.

11 | *Getting to Know the Clintons*

I n September 1992, Bill Clinton's presidential campaign organization asked if their candidate could deliver a major address at Merck's company headquarters in Rahway, New Jersey. Merck had never before hosted a presidential candidate there, and after some probing, we learned that Clinton's team had targeted Merck for the candidate's first important speech on healthcare reform.

Why Merck? I thought they'd chosen our company in part because of its reputation within the pharmaceutical industry. Although I hadn't been active in Democratic politics, I was a significant financial supporter of Bill Bradley and Frank Lautenberg, two Democrat senators from New Jersey. The other and more important reasons, I decided, were some of our company's recent activities. During the previous year, Merck had introduced its new policy on pricing, keying increases to changes in the Consumer Price Index. That innovation had received a great deal of favorable press as had our earlier decision to donate *Mectizan* to any program in the world capable of distributing the drug to people endangered by river blindness.

Merck was riding high, enjoying the kind of public acclaim for which every business and every CEO yearns. America's most admired corporation was an ideal platform for a major address on healthcare. Rather than announce their new proposals in a public health forum, we thought the Clinton team might want to use a corporate setting to suggest that their program had broad support, from business to organized labor, from conservatives to liberals. This was fine with us, even though we didn't know what, specifically, the candidate was going to say. Nevertheless, we quickly reached two decisions.

We decided to invite Clinton and welcome him graciously to Merck headquarters. But to balance the books, we extended the same invitation to the campaign of President Bush. We didn't actually think George Bush would accept our invitation (he didn't), but we certainly would have been happy to have the incumbent as well as his challenger speak at Merck. We thought exposure to presidential candidates in person would be good for our employees, who expressed great interest in seeing and hearing Clinton on our home turf.

On September 24, as scheduled, Bill Clinton appeared, along with his sizable entourage of staff members and supporters, many cars, and much equipment. He was accompanied by New Jersey Governor Jim Florio, whom I knew very well, and West Virginia Senator Jay Rockefeller. Of course I knew something about the Rockefeller family and its significance in modern American business and politics. From my long service on the Rockefeller University Board of Trustees, I knew David Rockefeller's side of the family. Besides, it would have been hard to live in New Jersey and not learn something about the other Rockefellers. On the other hand, I'd met Senator Rockefeller only in passing, and this day provided no opportunity for anything but more passing remarks. I'm not particularly good at badinage, and a great deal of this kind of socializing goes on in politics.

My wife, a natural diplomat, could do all these things effortlessly and gracefully. Throughout her academic career, Diana had been politically active, serving as president of her class and president of the student government at Barnard College. This was one reason she found it so easy to be the wife of a CEO and to handle the social obligations that role involved. She went far beyond the formal requirements of the task, taking an active part in building the kind of close relationships that help convert a collection of executives and their families into a coordinated team.

I have less aptitude along these lines than Diana, and so I tend to stick to a narrow circle of people who share my particular interests. But as CEO, I couldn't avoid involvement in politics, no matter how distasteful I found it. Before deciding to donate *Mectizan*, for instance, I had tried to persuade two federal agencies to fund the project. I explained to Donald Regan, Chief of Staff for President Ronald Reagan, that it would be a relatively inexpensive type of foreign aid and would have a significant impact on some of the poorest nations in the world. Meeting in Regan's White House office accompanied by Merck's head of public affairs, Al Angel, I laid out the problems of river blindness and said, "The powerful, wealthy United States is not always looked on with favor in these nations. By conquering river blindness, the State Department or A.I.D. can improve our image abroad at very little cost." My proposal was that the U.S. government should buy the drug from

Merck and distribute it free in Africa, eradicating a terrible human scourge.

Regan became very excited about this proposition. I said, "Merck has spent a substantial sum to develop the drug. But we will sell it to the government at a very low price. We're projecting a cost of only $20 million a year in the early going." Regan said, "The U.S. government should do this!" and told his aide to take care of it.

I was elated until we stepped out of Regan's office. The aide looked at me and said, "While we would like to do this program, we can't afford it." My department, he continued, "is broke." I couldn't believe a subordinate would not move forward with the plan his boss had just told him to make happen. But that, I learned, is how the government runs.

I wouldn't give up. On another trip to Washington, I visited with John Whitehead, Deputy Secretary of State. John seemed even more enthusiastic than Regan had been, but the results were similar. When we left Whitehead's office, his aide told me, "There are simply no funds available in the State Department for dealing with an African parasitic disease." Those who might be wondering today why the U.S. government didn't provide aggressive leadership in dealing with the early years of the AIDS disaster in Sub-Saharan Africa should look back to what happened with river blindness. We were stonewalled in Washington and in the European offices we visited to pitch our proposal for an effective, proven treatment. In the end, we decided the only way to ensure optimal distribution was for Merck to donate the drug for free. Much later, after the *Mectizan* donations were successfully under way, the World Bank Group began to provide some financial support for the necessary infrastructure, but the U.S. government still didn't budge. And Merck continued to donate *Mectizan*.

Not all of my political encounters involved subjects as positive as a pill that prevents widespread blindness. From time to time, in fact, I've been upset by the slimy behavior I've encountered among politicians. I've been invited to break the rules on campaign contributions, for instance, and in general, I've been disturbed by the lack of sincerity and intellectual depth in politics. But whether I liked it or not, I had to do what every other CEO has to do: swallow hard and get involved in the right way. That meant handling campaign contributions through political action committees and personal contributions – all strictly by the rules. It meant supporting lobbying groups to pressure the state and federal governments on significant public policies affecting our industry. Luckily, what Merck considered the right side of health issues usually coincided with the long-term interests of the public – in my opinion.

At any rate, you have to be personally active in politics. If you're running a large company with many employees and with plants in several states and other countries, with operations that are sensitive to changes in taxes, environmental regulations, and other public policies, you'd better be getting good political advice, which entails developing relationships with people who can get things done. If you don't do these things, your business will suffer. I was active, even though I knew that it wasn't my strong suit as a CEO.

My limitations in this regard didn't stem from lack of interest in political ideology. I had a position that I'd given a great deal of thought to over the years. I was conservative insofar as I believed and still believe in market competition free of government price controls. It's competition that brings out the best in us as individuals and the best for our organizations and societies. But I was liberal on social justice issues such as civil rights and affirmative action. I strongly supported the Food and Drug Administration, which regulated our industry, and I lobbied to increase their budget so that they could build first-class facilities and employ some top scientists with a deep understanding of complex drug application filings. I was liberal on matters of environmental policy. I was even liberal on many aspects of public health, the subject Clinton was going to address.

In all these regards, I was more liberal than most of my fellow CEOs, especially those heading Fortune 50 companies. I've met a few who would like to see the United States return to 1900 and do away with big government, taxes, and regulation entirely. Most are more thoughtful than that, but on balance they're quite conservative, especially in private. Few would have been receptive to having the Democratic candidate for president speak at their corporate headquarters. But I was pleased to have Clinton deliver what I was certain would be an important political address at Merck.

* * *

That September day the weather was beautiful, sunny and dry, as it often is in the fall in New Jersey. Clinton spoke in front of the original Merck administration building surrounded by huge trees that dated back to the company's move to Rahway in the early 1900s. Thousands

Presidential candidate Bill Clinton spoke at Merck on September 24, 1992.

of excited employees poured out to hear the talk. We knew very little about this particular candidate, but what little I knew seemed interesting. He was smart, well trained, had already been a governor, and had some new ideas about reforming healthcare in the United States. I was anxious to meet him. My initial response to the man was very positive. I thought, "Maybe I can really get behind this candidate and work to improve healthcare in this country."

I agreed with a number of things Clinton said that day. He mentioned some of the strengths of the U.S. system but noted that our pharmaceutical companies were investing too little in the discovery of important new drugs and too much in low-risk projects to develop drugs similar to existing products. The exception, he said, was Merck, which had invested heavily in research and contributed many breakthrough products. His reference to Merck was important to this crowd, standing right across the street from the labs that had given the world some of its most important new therapies.

Several of Clinton's remarks made me nervous. I didn't think he had any understanding of how so-called me-too drugs actually improve clinical practice and results, and his "except for Merck" remark, obviously added just for this occasion, also worried me. It ignored the serious R&D investments by other companies such as Pfizer. As he talked on, I saw that innovation was a minor counterpoint to his central theme: our country's problems. One involved access to healthcare. He noted that 25 to 30 million Americans had no medical insurance, and he wanted to extend coverage to more people. He didn't say how, but I strongly supported this goal. He talked about costs, noting that healthcare in the United States soaked up about 13 percent of our gross domestic product – the highest percentage among the major developed nations. He criticized the high prices charged by physicians, hospitals, and pharmaceutical companies, saying those prices had to be controlled.

This last point really worried me. Clinton made it clear that he was leaning toward government price controls. I was deeply concerned that Congress might create what would become a rigid set of bureaucratic controls that would inevitably corrode the research-intensive component of our pharmaceutical and biotech industries. It was no accident that the United States was producing such a high percentage of the basic pharmaceutical innovations in the entire world. This country had created a remarkable combination of government, nonprofit, and private organizations, all of which were involved in an exciting, effective search for new therapies and preventive medicines, including vaccines.

Other countries, even those with superb scientific establishments, had fallen behind the pharmaceutical industry in the United States. In many cases, foreign manufacturers had to contend with price controls, government purchasing of drugs, and other regulations that severely limited their ability to earn the profits that sustain large-scale, modern research laboratories. In other cases, political hostility to the use of recombinant DNA technology and research in genetics created an environment hostile to scientific progress. In some countries, the links between university research and industrial research were much less fruitful than they were in America.

In 1992, Merck, as well as every other company doing pharmaceutical research, was struggling to keep up with the vast array of new scientific frontiers being opened for exploration. The combination of molecular genetics and enzymology promised to yield cures for a variety of deadly diseases such as cancer and AIDS. Spurred by the opportunities to profit from successful innovations, all of the major foreign pharmaceutical companies had established, or were developing, beachheads in the United States. In fact, our home state of New Jersey was the country's leading center for pharmaceutical research and development.

Innovation in this industry was a complex, cooperative undertaking. Merck repeatedly turned to academic scientists, as it had to me some years before, seeking advice and assistance. As mentioned earlier, one of Merck's most important innovations, the hepatitis B vaccine, *Recombivax HB*, was a product of cooperative research between industry and academia. Dr. William Rutter of the University of California in San Francisco and Dr. Ben Hall, from the University of Washington, made vital contributions to this breakthrough vaccine.

Recombivax HB was like the tip of a great mountain that consisted of layer upon layer of private, public, and nonprofit institutions. Understanding that, it was impossible to ignore the significant role the U.S. government played in drug discovery. After all, the great majority of our fundamental research was sponsored by the National Institutes of Health and the National Science Foundation and carried out at universities. But anyone who knew anything about medical research knew that this basic research was transformed into effective therapies that improved human lives primarily in pharmaceutical company research labs. As CEO of Merck, it was impossible for me to accept a new system of political economy that would threaten the pharmaceutical industry's ability to remain an effective partner in the process of medical innovation.

That's why I was so concerned when Clinton repeatedly attacked our industry. Each time, he carefully added that his host, Merck, was a wonderful exception. Happy as I was to hear this praise, I knew that it was a throwaway formality, like tagging "Best regards to your family" on a business letter. As he was talking, I kept thinking that he was missing opportunities to mention the past and potential contributions of Merck and the rest of the industry to the quality of life in America. Our drugs were helping millions of people lead a better, and often longer, life. Clinton also seemed unaware of the fact that new drugs and vaccines help control the costs of healthcare. On all these points, there were thorough, quantitative studies of the savings – some conducted by agencies in the government Clinton wanted to head.

* * *

After Clinton's speech, he and I talked privately for about an hour in a small office in the administration building behind the stage. "I want your advice," he said earnestly, looking directly into my eyes. "I really appreciate what you've done with your research and your pricing policy, and if I'm elected, I'll want you to come in and advise me." I was wary, given the tone and message of his speech. One slip, I thought, and Merck might no longer be called the exception to the rule. But I was impressed with his openness, his willingness to reach out for information, and his very warm, charismatic style. He had clearly demonstrated to his Merck audience what an effective politician he was. I agreed with many of Clinton's objectives, and I wanted him to have the chance to solve some of the country's healthcare problems.

During this conversation, he questioned me about the industry. "How close are we to a cure for AIDS?" he asked. "The earlier drugs," I said, "slowed the onset of AIDS symptoms, but they worked only temporarily. The virus became resistant and most of the patients died." Our scientists were trying a new approach, I explained, but we still didn't know if it would work. "The best long-term objective is a vaccine against HIV, but that's many years away."

"How about cancer?" he asked. "The current drugs make people very sick." I told him that scientists were generating a new understanding of how normal cells are transformed into cancerous cells. Some specific enzymes and cellular receptors were being targeted. "But we're ten or twenty years away from truly effective drugs."

"What proportion of our drugs is invented in industry rather than universities?" he asked. "Most drugs," I said, "come from industry. The universities provide the foundation for drug discovery, but they can't make the enormous investments required for applied research."

Clinton's next question didn't surprise me: "Why do new drugs cost so much?" My answer was that the prices had to cover years of expensive research and development. On average, it takes ten to fifteen years to create a successful drug, and the costs run around $800 million. Sometimes it takes even longer, as was the case with the hepatitis vaccine. In addition, most research for drug discovery fails. The industry had, for instance, spent over $1 billion on AIDS research – and no vaccine had yet passed through clinical trials. The antiviral drugs being developed might control the disease, but they would neither eliminate it nor prevent it from being transmitted. The average cost of R&D includes successes and failures, but because most research fails to achieve a product, much of the overall cost relates to failed projects. The problem, of course, is the difficulty in identifying the losers early. But pharmaceutical companies have to recover long-term, risky investments and earn enough profits to fund future research.

Not satisfied, Clinton asked, "Isn't the pharmaceutical industry wasting a lot of money to make minor changes on another company's breakthrough drugs?" I explained that breakthrough products are seldom optimal. Further research can often yield an improved drug with fewer side effects or a longer duration of action. "When that's true, you can sometimes take a drug once a day, and that increases patient compliance. So the outcome for the patient is improved."

This was a relaxed, serious exchange of ideas. I was convinced Clinton would take a partnership approach to reform. I needed to see him again to argue against some of his ideas, but I wanted our first meeting to be positive. I thought he'd listen to advice. We might, I mused, be able to convince him that price controls would choke off the research that was giving us new therapies that were saving lives and money for America.

I was hopeful, earnest, and politically naive. I was receiving some good political advice from experts, but I was personally more trusting than I should have been.

* * *

Shortly after being elected, Clinton held an Economic Summit in Little Rock, Arkansas. The stated objective was to formulate policies for the incoming administration, but even to a politically naive participant it was obvious that the Clinton team also wanted to drum up support for some reforms they had already pretty much defined. Attending one of the sessions on December 13, 1992, I found myself sitting at the round table directly opposite the President Elect and next to Ron Brown, later the Secretary of Commerce. Clinton was the master of this situation, demonstrating the kind of political skill that had helped him win the election. He was agile and smooth and seemed open to advice. He was extremely comfortable with give-and-take on hot political issues. I was once again impressed by the way he dealt with the different people around that table, including CEO Robert E. Allen of AT&T, President Johnnetta B. Cole of Spelman College, and Chairman John S. Reed of Citicorp.

During my turn at bat, he pointed out the importance of vaccines in preventing disease. He asked my opinion about vaccination of children in the United States. "Prevention of disease by vaccination," I said, "is the most efficient way to improve health." I described the progress Merck research had made in developing new vaccines against hepatitis B and *Ha. influenzae*, type b (Hib). This had taken many years, I said, and had cost many millions of dollars.

Our exchange was friendly, even informative. I left the conference quite excited. "Bill Clinton," I said to myself, "is truly interested in improving health and he's going to give it a high priority in his administration. He's smart enough to understand the issues and he's eager to get going."

* * *

In January 1993, I learned just how eager he was to "get going" when the President blindsided Merck – and me personally – by attacking us for charging such high prices for our vaccines that American parents couldn't afford to get their children the shots they needed. I was angry and discouraged. What Clinton said wasn't true – then or now. We in the industry, along with most public health authorities, knew why the United States had worse vaccination rates for preschool children than many developed countries. The Johns Hopkins School of Public Health was just north of Washington, in Baltimore, and several people on the faculty there had a great deal of experience with vaccination programs. They would have been happy to explain what needed to be done. One or two phone calls would have put the President on the right track, but apparently no one made those calls. Nor did his closest advisers pay any attention to the smart, well-informed people in the administration who understood this situation very well.

Instead of doing his homework, Clinton came out blasting the industry. Our prices, he said, were "shocking." America's current situation was "unconscionable." The President warned: "We are running the risk of new epidemics spreading out in this country."

Yes, we had a national problem. Years later, we still do. But the President's blunt accusation that Merck and the other vaccine producers were making "profits at the expense of our children" was wrong. That kind of political rhetoric appealed to many people. Even though the idea was false, it grabbed headlines and was quickly endorsed by the *New York Times*. What a sorry mess, I thought. We weren't going to solve America's healthcare problems with divisive political slogans that vilified companies like Merck, which was investing heavily in the development of new vaccines. If we were going to solve serious problems, we needed a partnership, not a political slugfest.

Both the President and the First Lady continued, however, to speak with compelling passion on this issue. They were deeply concerned, they said, because American children, especially those living in inner cities, were tragically undervaccinated. Both apparently believed that vaccination rates were low because our prices were high, as did Donna Shalala, Clinton's Secretary of Health and Human Services. I knew they were wrong, but just in case, I went back to our vaccine experts and got up-to-date information. As they explained, the worst problems were in urban centers where people relied heavily on hospital emergency rooms and clinics for their everyday healthcare. The clinics all used vaccines purchased by the government at about half the market price, and clinic physicians and nurses gave the shots to the children free. Price was not an issue.

Nevertheless, many parents do not take their children for the free vaccines until they reach school age and the vaccinations are required for entry into school. Virtually all inner-city children get their shots by age four or five. The heart of the problem is children under age two. They are susceptible to diseases preventable by vaccination, but too many of them aren't getting their shots.

Why do parents wait? Some just don't get their acts together, but most find it hard to get to a clinic because of their jobs. They can't afford to sit for hours waiting for the shots. It seemed evident to us even back then that the United States needed new ways to help clinics, health maintenance organizations, emergency wards, and private physicians vaccinate preschool children. Something had to be changed.

We knew the problem wasn't Merck or the three other companies that supply most of the world's vaccines. I visited several Democratic leaders (including Ted Kennedy, Bill Bradley, Dan Rostenkowski, John Dingle, Frank Lautenberg, and George Mitchell) to explain this situation. I told them we wanted the federal government to put its money where it would do the most good. What America needed was a better tracking and distribution system for vaccines to ensure that more people would be vaccinated. Merck was already helping by providing support for local programs focused on this aspect of the problem. But increasing the supply of free vaccines was not the answer. "In some urban centers where too few children are being vaccinated," I said, "there is enough free vaccine to vaccinate every child *twice*!" All the politicians I contacted seemed to understand, but as Bob Rubin said to me in a moment of candor, "What the President wants to do is bad national policy, but he *is* the President and that's what he wants to do." (Of course now he says he doesn't remember saying that, but he did.)

Indeed, Clinton did exactly what he wanted to do. It was virtually impossible for a politician to oppose anything that promised to help children, and the Administration's vaccine program sailed through Congress on the winds of political rhetoric. The Vaccines for Children program pumped more federal money into a system that badly needed an improved infrastructure, not cheaper vaccines. Before long, even the government began to recognize that the plan was based on false assumptions. The Government Accounting Office (GAO), which evaluated the Clinton policy, concluded that the price of vaccines was not preventing children from getting their shots. As the GAO discovered, neither the Clinton rhetoric nor the goal of increasing the supply of free vaccines was justified.

By that time, however, we had been badly bruised. I hated the fact that the media and Washington, DC, identified Merck – and the other vaccine producers – as an opponent of reform. Actually, we were proponents of a new program to make vaccination more accessible to inner-city children at an early age. Merck also favored expanding medical insurance coverage, improving the quality of care, and limiting liability and bureaucracy, which were all changes that would allocate U.S. healthcare dollars more efficiently.

But that message didn't get through. I tried several times to act on the President's general invitation to "come in and advise me," but his office was never able to schedule a private meeting to talk about either vaccines or the general issue of healthcare reform. I saw him from time to time at fundraisers and other large occasions, and he continued to be extremely cordial. "Roy," he would say, "I really want you to come and visit." But the next Clinton with whom I consulted privately was his wife, Hillary Clinton. I had tea and talk at the White House. That conversation was an eye-opener.

* * *

Hillary and I talked about the administration's proposition to restructure the nation's entire healthcare system. This was a typical gathering of its kind, but with a not-so-typical ending. The First Lady brought her entourage, including Ira Magaziner, her adviser on healthcare reform; Chris Jennings, a member of her reform team; and Melanne Verveer, Hillary's chief of staff. I brought along four Merck people, including Judy Lewent, our chief financial officer, and Teel Oliver, the head of Merck's Washington office. Hillary sat on my left so we could address each other directly. She briefly summarized the President's plan, which we already understood very well – a series of new government organizations that seemed headed to thoroughgoing price control – and occasionally called on Ira Magaziner to fill in some details of projected costs.

Then I summarized our plan: I wanted to see broader coverage by insurance and better management but with control left in the hands of the industry. I asked Judy Lewent to discuss the costs of drug research and development and the high-risk nature of the investments made in the pharmaceutical industry. We talked for about an hour. I emphasized the savings to individuals and the nation as a whole if we had a vaccination program that reached all children. We could take vaccines into the neighborhoods with mobile clinics or work through existing clinics and schools. I discussed the dramatic improvements in health produced by the combination of government and industry investment in biomedical research. I concluded, "It's our hope that all Americans can benefit from the fruits of this productive, cooperative enterprise."

Despite my disappointment over the vaccine controversy, I was at the White House because I was *still* looking for a partnership in reform. Near the end of the discussion, however, the First Lady made it clear that we were not there to exchange ideas. In her mind, our meeting was, like a court of law, fundamentally adversarial.

She said, "Well, Dr. Vagelos, do you think you can support the President's plan?" I was stunned. "Of course not," I replied. "I just told you that we can't support the plan because it's very different from what I think would be best for the country." She quickly countered with a suggestion: "In that case, you could be neutral." Again, I was surprised. I thought I had made myself abundantly clear. "What do you mean by being neutral?" I asked. "You just will say nothing," she replied. "No, I can't be neutral because I head the largest pharmaceutical company in the world and we have a position which I represent. I will talk about it to the media and others if asked." She then slammed the door on our talk: "Well, if you can't be supportive and you can't be neutral, then you are an enemy and you won't have any input."

In this she was half right. We certainly had no "input." Given my medical training, my experience as head of Merck, and my willingness to help, I thought an administration struggling to solve a great national problem should at least have listened to my ideas. But two things were apparent after our meeting. The White House – at least the part running healthcare reform – had never really wanted our advice, and the door the First Lady slammed would not be opened to me during the remainder of the Clinton tenure. Hillary Clinton is unusually intelligent, articulate, and energetic – but completely unreceptive to any discussion of ideas different from her own. I also began to realize that her ultimate objective was not universal vaccination of American children. What she really wanted to do was punish the American pharmaceutical industry through price controls.

But she was wrong about my being an "enemy." I certainly wasn't an enemy of the millions of Americans who need healthcare. I had spent my entire career – as a physician, a research scientist, a teacher of medical students, a research leader, and an executive in the pharmaceutical industry – trying to help patients in one way or another. Out of those experiences came my ideas about the kind of partnership that can help us realize the system of healthcare the United States deserves.

At Merck, we had been thinking about healthcare reform long before Bill Clinton was elected president. A few simple statistics demanded that something important be done. The United States was spending a higher percentage of its gross domestic product on healthcare than any nation in the world, but the results for a significant part of the population were discouraging. U.S. infant mortality was comparable to that of many developing countries, and life expectancy was far too low for a nation with our sophisticated medical establishment. Millions – 54 million at that time – had no health insurance at all, and others had no protection against a catastrophic illness and the bills it would produce.

We explored reforms we thought would have a good chance of being implemented. Our approach was incremental. We started with things we could do ourselves – first by limiting price increases and then by offering all Medicaid programs the lowest price we gave to any customer. Both these initiatives had ripple effects in the industry and the government that multiplied their impact. In 1990, Congress adopted a provision about Medicaid patients similar to the Merck plan.

Nonetheless, much more still had to be done. In 1991 we had proposed to the industry a plan to constrain price increases in a competitive, market-oriented system. And the industry accepted it. We wanted to balance universal access, individual choice, and continued innovation. That was a tall order, but we believed balance could be achieved through "managed competition." Management by industry itself is needed, but so is increased federal funding to spread insurance coverage and thus access. One critical issue, for example, is covering prescription drugs for the Medicare population.

I still think something along these lines could be implemented today. But there would have to be dialogues more productive than the one I had with Hillary Clinton, who didn't want to listen to information that was inconsistent with her plan and who divided the world into "supporters," "neutrals," and "enemies." Hillary Clinton is certainly not the only American political figure unwilling to base public policy on solid data. But in this case, she had as First Lady taken over the healthcare issue, a field in which I'd invested my entire career, and so her closed-mindedness riled me more than most.

The Clinton Plan created so many enemies that it went down to defeat. The problems we had discussed – for instance, the lack of medical insurance for a significant portion of our population – simply continued to grow. I hope the future will lead to creative compromises that change the current system as more and more Americans come to understand that our citizens' health needs to be protected as much as our national security.

12 | Partners

I n 1994, my retirement from Merck was celebrated in the lavish style characteristic of today's successful American corporations. There was the magnificent dinner complete with a small band and huge floral centerpieces. And, of course, the made-to-order video with shots of my friends, family, and colleagues from around the world saying nice things about me and what we had accomplished in the past nine years. The outdoor phase of the retirement ceremonies was held on a sunny October day in Rahway. Dr. Bruce Alberts, President of the National Academy of Sciences, lauded my scientific and academic accomplishments. New Jersey Governor Christie Todd Whitman helped dedicate Merck's Rahway site as the "P. Roy Vagelos Research and Development Center." I appreciated their kindness, but I could hardly stand any of this praise. I couldn't wait to leave and jumpstart the next phase of my life.

It was of course comforting to know that Merck was in good shape. The Clintons' bashing had caused the stock price of Merck and all the major pharmaceutical companies to drop. Merck slid from $54 to $29 a share, but it was slowly recovering – as we knew it would. Merck's core business was fundamentally very strong. Perhaps the best news accompanying my retirement was our progress in developing an effective treatment for HIV infection and AIDS, the kind of achievement that makes work in the pharmaceutical industry unusually rewarding. After experiencing numerous devastating setbacks and devoting eight years of intense, multiteam research to the effort, Ed Scolnick and his talented scientists made a breakthrough and had a promising antiviral compound in hand. The outlook for a vaccine was still bleak, but we succeded with indinavir sulfate (*Crixivan*), a protease inhibitor that prevented viral replication. As became apparent later, it was especially effective when combined with other antiretrovirals in a drug "cocktail." *Crixivan* was an important discovery for infected patients in industrialized nations who were facing almost certain death when their infections progressed to AIDS.

Merck researchers were among the first to focus on the HIV protease, an enzyme critical to the replication of the virus. The credit for focusing on the protease and other molecular targets should go, however, not to any single organization but to the combination of public, private, and nonprofit institutions and their thousands of individual researchers. The invention and development of the protease inhibitors gives you a good sense of the strength of this partnership – a combination that has made the United States the most important source of the entire world's new pharmaceuticals in recent decades. The government played a major role in identifying and achieving a better understanding of the disease. University and NIH scientists made significant contributions, as did large pharmaceutical companies and small biotech firms.

The spirit of cooperation intensified as the true proportions of the pandemic became evident, and, as I noted before, in 1993 Merck led the drive to create an Inter-Company Collaboration for AIDS Drugs Development. For three years, companies that were normally competitors exchanged information that facilitated clinical trials of their various drug candidates, especially those to be taken as components of "cocktails." The collaboration also provided a convenient forum in which AIDS activists could meet representatives of the leading pharmaceutical firms conducting research on HIV.

Merck finished third (right behind Hoffmann-La Roche and Abbott) in the race to bring out a protease inhibitor that enabled a patient's immune system to cope with the infection. The new drugs didn't cure the infection. It is very important to keep that in mind. But when used in a triple combination they significantly decreased mortality and morbidity. Critically ill hospitalized patients were able to return to work and live a more normal lifestyle. The new drugs were inconvenient – the dosages and combinations had to be varied, and the times of administration had to be precisely regulated. Efavirenz, another MRL discovery, simplified treatment, but the problem persisted. In addition, all the combinations caused side effects.

Most important, the patients and their physicians knew that the pattern of resistance developed by the virus against all previous drugs indicated that the same thing would happen with the protease inhibitors. It was only a matter of time. These breakthrough drugs were thus a stopgap. Better drugs would be needed soon if the disease were to be controlled while a vaccine or another type of drug was being developed. After a decade of basic research, the molecular biology of the virus was well understood, and other molecular targets for drug discovery (in addition to the reverse transcriptase and the protease) were identified. The process of discovery was taking longer than I had originally envisioned, but I was still convinced that we would be able to develop either a vaccine that would prevent infection or a drug that would actually cure it. I'm still optimistic today.

***

The drugs that made up the life-sustaining "cocktails" were priced for the developed world at a level to permit a decent profit and to allow AIDS research to continue. But that price was far too high for the developing world, particularly in Africa, which had the highest percentage of HIV infection of any continent. The *Mectizan* donation program to eradicate river blindness could not be replicated because HIV infected a vastly larger population and the cocktails required daily complex drug treatment, probably for life. It was, nevertheless, incumbent on the pharmaceutical industry to come up with a pricing plan that would get the drugs to these people. The U.S. or other governments, the World Bank, IMF, or large foundations would then have to work with us to build the infrastructure required to distribute the drugs throughout Africa's rural societies. Although the response of funding organizations had been very disappointing at the start of the *Mectizan* program, many joined us later, and so I assumed a similar response would be forthcoming for HIV drugs. Appropriate medicines were available and being widely used in the United States and Europe. I saw this as an exciting opportunity for cooperation between industry and some of the governments and foundations of the developed world. I was, however, disappointed with the reactions of both the governments and the pharmaceutical industry, including Merck, which for several years made no serious attempt to control the mounting pandemic in the developing nations. Many millions of people were infected and many thousands were dying. The industry initially refused to reduce prices or to permit the manufacture of generic copies of its patented drugs. After several years of growing negative public reaction, especially in the United States, the industry capitulated – having sustained a badly tarnished image – and arranged to make its medicines available at low cost.

The long-term hope, of course, was that scientists would find a way to produce an effective, safe vaccine. Merck never stopped looking, but in 1994 we projected that a vaccine was still many years and many wasted lives away. When a vaccine is finally developed, I'm certain it will be a product of the kind of public–private partnership that produced all the important new U.S. therapies of the twentieth century.

* * *

Throughout these years, Merck was continuing to make significant investments in the partnership principle. Scientists in private, public, and nonprofit organizations were studying the sequence of the human genome in an effort to understand the function of all the genes in the body. Several biotech companies were racing in parallel with their own studies to obtain the DNA sequences that would allow the discovery of new drugs. These firms intended to patent the information derived from DNA sequencing so that academic researchers or pharmaceutical companies could not access it without a license. Some large companies made major deals to get proprietary rights to such information.

Scientists and top management at Merck took a different position. We saw the DNA sequence as early but important information that should be readily available free to all scientists – academic and industrial – unimpaired by licensing requirements. To support that goal Merck helped finance a major gene sequencing operation at Washington University, where Dr. Robert Waterston put together a consortium of university laboratories. This project developed information that was made available at no charge via the Internet to all interested scientists.

I was pleased with that outcome and with the condition of the Merck pipeline, which was full of exciting new products when I was retiring in 1994. In addition to *Crixivan*, Merck was introducing *Fosamax*, a new treatment to prevent bone loss in postmenopausal women. *Fosamax* put Merck into a completely new therapeutic field, and we had trained and prepared our marketing and sales groups for this transition well in advance. The other promising drug was *Cozaar*, an antihypertensive drug that was clearly (at least to me) going to become the next market leader in the cardiovascular field, where Merck had been dominant for many years. Most of our top management also thought *Cozaar* would keep us at the front of the pack, but our marketing group was not enthusiastic at the start because the new drug served the same patient population as *Vasotec*, a great success story. They wanted to press on with the proven leader. But *Cozaar* had a significant advantage over *Vasotec* and all other drugs in that class: it didn't cause the irritating cough that occurred in a small percentage of the patients.

I put myself in the position of a prescribing physician. Would I prescribe an excellent drug that normalizes blood pressure but causes cough in a small number of patients, or an equally effective drug that doesn't have this side effect? Since there was only one possible answer, I pushed the marketing people rather hard. They responded, with some grumbling, and ultimately *Cozaar* became the market leader. But that wouldn't have happened without pressure, and this is why all institutions – businesses, universities, and government agencies alike – need strong leadership if they are to remain innovative.

* * *

Pleased about our pipeline, I approached retirement with only three major regrets. One was highly personal. Company policy required me to stop doing what I loved, and I found that very upsetting. Merck had become the largest pharmaceutical company in the world based on an unprecedented flow of important new products. It was "most admired" not only in the annual *Fortune* survey for many years but also in the minds of biomedical scientists, patients, and physicians around the world. It was also most admired by buyers of pharmaceutical company stock. Year after year it had the highest market capitalization and the highest price-earnings ratio of all the major firms in the industry. I loved the opportunity I had to play a role in building that kind of organization at Merck.

As retirement loomed, the shadow of my late father fell over my shoulder. I remembered all too well what happened when Herodotus had approached the age of sixty-five. He and my mother had worked hard to build up Estelle's Restaurant, but my sisters and I finally convinced them to retire. Grudgingly my father agreed to step down. He tried to busy himself around the house and get more involved in social activities, but he was obviously disgruntled. He missed the daily demands and above all the social contacts of his small business. The shopping, the food preparation, and the banter with customers and salespeople had made him happy.

One year after he retired, he developed colon cancer. After an operation and bouts with phlebitis and pulmonary emboli, he was finally able to return home to convalesce. As soon as he felt stronger, he announced, "Retirement is not good for me!" He went back to work with a smile, managing until he was seventy-eight the restaurant he and my mother had sold. Then he became a cashier at the Grand Diner in Rahway (at the corner of Grand Avenue and Route 1), staying in that job until he was eighty-five. I thought about Herodotus a great deal when my own retirement was approaching, and I decided, "Retirement is not good for me either!"

My second regret was that I was never completely satisfied with the level of innovation in our marketing efforts. Although Medco was making tremendous strides in lowering the costs of distribution, the old system of personal "reps" remained intact and continued to play a large role at Merck and throughout the rest of the industry. We had introduced laptop computers and emphasized the role our reps played as a source of up-to-date information for physicians and other healthcare professionals. We had the highest standards in the industry, I believe, for what we would say about our products and those of our competitors. But the system was still fundamentally flawed.

We sent our well-trained reps to wait in physicians' offices for hours hoping to spend a few precious minutes with the doctor. When I was a practicing physician, many years ago, I never talked to the reps because I didn't want to waste my time. So you can see how conflicted I was. As CEO, I had for years presided over a system I knew was inefficient. I also knew, however, that if a drug company didn't market its products aggressively, using the traditional approach, it could not maximize sales. At least not under existing market conditions.

We experimented with some new approaches. Before the advent of the Internet, Merck and other companies had tried to reach practicing physicians by placing a computer in their offices and a satellite dish on the roof so that a busy physician could obtain product information any time he or she wanted. This system was intended to inform physicians and at the same time break the traditional sales rep paradigm, thereby saving millions of dollars in drug promotion costs (which are covered in the product prices). The problem was that after we installed the equipment in offices of a select group of physicians who had agreed to participate in this educational experiment, they simply wouldn't turn on the computers. They preferred the coffee and donuts, the pizzas and free samples, and the personal contact provided by a sales rep. The tug of tradition was very strong. In Eastern Europe we tried employing only physicians to represent our firm rather than a traditional sales force. But we knew that approach would never work in markets where traditional sales forces were already deeply entrenched.

After I retired, Merck-Medco moved aggressively to increase communication from the company to the physicians and patients who needed information about our products and the diseases they target. Merck-Medco skillfully employed the Internet to improve our communications capability, but they carefully avoided any suggestion that this information technology would substitute for the traditional "rep" system. The Internet may ultimately provide the breakthrough innovation I was looking for. In the meantime, all the major pharmaceutical firms, including Merck, have ramped up their sales forces, sending out new cadres of reps to deliver their samples, gifts, and pizzas and then to wait dutifully in doctors' offices for a moment's opportunity to pitch a new product.

Even more disappointing to me was the problem of developing my successor. One of the most important responsibilities for any CEO is to prepare for an orderly succession, normally by grooming an heir apparent. I had done just that at MRL, where Ed Scolnick was heading our formidable drug discovery program. As CEO, I had begun identifying and developing successors long before others were thinking about my retirement. All went well, and the Board of Directors and I were anticipating a smooth transition, but my plan crashed when our lead candidate left Merck for personal reasons. The Board launched a search that began by reviewing the firm's top executives and continued with a survey of business leaders outside of Merck. They selected Ray Gilmartin, who was then heading Becton–Dickinson, a medical equipment firm. Although Ray had no experience in pharmaceuticals, he was a talented business strategist with a special ability to encourage a cooperative team approach to any business activity.

Once Gilmartin had taken over and the transition was completed, I stepped aside. I resigned from the Merck Board, although I was urged to remain as my predecessor had. But I didn't want to sit on the Board of Directors and have Ray and others in the company think I was looking over their shoulders, possibly being critical of what they were doing. I also wanted to get on with the next phase of my own life, and I wanted to be completely independent. I was anxious to try some new ventures, unencumbered by the past.

* * *

University of Pennsylvania commencement, 1999; Roy appears on the far right behind Judith Rodin (seated), President of the University.

As the memories of my retirement ceremonies happily faded, Diana and I set out on several new careers. I immediately became Chairman of the Board of Trustees of the University of Pennsylvania. After graduating from Penn in 1950, I had spent very little time there, although I occasionally delivered lectures in biochemistry at the School of Medicine. But then our younger daughter, Ellen, changed all that by attending Penn. In high school, she was a star on the field hockey team, and Diana and I had loved watching her compete. It was even more fun to watch her and her team at Penn's Franklin Field. That reconnection with my alma mater had led to my becoming a trustee.

Until I retired, my heavy obligations at Merck had limited my efforts as a trustee, but I was able to focus some attention on Penn's chemistry department. The faculty was strong, probably stronger than when I had been a student, but the department's facilities were visibly inadequate. They needed new laboratories. Over several years, while the university developed plans for a new building, I led a small group of faculty and administrators on fundraising visits to chemical and pharmaceutical company headquarters. I pitched the importance of supporting this stellar chemistry faculty with a new lab. The federal government agreed to contribute, as did several of the companies we had approached. Then Diana and I did our part by making a major gift that would get the job finished. Architect Bob Venturi designed a marvelous building that was perfect for the kind of scientific research essential to a first-class university.

I also helped select a new president for the university. The search committee, chaired by Alvin Shoemaker, then Trustee Chairman, identified Dr. Judith Rodin, who had been an outstanding Penn undergraduate. After earning a Ph.D. at Columbia, she had gone on to a career in psychology at Yale, where she became chair of the Psychology Department and, briefly, provost. I was asked to investigate her research accomplishments as part of the search committee's due diligence. Our conclusions were that her work was stellar – as was the candidate in every regard. She became president of Penn in June 1994.

When I took over my new responsibilities as Chairman of the Trustees, in November 1994, I knew that campus safety was a major problem. A student had been murdered not far from Penn shortly before President Rodin arrived, and she and the trustees quickly acknowledged the gravity of a situation that Penn shared with Yale and other urban campuses. Penn's administration had responded by improving the lighting on campus and increasing the number of security guards. But the problem was too complex to be solved that simply. The West Philadelphia neighborhood surrounding Penn had deteriorated over the years. Although it had once been home to many of the faculty and staff, over a period of about thirty years the faculty had gradually moved out to the suburbs and many of the houses had become run down. Unscrupulous landlords tried to squeeze the maximum profits out of their aging buildings, investing very little to maintain their property or the neighborhood.

Much earlier, the University of Chicago had undergone a similar neighborhood disintegration with a nearly identical impact on the school. The trustees and administration reacted forcefully, launching a major program of investment in local revitalization. They turned the neighborhood around and saved the university. President Rodin and the trustees now moved aggressively to implement that same policy at Penn. The university invested in housing renovation, offered low-cost mortgages for faculty and staff living in the area, and subsidized the rents of new retail shops. Penn also subsidized the construction of a new public grammar school as the focus of area rehabilitation as well as a way to attract young faculty back to the neighborhood. Penn contributed the land, the city paid for the new building, and Penn committed to paying $1,000 per student to ensure optimal support of the instructional programs. The Penn Graduate School of Education took a leadership position in helping to select faculty and establish an optimal curriculum.

Another hot button for me in my new role as Chairman of the Trustees was the need to increase endowment to support undergraduate scholarships. Penn was woefully underendowed compared with other Ivy League universities, and we shortly launched a major drive to strengthen our scholarship program. I made numerous visits to alumni to explain the situation. Unless we could provide competitive scholarships to top students who needed help, we would continue to lose them to Harvard or Columbia or Yale or Princeton. That was unacceptable. Working with the university staff and the other trustees, we were able to sell this program and increase the endowment by $85 million by the time I stepped down as chairman in 1999.

I thought we had made a respectable beginning, but more had to be done. Diana and I decided to intervene directly. Of particular importance, we felt, was the training of undergraduates for careers in scientific research and medicine – the careers I had adopted after leaving Penn. Although the university attracted some top students, no program brought together all the basic disciplines required to train the basic life scientists of the future. Fortunately, one chemistry professor, Dr. Ponzy Lu, had particularly close relationships with both undergraduate and graduate students. Dr. Lu stitched together a Molecular Life Sciences Program that immersed Penn students in science. Rigorous and demanding, the program included advanced math and science courses as well as seminars and special laboratory work. The students were given certain privileges as well as a heavy workload. They could, for instance, take courses and lab work in any of the schools of the university, including the School of Medicine. Diana and I decided to endow this exciting program so that talented students from anywhere in the United States could participate regardless of their families' financial resources.

At Penn as at Merck, I encountered problems I couldn't solve. One very close to my heart was the financial difficulty at the School of Medicine. Under the outstanding leadership of Dr. William Kelley, the medical school was up near the top in the national rankings, but the economics of healthcare deteriorated dramatically in the late 1990s. The school's finances suffered severely. Government payments under Medicare and Medicaid were being drastically reduced. Payments for patient care by Philadelphia HMOs fell at the same time, and the city didn't cover increases in indigent care. Like every other academic medical center in the United States, Penn's School of Medicine was being crushed by rising costs. The losses at Penn were particularly steep and troublesome to me, but I had to leave that problem in the lap of the next chairman.

At the age of seventy, I had to step down from the university: my second encounter with statutory retirement. This time I was better prepared for the emotional shock. I had prepared myself by visiting faculty and students in all twelve schools at Penn. I had been able to lecture in Arts & Sciences, the School of Medicine, and the Wharton School. In particular, I had enjoyed my informal talks with students who, like the young Roy Vagelos, were full of enthusiasm and dreams.

Retirement was also less painful this time because I was already deeply involved with three other important activities. In 1989 Ray Chambers and Larry Goldman (chairman and president, respectively) of the New Jersey Performing Arts Center (NJPAC) had invited me to join their board as cochairman. The facility was the dream of Governor Thomas Kean, who believed it would bring world-class performing arts to the New Jersey side of the Hudson River. It would be a center for educating children in the arts and would, he hoped, catalyze the rehabilitation of Newark, the state's largest city. Newark had never really recovered from the fires and looting during the race riots of 1967. I especially liked the educational and city revitalization aspects of the project, and I was certainly taken with the idea of seeing topnotch performances without having to negotiate the Lincoln Tunnel. For several years I worked with the Board to plan and finance this center. They had come to me for financial support from Merck and for help in recruiting other New Jersey corporations. I delivered both. With heavy contributions from the state government, NJPAC was built right in the middle of Newark and initiated performances in 1998.

Diana was attracted to this project because of Newark's rich cultural history as a center for jazz, because of the center's focus on children, and because of its effort to help rebuild the city. She became the founding president of the Women's Board of NJPAC, which arranged the

Roy at the New Jersey Performing Arts Center (NJPAC) with Christie Whit-man, New Jersey Governor; Art Ryan, CEO of Prudential; Sharpe James, Mayor of Newark; and Lawrence P. Goldman, CEO and President of NJPAC.

opening, major fundraising galas, and educational programs for their membership. After decades of marriage, Diana and I were at last work-ing on a joint project outside the family. She also became a Director of NJPAC and the chair of the education committee, which has sponsored to date dance, music, and theater programs for 125,000 children and their families.

Keeping to my usual schedule of shifting interests every ten years, despite my great enjoyment of NJPAC, I resigned from the board in 1999 to take on an entirely different and fascinating enterprise. After my Merck retirement, Diana and I, like many other Americans, be-came interested in exploring our roots by renewing our knowledge of Greece, in particular, its language, history, and archaeology. A medical school classmate, Dick O'Connor, had spent many summers digging on the island of Ithaca to search for the palace of Odysseus. We now traveled with him to various archaeological sites throughout Greece and became even more excited about the country's rich history. In an

Roy and Diana attending a gala for the New Jersey Performing Arts Center.
He was Co-Chairman of the NJPAC Board of Directors. She was First Vice
President of the NJPAC Women's Board Association.

effort to promote further explorations, I served for a time as president
and CEO of the board of the American School of Classical Studies at
Athens. Although the major programs of the American School were
traditional excavations and analyses of literature and artifacts, my interest was what might be learned about the origins and relationships

of the ancient peoples through studies of their DNA. Preliminary work was being carried out in the University of Michigan laboratory of Dr. Andrew Merriwether, who was determining whether the DNA in ancient Greek skeletons was sufficiently preserved to warrant a major study. That brought me full circle, back to chemistry, in the hope that science would open a new chapter in my continuing need to be involved in discovery.

*   *   *

Science was also at the heart of my post-Merck business ventures. Leaving one of the world's leading multinationals, I became deeply and enthusiastically involved with a pair of tiny research firms. There were plenty of opportunities to take a grander, less risky route, but even at age sixty-five, I was still looking for challenges. The first of these business upstarts was Regeneron, which approached me about joining its board shortly before I retired from Merck. I hesitated until I received calls from three Nobel laureates who were already directors. Dr. Michael Brown and Dr. Joe Goldstein were old friends whom I knew very well from their involvement at Merck as consultants and their path-breaking work on cholesterol control. The third was Dr. Alfred Gilman, who had mentored Regeneron's talented CEO, Dr. Len Schleifer, during Len's graduate training at the University of Virginia. Trying to escape my despondency over retirement, I visited Regeneron, in Tarrytown, New York, and met George Yancopoulos, an M.D.-Ph.D. from Columbia who had joined the company shortly after it was established in 1988. The firm was completely focused on degenerative diseases of the nervous system (such as Lou Gehrig's disease), the most difficult diseases to attack therapeutically. George explained that he and his team were working on the structure and function of both receptors and natural substances called ligands that are released by cells and that trigger the receptors' reactions.

Regeneron had suffered one major clinical failure and its stock price was down around $3, but I was impressed by the clarity of George's scientific thinking, the work he and his team had done, and their plans. They had developed some of the most powerful technology platforms I had ever seen – platforms now known as "targeted genomics, functionomics, and designer protein therapeutics." While other scientists were doing gene sequencing with no knowledge of what these genes did, George's scientists were targeting specific genes, isolating the gene products, and demonstrating their functions. He was several years ahead of the field.

The problem was that Regeneron had focused this sophisticated science on the most difficult diseases in the world: those poorly understood at the molecular level. I felt Regeneron was in a position to do what Merck had done two decades earlier, but only if the research objectives were reshaped. I joined the board as chairman, and in the next eight years we refocused the research on projects more likely to produce positive results in a reasonable amount of time. With my encouragement, Regeneron soon concentrated on obesity, rheumatoid arthritis, asthma and allergic diseases, as well as cancer.

Like most such entrepreneurial ventures on the cutting edge of biotechnology, Regeneron is still looking forward to launching its first breakthrough product. But in contrast to most of its biotech and pharmaceutical competitors, Regeneron has a full pipeline of attractive product candidates and a research organization that is the envy of the industry. Alliances with larger pharmaceutical and biotechnology companies – including Amgen, Procter & Gamble, and Sumitomo – along with stockholders in the company, supplied the capital needed to support our long-term research projects. I am continuing to help the firm reach its objectives in any way I can.

My other entrepreneurial venture involves a small startup, Advanced Medicine, Inc., in South San Francisco. Dr. James B. Tananbaum, a former associate at Merck, was interested in building a company based on a novel approach to drug discovery developed by Dr. George M. Whitesides of Harvard's Chemistry Department. The approach involves multivalency, linking two molecules of a drug to align them strategically with two target molecules – either an enzyme or a receptor. The idea is to take a marketed drug, such as an antibiotic or a drug for asthma, for example, and improve it so that it reacts more strongly with its normal target (and thus be able to work at a lower dose), reacts more selectively (thereby reducing side effects), or reacts for a longer duration (so less frequent dosing would be required).

Tananbaum, Whitesides, and I discussed the feasibility of such a company, which I liked very much because the technology promised to lead to the discovery of improved medicines. Since this approach would not compete with that of Regeneron, I joined Advanced Medicine as chairman of the board when the corporation was organized in 1997. One of the dominant scientific disciplines required in its research was chemistry, and we shortly recruited Dr. Burton Christensen to lead that effort. Burt had been one of the most senior chemists at Merck and had fathered several important drugs before his retirement. He had been a consultant at Advanced Medicine, but now we persuaded him to move to South San Francisco and lead our search for superior small-molecule medicines.

This little company was being leveraged by some talented leaders. In 2001 Tananbaum returned to venture capital work and was succeeded as CEO by Rick Winningham, who had spent fourteen years as an executive at Bristol Myers Squibb. That year, I was able to recruit Dr. Patrick Humphrey, the Glaxo SmithKline research executive who had led the group that invented *Imitrex*, the first modern medicine for effective treatment of migraine, and *Zofran*, the breakthrough medicine for preventing the nausea that often accompanies chemotherapy. In 2002 Pat succeeded Burt as head of the firm's research laboratory. That year the company name was changed from Advanced Medicine to Theravance Pharmaceuticals, Inc., just as it was putting its first product candidates into clinical trials.

Why could our small company attract senior pharmaceutical leaders like Christensen, Winningham, and Humphrey? Why could they in turn recruit top young scientists beginning their careers? This was a pattern I had observed earlier at Regeneron. As I've indicated in the previous chapters, recruitment has always interested me because I am so certain that it is the key to effective corporate innovation. Recruitment had been very difficult when I joined the pharmaceutical industry because, in the 1970s, academics looked down on commercial enterprises. I was one of the first senior university scientists to join a major company in a leadership position. I entered the industry when it was smaller, when it was still obvious, at least to me, that I could have a major impact on the company I joined by introducing new ideas for drug discovery. Top management brought me in as a change agent and was completely supportive of what I wanted to do. In effect, they put the future of the company in my hands.

Today, however, pharmaceutical companies are much larger, and this size has created problems for them. There are two in particular. First, it is difficult to continue adequate sales growth when sales are already very large. Growth, however, is what attracts investors and capital, leading to a high price-to-earnings (P/E) ratio. A high P/E allows greater flexibility in corporate strategy (such as the ability to make acquisitions using corporate stock). A low P/E ratio signals vulnerability to acquisition by another company. The problem of trying to increase already sizable sales is exacerbated when company patents on major products are expiring.

The pharmaceutical industry of the 1980s and 1990s was one of the great growth sectors of the U.S. economy. With the flow of new products and the ability to raise prices, many drug companies enjoyed double-digit revenue and earnings growth for many years. If, however, the progression of major new products through the pipeline is inadequate to replace older products losing patent protection, then these large companies need other strategies for growth. They can license or acquire products from a small company that lacks the ability to develop, produce, market, and sell the products itself. Most large companies – those facing patent expirations as well those merely looking for additional sales growth – are constantly seeking licensing and acquisition opportunities, thus driving competition and yielding inflated values for the best licensing candidates.

The second critical problem for the large companies is their inability to attract top talent to their labs. Drug discovery requires outstanding scientists who believe in their research strategy, give the work their best efforts, and have the potential to affect the future of their company. These scientists are the intellectual capital absolutely necessary for the growth of any biotech-pharmaceutical company. Of late, more and more of them have gone to small firms, and they have shifted the primary site of innovation to those small biotech enterprises. The best scientists like working on new approaches based on strong scientific principles likely to produce results in the near future. Small companies are less politically complicated than big pharmaceutical firms and less structured internally. There's little bureaucracy and few papers to fill out or permissions required to pursue a lead. That appeals to university-trained scientists, and the effects can be seen in the pharmaceutical industry today.

The trick for the small company is acquiring enough capital to sustain the business until it launches its first product. To do that, the company must have a strategy likely to yield an important product, preferably more than one in order to constitute a pipeline. Recruitment is easier in this setting because early joiners, who are usually risk takers, receive significant equity ownership in the form of stock or stock options. Anyone joining up understands that the company must develop a product to survive. The awareness that no one can afford to fail generates a tremendous incentive. People usually must pitch in on more than one task. Interdisciplinary cooperation is easy and necessary. Everyone succeeds or fails together. The atmosphere is high pressure – there is no room for weak performers who like short days.

The smartest young people in science are excited by the idea of this kind of drug discovery. Along with intellectual satisfaction, it brings the opportunity to improve people's health as well as to reap major financial rewards. In a small company, researchers are big fish. Since sales are zero and earnings are negative at the start, the introduction of a product causes rapid sales and earnings growth, which leads to rapid stock price appreciation. That same product introduced in a multibillion-dollar company will have only a modest effect.

The trade-off for the scientists is lack of security. Many small companies fail to create a product. But top science graduates have great self-confidence and do not seek security, and so the top talent often goes to small biotech companies rather than big pharmaceutical firms. With more mergers occurring in the future, only a handful of mega-multinational pharmaceutical companies will remain, but numerous start-up and small companies will continue to grow and establish relationships with big firms for their nonresearch capacities. Much product innovation will come from the smaller organizations; discovery research will be largely outsourced by the large businesses, which will become solid investments but will no longer be major growth companies. The large firms will maintain the development organizations to conduct large-scale drug trials and regulatory groups to negotiate drug approvals with the FDA and regulatory agencies around the world. Production, marketing, and sales will be the province of these large companies. Meanwhile, the joy and excitement of drug discovery will have migrated to the minds and souls of scientists in the small biotech firms. This is my vision of the future of R&D in this industry.

Of course a small number of the successful biotech companies will pursue the dream of the earlier pharmaceutical giants, building manufacturing, marketing, and sales capabilities along with their development capacities. I anticipate that some of these companies will apply the ingenuity and innovation that initially led to their success in drug discovery to marketing and sales, thereby revolutionizing the entire industry from start to finish.

After spending more than eight years as an active entrepreneur, I'm convinced that firms like Regeneron and Theravance will continue to be vital contributors to pharmaceutical innovation for many decades

The Vagelos family at Martha's Vineyard, August 2002.

to come. The U.S. industry will benefit, as it has in the recent past, from the large number of small firms that have sprung up in this country. Modern medical science and technology are exploding with new ideas and new approaches to discovery, development, and production. Molecular biology, the new information made available from the complete sequence of the human genome, functional genomics, rDNA technology, and many new approaches in chemistry are opening so many pathways to innovation that we will need even more small entrepreneurial companies to ensure that the most promising paths are fully explored. The United States, with its practice of corporate collaborations and its good venture capital system, is unmatched in its ability to encourage this fruitful combination of start-up firms and large pharmaceutical companies operating in a supportive environment of government-sponsored research and strong research universities.

* * *

As should be clear by now, my fears about retirement were unwarranted. Diana and I have remained busy, happy, and optimistic. We hope that our current work at Regeneron, Theravance, and the New Jersey Performing Arts Center will be as rewarding for us, for our colleagues, and for society as were our previous careers at NIH, Washington University, and Merck & Co., Inc. At every step, the successes we achieved were a product of a unique society that opened its doors to immigrants and their families, that rewarded hard work and good ideas, that created and sustained the most innovative medical, scientific, and pharmaceutical establishments in the world's history. We are grateful that we could be partners in the vast complex of partnerships that make that system a success.

Index